Company Houses
Company Towns

Heritage and Conservation

Edited by
Andrew Molloy
Tom Urbaniak

Company Houses
Company Towns
Heritage and Conservation

Edited by
Andrew Molloy
Tom Urbaniak

CAPE BRETON UNIVERSITY PRESS
SYDNEY, NOVA SCOTIA

The editors and contributors wish to thank the many contributions
and funding provided to make this book possible, including the Social
Sciences and Humanities Research Council of Canada.

Cover Images: Front cover, see articles pp. 46, 76;
back cover, see articles pp. 219, 46, 117.
Cover design: Cathy MacLean Design, Chéticamp, NS.
Layout: Mike Hunter, West Bay and Sydney, NS.
Copyediting: Robbie McCaw, Ottawa, ON.
First printed in Canada.

Includes bibliographical references and index.
Issued in print and electronic formats.
ISBN 978-1-77206-049-2 (paperback).--ISBN 978-1-77206-050-8 (pdf).--
ISBN 978-1-77206-051-5 (epub).--ISBN 978-1-77206-052-2 (kindle)

1. Company towns--Canada. 2. Historic buildings--Conservation
and
restoration--Canada. 3. Architecture--Conservation and restoration--
Canada. 4. City planning--Canada. 5. Urban renewal--Canada. I.
Molloy,
Andrew, 1960-, editor II. Urbaniak, Tom, 1976-, editor

HD7545.A3C64 2016   307.76'70971   C2016-902113-0
                                                 C2016-902114-9

Cape Breton University Press   Sold and Distributed by
PO Box 5300   Nimbus Publishing
Sydney, Nova Scotia B1P 6L2   3731 MacKintosh St
Canada   Halifax, Nova Scotia B3K 5A5
                                      Canada

Contents

Preface

Memory, Diversity and Regeneration

In his 1971 classic, *Minetown, Milltown, Railtown*, sociologist Rex A. Lucas argued that Canadian company towns have "few past memories" and a "short past." They depend on "impersonal forces" (Lucas 1971: 20).

The authors in this book present a different portrait. Yes, company towns have appeared, lived and declined because of global economic forces. But they reflect these forces in distinctive—and personal— ways. They have inspired attachment and a sense of place. They can be tight-knit but also quintessentially global. They served far-off markets while housing a mosaic of newcomers from around the world. They speak to the diversity of Canada and the immigrant experience. Their landscapes are a kind of language that conveys rich and layered stories. They are hands-on classrooms of culture, economics, architecture, politics and sociology. These company towns mean a great deal to the people who put down roots there or passed through them. The houses became homes.

Taken together, the case studies in this book speak to the enduring value of these places. Richard MacKinnon reveals how the architectural styles of the thousands of company houses in Cape Breton, even the most modest, reflect the aspirations of the industrial revolution and the resistance to some of the effects of heavy industry. Impersonal building plans were personalized over time by coal and steel workers and their families. Alex Forbes assesses the formidable personality of Alexander "Boss" Gibson and his vision for Marysville, New Brunswick. Gibson's patriarchal, but also benevolent and complex, behaviour moulds the character and culture of the community generations after the founder's death. Gail Weir shows that a post-industrial cultural landscape—Wabana, Bell Island, Newfoundland—can become a storytelling landscape, a landscape that reveals important facts and nuances about the lives of the iron-ore workers and their families, including her own family. Today, this landscape—and the people who live in it and on it, and who study it—share those stories with visitors, including tourists.

Affirming collective identities is a struggle. Lucie K. Morisset and Jessica Mace document how the strong sense of identity of Arvida, Quebec, survived municipal amalgamation and the attempts by public bodies to subsume the autonomy of the city founded by a large aluminum company. The seeds of Arvida's sense of self were embedded in the original utopian designs. These designs and ideals are now celebrated as Arvida seeks international heritage recognition. Tom Urbaniak looks at contested interpretations of cultural identity in Kaszuby, Ontario, a non-industrial "intentional community" in eastern Ontario. It is a more recent kind of "company" town that nonetheless draws on the names and symbols of the 19th-century Polish Kashub settlers and their descendants. It is also a window on how globalization can actually contribute to the resurgence of local and regional cultures and identities.

Today, the health and survival of these towns requires a different kind of entrepreneur – a social entrepreneur, a policy entrepreneur, a network of activists and grassroots risk-takers who can create the soil for new things to grow, albeit with reference to the old. Barbara Hogan, Lyn Bleiler, Anne Leckie, Rob McIntyre and Marc Johnston take us to Elsa, referred to as Yukon's last company town. Can environmental remediation revive its prospects and help save some of its vestiges—and with those vestiges the enduring memories of a remarkable cross-cultural experience? And by reflecting on a demonstration project in which they were involved, Andrew Molloy and Tom Urbaniak profile the difficulties but also very real opportunities to revitalize homes and neighbourhoods in the post-industrial Cape Breton Regional Municipality.

This book suggests that heritage status and recognition can affect quality of life and community survival. Heritage designations—local or national—have helped some of these communities. Marysville's status as a national historic district is a form of certification, an affirmation of legitimacy. The national recognition did not trigger strict local regulations, but it has reinforced careful stewardship and public attention whenever the fabric of the community is threatened. The Wabana Iron Ore Mines National Historic Site appears to be slowly doing the same for Bell Island, along with other designations, murals, publications, an interpretive museum and even dramatic productions. In Glace Bay, the heritage designation of a company house—the first such designation in the region—gave a boost to the volunteers who were renovating it for affordable housing. It sent the message that this is living history in an evolving community, not just a static artifact.

Long after the company captains and their enterprises have left the scene, a place's character, values, behaviour and politics are influenced by its founding moments, its founding organizations and its early inhabitants. The overarching role of "Boss" Gibson arguably makes contemporary Marysville more amenable to leadership from benevolent public dignitaries as opposed to upstart small businesspeople. It would be hard to live and work in Kaszuby without understanding the hardship of the Polish Kashub settlers and the longings (sometimes wounds) of the more recent immigrants, their enduring cultural project and the deep pride that their histories have engendered.

And so the ability to make a successful transition has much to do with the DNA of a place. What were its founding moments? What were the early institutions and organizations that forged a spirit of place? How have these shaped the character of the community and made it more or less entrepreneurial when faced with the sometimes-urgent need to re-orient the local economy and find new vocations?

In Arvida, the aluminum company created civic organizational structures, public places and public art. A form of democratic engagement, as well as private ownership of homes, but subject to aesthetic covenants, was encouraged. In Glace Bay, Nova Scotia, and Bell Island, Newfoundland, the founding elites were less public-spirited. When mines closed there, and with them the vibrant labour unions, much of the infrastructure for creative regeneration and community-building had to be built from the bottom up, a process that is still ongoing.

These sorts of economic and social considerations are seeping into the consciousness of those who work on and champion heritage conservation in Canada. Heritage conservation—even architectural conservation—is about much, much more than buildings, although buildings are crucial to the mix.

The National Trust for Canada has adopted strategic directions that link the power of place to the regeneration of struggling communities, youth engagement, cultural diversity and the creation of economic opportunities. Over the past few years, these emphases have resonated at national conferences, headlined by the likes of centres for social innovations, the economic success story of Membertou First Nation in Nova Scotia and the development of the local-food movement. Even when dealing with buildings, "we are in the people business" is a refrain often heard from the Trust's volunteers and staff.

These kinds of directions require a thoughtful and organic approach to public policy.

Being thoughtful about public policy sometimes means fewer regulations, not more, to encourage the regeneration of historic communities. Take the cumbersome provincially mandated tax-sale system in the Cape Breton Regional Municipality, which made it difficult for a willing non-profit housing organization to acquire and renovate any of the 800 vacant homes in the municipality, a municipality where there is a demonstrated need for decent affordable housing. Under the operative provincial legislation, deteriorating properties languish for years without municipal ability to transfer title to willing organizations. Consider how by-laws in many municipalities thwart the adaptive reuse of a building because of requirements for building setbacks, parking, or even the exigencies of officials who are not familiar with the alternative measures enabled by "objectives-based" (as opposed to literally based) building codes.

At the federal level, it took the 2004 intervention of the auditor general to hold the government of Canada accountable for the environmental-liability costs associated with a number of abandoned mines. This made it possible for a new mine owner in the Elsa area to operate without assuming the liability of long-gone previous owners. Besides providing employment opportunities, the new owner has repurposed some of the remaining buildings in Elsa.

Another take-home message is that places need champions. In the 1950s, Fr. Rafal Grzondziel helped Kaszuby, with its marginal farms and out-migration, to find an additional vocation through a connection with the Polish Scouting movement. In the 2000s, local leaders championed the area's longstanding Kashubian language, customs and culture. In Marysville, the intervention of a provincial politician who threatened to resign pushed the government of the day to take over the former cotton mill and convert it to government offices.

When we think of the future of company towns, we need approaches that can bring together champions, diverse policies, local wisdom and, sometimes, technical expertise. In that regard, organizations like the National Trust are rediscovering and updating some of the tools in their toolkits. The National Trust's "Main Street Canada" program involves not just downtown thoroughfares and abutting buildings but regions and systems and economies. The national crowdfunding "This Place Matters" program is proving to be a catalyst for new ideas.

As we mark the 150th anniversary of Confederation in 2017, we should think of how these efforts can be tied together in a national project of regeneration, one that creates opportunity, one that is not so quick to accept obsolescence and a throwaway culture. Adaptation, creative planning, re-purposing, the cultivation of new small businesses, the arts and the challenge of "place-making" can be part of the equation of equity, opportunity, diversity and beauty.

The places in this book, the people who gave them meaning, and the people who cherish them still, can be part of that national project of regeneration. They should be part of our national legacy.

—

The editors would like to thank the contributors for their dedication, rigour, patience, and their passion for understanding communities and for applied research as a means of public service.

Mike Hunter of Cape Breton University Press provided exceptional support for this project over a period of almost five years. We are grateful to Cape Breton University for its support, to our students and colleagues for creating an excellent working environment, and to Academic Vice President Dale Keefe for his encouragement. Alison Etter gave thorough feedback and editorial advice on major components of this book. We are also fortunate to work with selfless volunteers and activists locally and nationally. We feel blessed to know them and we continue to learn from them.

Tom Urbaniak
Andrew Molloy
Sydney, Nova Scotia
September 2016

Reference

Lucas, Rex A. 1971. *Minetown, Milltown, Railtown: Life in Canadian Communities of Single Industry*. Toronto: University of Toronto Press.

Chapter One

Richard MacKinnon

A Typology of Cape Breton Company Housing

The built landscape reveals much about human beings and their relationship to land, work and culture. Architecture has been explored from a variety of perspectives, including art and architectural history, cultural geography, folklore, archaeology and industrial archaeology. While each of these disciplines studies what we call "architecture," each has its own way of interpreting buildings and landscapes. Despite the variety of methodologies and approaches, one of the first steps required for most studies is the conception of a typology of buildings in a specific cultural region. Cultural geographer Fred Kniffen's seminal study in the 1960s demonstrated the value of this kind of detailed work to scholars. For Kniffen, "folk housing" includes all human habitations, barns and outbuildings of the folk or common people. Kniffen set up a typology "quantified as to numerical importance and qualified as to areal and temporal position, and to seek out origins, routes of diffusion, adaptations and other processes affecting change or stability" (Kniffen 1965: 550). His study was a massive undertaking, taking into account "the whole eastern United States from the Gulf to the Lakes and from the Atlantic to the Mississippi" (550).

This chapter is more modest; it attempts to provide a typology of the extant company housing on Cape Breton Island, Nova Scotia. Now a largely deindustrialized region, Cape Breton was once heavily industrialized, complete with coal mines, quarries and steel mills.

Although much of the mining and steel infrastructure has been dismantled since 2000, the houses of the former industrial workers are evident throughout the landscape, revealing much about the region's industrial past.

Geographers such as Yi-Fu Tuan, Donald Meinig, Edward Relph and J. B. Jackson study cultural landscapes and eloquently discuss how human beings transform spaces into meaningful places (Tuan 1974, 2004; Jackson 1980, 1994; Jackson and Zube 1970; Meinig and Jackson 1979; Relph 1976, 2000). These explorations under their purview of cultural landscape include: nature, the forest and the various ways human beings transform land and waterscapes; the naming of landscape features; and the spiritual nature of land and seascapes. What is also termed "the built environment," and corresponding spatial relationships, are also a major component of their gaze. The built environment includes all structures made by human beings, including all forms of architecture, from skyscrapers to churches to homes and outbuildings.

An ethnographic approach to the built environment, which includes conducting fieldwork by taking photographs and doing measured drawings of floorplans, is a technique often employed by folklorists who have studied vernacular architecture and the built environment. Extending the scope of research beyond the library or the archive to include fieldwork allows researchers to traverse the landscape to look at, photograph and measure buildings in an attempt to understand these unique cultural artifacts. Folklorist Henry Glassie, who has explored architecture, material culture, oral tradition and landscape in areas as diverse as Ireland, Afghanistan, Turkey and the United States, has influenced the scope of this research immensely. He has demonstrated that it is important to examine both tangible and intangible culture in order to understand the personality of distinctive places (Glassie 1969, 1972, 1975, 1982, 1999, 2000). One of the few Atlantic Canadian studies to explore traditional buildings and culture in a similar way is found in Gerald Pocius's *A Place to Belong* (1991). Pocius recorded and analyzed the buildings, spaces and traditions of a Newfoundland fishing outport prior to the contemporary demise of the East Coast fishery. The cultural-landscape patterns, usage and built structures that he records represent at least a 400-year history that, with the collapse of the regional fishery, has suddenly been shaken. Pocius's book includes examples of unique vernacular building types distinctive to Newfoundland, such as fishing stages and flakes (for drying fish) that are no longer part of the landscape, and contains considerable local and traditional environmental knowledge. However, he clearly points out that the people of this outport community live in two worlds: one modern, with satellite dishes and contemporary popular culture, and one past, which is continually being re-enacted through stories, songs and oral history. When people are asked, "Where are you from?" they respond by saying, "I belong to Calvert." The book explores the myriad ways people "belong" to this place and provides a clear understanding of how people in rural communities develop a sense of place. Architect Robert Mellin (2003) also provides a model for studying the built landscape through his detailed survey, including photographs and measured drawings, of all buildings in the Newfoundland outport of Tilting, Fogo Island.

In most studies of Atlantic Canadian architecture, with a few notable exceptions, the housing of miners and steelworkers is ignored (among the exceptions, Latremouille 1988; MacKinnon 1982a, 1996, 1998; MacLeod and St. Clair 1992, 1994; Ennals and Holdsworth 1998; Holdsworth 1984). Usually, the architectural books of the region focus on the homes of well-known or affluent citizens, political leaders or captains of industry (Byers and McBurney 1994; Comiter and Pacey 1988; Pacey and Comiter 1994). Churches and houses of worship feature prominently in many regional architecture studies (Pacey, Rogers and Duffus 1983; Hyde and Bird 1995). In the British Isles, however, there have been numerous important studies of the buildings of industrial communities, including those found in coal-mining districts.

As with the British Isles, Cape Breton Island was heavily influenced by the Industrial Revolution, which began in the 18th century and continued throughout the 19th and early 20th centuries (Frank 1971, 1983, 1986, 1999; Hornsby 1992; MacGillivray 1974; Muise 1980). The first commercial coal mine in North America began production in Cape Breton, at Baie de Mordienne (now Port Morien), around 1720. Known locally as "the French Mine," this primitive drift mine supplied coal by boat to the burgeoning Fortress of Louisbourg on the Atlantic coast. As geographer Stephen Hornsby notes, "Between 1786 and 1827, the [British] Colonial Government and local entrepreneurs alternated in operating a small coal mine at Sydney Mines on the north side of Sydney Harbour" (Hornsby 1989: 423). Throughout the 18th century, coal mining was in its infancy; mining technology was simple and the Sydney mines only employed "about 50 seasonal workers" who produced no more than 13,000 tons of coal per year (ibid.).

As the 19th century unfolded, mines expanded throughout Nova Scotia, and as historian Ian McKay has noted, strikes, labour unrest and struggles for better pay and working conditions became common (McKay 1986: 18). Richard Brown, a 19th-century Sydney Mines coal master, lived in an ornate mansion while miners lived in poorly constructed brick-and-wood row housing in close proximity to the mine. Class structure was clearly defined in the industrial landscape; this was true not only in Cape Breton, but in most of Nova Scotia's coal communities during the 19th century.

What kinds of buildings were lived in by Cape Breton's working-class families?

Typology of Company Housing in Cape Breton

To begin to develop a typology of workers' housing for Cape Breton, I will focus on the island coal towns of New Waterford and Sydney Mines, and the steel city of Sydney. While this will not provide a complete typology for the island, the patterns common in these communities are a representative sample of the kinds of dwellings commonly found throughout the region. These communities represent single-industry towns of the 19th and 20th centuries, or what are sometimes called company towns.

> A company town is an entity created by a corporation for the purpose of encapsulating the work and leisure of employees into one environment, with residential and commercial ownership in the hands of the company. (Katers 2010)

New Waterford

Like many industrial Cape Breton communities, the town of New Waterford owes its existence to coal. It's been a mixed blessing, causing the community to flourish during boom times and suffer greatly during busts or, particularly, during disasters, such as the New Waterford mine explosion of 1917, when 65 men and boys of the community met their deaths in the No. 12 colliery.[1] Geographically, the town is laid out on a grid pattern along the eastern mouth of Sydney Harbour. The grid—a form of community development that dates back to Roman times—was a common form of spatial layout for many of the company towns in Atlantic Canada. Thus, one finds First, Second and Third Streets, for example, in New Waterford, but also in other mining towns in the Atlantic region, including Inverness and Stellarton, Nova Scotia, and Wabana, Bell Island, Newfoundland. New Waterford's population is largely made up of Scots, Irish and Acadians, but also includes minority Italians, Ukrainians, West Indians and Newfoundlanders who came to mine the coal in the early years of the 20th century (Boutilier 1963, 1988). Italians, eastern Europeans and Caribbean blacks settled in the area of town known as "No. 14 Yard," alongside the now-defunct No. 14 colliery and in close proximity to the Lingan and Phalen collieries, closed in 1992 and 2000, respectively (see figure 1). Many Gaelic families moved to New Waterford from the town of Inverness on the western side of Cape Breton in 1938, when mines started closing in that region. These people settled in an area adjacent to New Waterford known locally as "Scotchtown" (Boutilier 1963, 1988).

But coal mining had actually become important near New Waterford soon after Europeans began to visit Cape Breton Island.

Fig. 1 – Company houses near the Dominion Number 14 coal mine and yard, New Waterford, ca. 1910. Beaton Institute, Cape Breton University: Mines and Mining. 80-852-5032.

DOMINION NO 14 COLLIERY NEW WATERFORD N S CANADA

Fig. 2 – Lingan Colliery, 1873. Canadian Illustrated News. *77-469-603. Beaton Institute, Cape Breton University.*

In the 18th century, coal there was dug along the coastline, near Baie de L'Indienne, a few miles from the present-day town of New Waterford. Coal dug from primitive drift mines located near the bay's cliffs, where coal seams were exposed, provided fuel for the stoves of Louisbourg in the early years of the 18th century. In 1827, the General Mining Association, a British company, started mining in Lingan and continued mining until 1886 (figure 2). The General Mining Association also operated the Victoria mine in Low Point by 1865, and continued mining there until 1882, when a new mine was established in nearby New Victoria (Hornsby 1992: 178). Another GMA mine was developed in 1867 at the site of Barrachois Cove, within present-day New Waterford (Boutilier 1988: 2). The company had a monopoly on all the coal seams of Nova Scotia until the mid-19th century.

While some housing was constructed in the Lingan area by General Mining in the mid-19th century, none of the buildings are extant. Much of New Waterford's existing housing was not constructed until the boom-town environment of the early 20th century. In 1907, DOSCO (the Dominion Steel and Coal Corporation) opened No. 12 colliery in New Waterford and began building "company houses" there. By the time New Waterford was incorporated (1913), there were three other collieries operating within the town limits: Nos. 14, 15 and 16. By 1915, most of the town's company houses were completed (Boutilier 1963; Boone 1990; Muise 1980). Housing was rented to miners, with rent deducted from their paycheques, a practice locally referred to as "the check off." Maintenance of housing, fences and outbuildings was the responsibility of the company, which provided carpenters to do such work.

By the mid-1920s, the coal and steel industries were in trouble, and there was little incentive or money to improve industrial housing in Cape Breton. A royal commission on the coal industry in Nova Scotia, convened in 1925, reported that "the housing, domestic surroundings and sanitary conditions of the mines are, with few exceptions, absolutely wretched" (Royal Commission on Coal 1925). By the 1940s, Dominion Steel and Coal Company began to sell its houses to residents at a price of $550 per house (Boone 1990).

The typology used in this chapter was developed by travelling by car through the streets of New Waterford, taking photographs of buildings, and counting and categorizing buildings. I was born there, and have spent time in and visited many of these houses; my knowledge of the floor plans and layout of such homes comes from personal experience. The diagnostic architectural features I use in developing this typology include exterior features such as height, size and roof style, along with interior floor plans.

In order to follow my line of reporting here, it is important to understand a concept central to much folklore scholarship—the concept of types and versions. When folklorists study narratives, songs or buildings, they have found that there are distinct types, such as the tale of Cinderella, the 17th-century ballad "Barbara Allen" or the architectural type known as the English barn. What you have throughout the Western world are various versions or performances of this story, song or barn—some long, some short, some very detailed, some sparsely so, some large in size, some smaller. What you have is a distinct type with unique variations on the form, not unlike the manner of jazz music, where a musician takes a distinct form and improvises on that form within established precepts. Following this thinking, I suggest that there are five distinctive types of company-built housing extant in New Waterford, with their own variant versions:

1. **Two versions of single, detached houses built in rows**
2. **Four versions of duplexes (double houses) in rows**
3. **Boarding houses**
4. **Shacks**
5. **Management houses**

Type 1
1.1 – The single, detached, two-room floor-plan miner's cottage, with symmetrical facade.

1.2 – The single, detached, two-thirds Georgian floor-plan type, with three rooms.

Type 2

2.1 – Duplex, two-thirds Georgian plan, with back kitchen form.

2.2 – Duplex, two-thirds Georgian plan, with a central, triangular dormer cutting the roof line.

2.3 – Duplex, two-thirds Georgian plan, with shallow or mono-pitched roof.

2.4 – Duplex, two-thirds Georgian plan.

Type 3

Boarding houses, sometimes called "hotels" by town residents – built for single men, boarders and for families waiting to access other company-house styles.

Type 4

"Shacks" – temporary houses for single men near mine sites.

Type 5

Management houses

Type 1.1

This single, detached, one-and-a-half storey, two-room miner's cottage with symmetrical facade (see figure 3) was one of the earliest forms of company housing in New Waterford. Also seen in Bell Island and Sydney Mines, this type was made for miners' families and is found on Heelan Street and First Street (now Lower Wood Avenue), New Waterford, near the site of the former No. 16 mine (MacKinnon 1982a).

The Type 1.1 form is basically a two-room plan with a kitchen/dining area in the small rear extension and a parlour at the front of the home, facing the

Fig. 3 – Single, detached, one-and-a-half storey, two-room miner's cottage with symmetrical facade. Lower Wood Avenue, New Waterford. Photo by Richard MacKinnon, 2016.

road. There are two bedrooms on the upper floor. Some had wing-like side extensions that contained a small pantry off the kitchen and an entry porch. There are not many of these types still standing in New Waterford. Two are extant on Heelan Street and four are still standing on Lower Wood Avenue. In appearance, these houses are similar to the standard "I" house form, a common 19th-century vernacular form seen throughout New England (Soloman 1985; Kniffen 1986). One interesting decorative embellishment is the use of classical "returned eaves," a common feature of 19th-century Classical Revival architectural styles (Maitland 1984; Fredericton Heritage Trust 1982; Hamlin 1964 [1944]).

Type 1.2

The most common detached company-house form in New Waterford is the so-called two-thirds Georgian plan, with the front entrance in the short side of the house, facing the road (see figure 4). It possesses a main entrance on one side of the gable with a hallway and two rooms, a front room and kitchen, back-to-back off the hall (see floor plan figure 5). The kitchen usually contains a very small pantry at the rear or on the side. There is usually a small back porch, where coats are hung, and a coal shed in the backyard (in the past there would have been an outhouse as well). There are some slight variations on this plan. In

Fig. 4 – Type 1.2 Gable-entry, two-thirds Georgian workers plan. Photo by Richard MacKinnon.

some houses, the hallway is walled in, completely separating the front room and the kitchen; in others, the hallway is not walled in, allowing for a clear view from the front entry through to the rear kitchen. In some there are two upper-floor bedrooms; in others, there are three and sometimes four upper-floor bedrooms. The house dimensions were typically 27 x 21 ft., 25 x 19 ft., 23 x 17 ft., or 21 x 15 ft. (8 x 6.5 m, 7.6 x 5.8 m, 7 x 5 m, 6.5 x 4.5 m).

This form is comparable in plan to what Glassie (1986) calls the "two-thirds Georgian" house. Glassie argues that New England builders in the 18th and 19th centuries modified the Georgian house by constructing one-third and two-third portions of the form. Not only was the modified form popular in rural regions, but Glassie points out that when town builders searched for architectural forms, Georgian subtypes were chosen, indicating a traditional element in mid-Atlantic town plan-

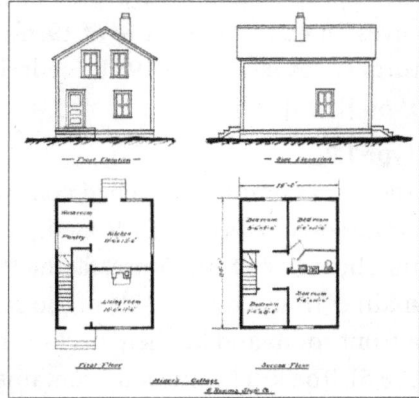

Fig. 5 – Miner's Cottage "Style F," 1906. Plan 567-Y. Beaton Institute, Cape Breton University.

ning: "the narrow, deep proportions of the one-third and two-thirds Georgian subtypes made them suited to small lots and crowded situations" (Glassie 1972: 403).[2]

This two-room floor plan was comparable to a common 19th-century floor plan found throughout much of eastern North America: the hall-and-parlour plan. However, these homes were markedly different from the majority of Cape Breton's 19th-century homes in that the front door is located in the gable end of the house, facing the roadway. This form is also called the "side-hall house" or the "gable-front house," with a main entrance off to one side on the end gable. The form is said to have emerged in North America as early as the 1830s (Glassie 1969: 54-56; Noble 1984: 107-109).

The Georgian subtype grew largely out of the late-18th-century interest in classical forms, which promoted the architectural style called Classical Revival so popular in religious, public and domestic buildings from the 1820s until the 1860s.[3] Thomas Hubka points out that New England farmers readily incorporated this form into their building repertoire after the 1830s, at a time when there was a considerable reorganization of space on New England farms (Hubka 1985: 38-39). Moreover, he argues that the primary appeal to Americans of the Classical style was nationalistic; it became a symbol of the new American republic, which was attempting to build a nation based on Classical ideals: "The image of Greece and Rome became a symbol of progress" (196). The adding of simple, rudimentary classic decoration in the form of returned eaves or raised cornices appears on many of the non-company houses using this style, giving a "temple front" appearance.

As the century progressed, it became one of the most common house forms throughout New England: "its basic form became a standard component of New England housing during the latter half of the nineteenth century" (39). Geographers Peter Ennals and Deryck Holdsworth (1981) have shown that this form was common throughout the Maritimes at the end of the 19th century. More than 130 houses of this type, with gabled roofs, gambrel roofs, half-hipped roofs, flat roofs and side additions, all dating from the end of the 19th century, are found in the rural communities of Inverness County, one of the noted source areas for the New Waterford mining community (MacKinnon 1982a). Mining families would have been familiar with this floor-plan type. Companies chose this plan because it allowed for the arrangement of more houses in smaller spaces. In New Waterford, these houses are situated on:

Street	No. of houses remaining	Mine
King Street (formerly 11th St.)	14	No. 14
12th Street	28	No. 14
Lower Plummer Avenue	6	No. 16
Park Street	14	No. 16
Ling Street	8	No. 12

This type of house was popular in New Waterford and in other mining communities such as Bell Island (see figure 6). Furthermore, when miners had the finances available to build their own houses, separate from the company-provided homes, this template was frequently employed.

Type 2.1

All Type 2 houses are duplexes set in rows and constructed on the grid-patterned streets of the town. Company-built duplexes constituted the majority of company houses in New Waterford, and are the most common company house form still extant. The basic duplex form has a gable roof and a three-room ground-floor plan of a front room, dining room and kitchen, with three bedrooms in the upstairs (see figure 7). The kitchen is situated in a back addition that was integral to the house at the time of construction. Families who lived in the two-room company forms preferred to live in this type, primarily because of the larger back kitchen, the extra bedroom and the larger space for living. This was also the most common form constructed in some of the nearby Cape Breton mining communities. A local history of Glace Bay states:

> Messrs. Rhodes Curry and Co. Ltd. were given a contract to build one thousand double houses; two new towns sprung up—Dominion Number four with 300 houses.... Dominion Number two with 300 houses.... The old collieries had their housing augmented, Caledonia getting some forty new double houses, Dominion about sixty and Reserve, sixty.... Eighteen large boarding houses were erected which could accommodate fourteen hundred men.[4]

Fig.6 – Bell Island, Newfoundland company house. Photo by Richard MacKinnon.

Fig. 7 – Duplex form has a gable roof and a three-room ground-floor plan of a front room, dining room and kitchen, with three bedrooms in the upstairs. Warren Avenue, New Waterford. Photo by Richard MacKinnon, 2016.

A social worker who visited industrial Cape Breton in 1925 provides a detailed description of these double houses:

The company owns the several hundred houses in which are housed the godly several thousand miners' families. These houses were built cheaply and quickly, with a view to hurried, raw, camp life for bachelors. If these bachelors took wives unto themselves, and if their children came to them, look out! Nobody cares. The houses are all of the same proportion, style and cheap lumber. Each house is of 8 or 9 rooms, divided by a thin wooden partition into two parts, and is called a double house. In each part of 4 rooms, one or two families live, no matter how large. Each shack is a straight up and down affair, painted a dull slate color originally, and is now a muddy dirt hue. On the inside the rooms are divided off by a single coat of plaster or wooden wall, and give one a "jack in the box" feeling of closeness. There are no porches; from the low wooden single doorstep, one walks in on the family to the kitchen or bedroom. (Gold 1925)

In New Waterford, these houses are situated on 8th, 9th and 10th Streets; George, Thompson and Acadia Streets for No. 14 mine; Mount Carmel Avenue (originally Church Street) for No. 14 mine; and on Plummer, Warren, Wood, Wilson and Duggan avenues for No. 16 mine. Houses of this kind are common in the nearby community of New Victoria, where the No. 18 mine and the Victoria mine were formerly situated.[5]

Type 2.2

This type is similar to version 2.1, except for the addition of a central Gothic dormer on the facade gabled roof (see figure 8). Its plan is almost identical to a three-room plan consisting of a front room (sometimes called a parlour), a dining room and a kitchen to the rear of the house on the ground floor, and three bedrooms on the upper floor. This form has a gabled roof with a large central dormer cutting the roofline. This shallow-pitched central dormer hints at the Gothic Revival style that began to appear in the Maritimes in the early years of the 19th century and was common throughout by the century's end (Penny 1989; Ennals and Holdsworth 1981). In New Waterford, this form is limited to Lower King Street, near the No. 14 mine. There are eight double houses still standing there. This type is also found in other Cape Breton mining and steel communities, including Glace Bay and the Victoria Road row in Sydney (figure 9).

Type 2.3

Type 2.3 duplexes, like other duplexes in the town, have a two-thirds Georgian floor plan with a front room, dining room and back kitchen on the ground floor, a stairwell leading to the upper storey and three bedrooms upstairs. Type 2.3 is marked by a shallow- or mono-pitched roof, reminiscent of houses constructed throughout

Fig. 8 – Duplex form with central Gothic dormer. King Street, New Waterford. Photo by Richard MacKinnon, 2016.

rural Newfoundland at the turn of the 19th/20th century (Mills 1977; Ennals and Holdsworth 1981). There is no agreement on the historical development of this form.

A study in Newfoundland (Pocius 1991) suggests that this flatter roof style arrived in Atlantic Canada at the end of the 19th century, when the late-Victorian Italianate and Second Empire architectural styles were sweeping North America. Their existence indicates a vernacular interpretation of these international styles. This flatter pitched roof emerged at the turn of the 20th century, when new forms of roofing materials, such as tarpaper and roofing felt, were made available to the general public. This may have enabled builders to deviate from established gable forms common in the region before this date. There are only two double houses of this kind still standing, both on Upper

Fig. 9 – Victoria Road (Sydney) duplex form with central Gothic dormer. Coke Ovens at rear. Photo by Richard MacKinnon, 1998.

George Street, near the original site of the No. 15 mine. Houses of this kind are also found in nearby Glace Bay, in the Hub and No. 2 mine areas, where large numbers of Newfoundland emigrants settled to work the coal mines (figure 10). More fieldwork might reveal that Newfoundland miners may have brought this style to Cape Breton, as this shallow, pitched-roof style was common throughout Newfoundland by the early 20th century.

Fig. 10 – Shallow- or mono-pitched-roof company house. George Street, New Waterford. Photo by Richard MacKinnon, 2016.

Type 2.4

This type of duplex was also very common. It is a scaled-down, smaller version of Type 2.1. Its floor plan consists of a front room, which takes up the entire width of the house, and a small kitchen situated in a small back addition. There are two

Fig. 11 – Smaller, scaled-down version of type 2.1 house, 13th Street, New Waterford. Photo by Richard MacKinnon, 2016.

bedrooms in the upstairs. Oral histories suggest these buildings are some of the oldest still standing in New Waterford.

Street	No. of houses remaining	Mine
Lr. King Street (formerly 11th St.)	8	No. 14
13th Street	12	No. 14
14th Street	2	No. 14
Lower Park Street	3	No. 16

There are two of these double houses that have been transformed into one-half units. Half of a duplex is sometimes torn down—after a fire, for example; the undamaged half is left standing as a single-family dwelling. In a sense, these houses are a half version of the standard "I" house, a common 19th-century vernacular form throughout much of eastern North America.

Type 3

I call this type a boarding house, although they were often called "hotels" by locals. With the boom of the early 20th century there was a shortage of housing for workers. The company, along with private citizens, constructed large two- and three-storey boarding houses to accommodate single workers, as well as families (figure 12). Miners would stay in these buildings until a duplex or detached company house became available for rent. Married men would often then send for their families. The wait could be a few months. Some of these buildings developed local names such as the "Red Onion," the "Victoria Hotel" or the "Acadian Hotel."

This form of housing was also common in the Whitney Pier neighbourhood of Sydney during construction of the steel plant, and in frontier mining communities (Black [n.d.]) (see figure 13). In New Waterford, there are two of these boarding houses still standing, although they have been extensively renovated as apartment buildings. One is at the corner of Arthur Street and Plummer Avenue, near the site of the former No. 14 colliery; the other is on Ling Street, near the former No. 12 colliery.

Fig. 12 – Scotia House on Lingan Road in Whitney Pier, ca. 1912. Photographer unknown. 91-649-22610. Beaton Institute, Cape Breton University.

This idea of constructing a large shelter for many workers was not new at the turn of the 19th/20th century. Seventeenth and 18th-century fishing establishments in Atlantic Canada regularly employed large "cook rooms" to house the migratory fishermen who regularly visited (Story, Kirwin and Widdowson 1982: 113). Early-19th-century miners' houses in Cape Breton were also referred to as barracks and cook rooms. J. S. Martell quotes Richard Brown as saying that before 1827 Irish miners lived in these kinds of houses near Sydney:

Fig. 13 – Boarding house, Dominion, n.d. Courtesy Len Stephenson collection, Dominion Historical Society.

All the men except the two overmen and four mechanics lived in two barracks or cook rooms (as they were called), where they took their meals and slept in the same apartments. Their sleeping berths were ranged along the sides of the two rooms in tiers, one above the other, as in a ship. It may easily be imagined what sort of a place the cook room was, where forty men ate, slept and washed—when they did wash, which was only once a week—in a single apartment. In winter, it is true, they had abundant means of making it warm enough, which is about all that can be said in its favor; in the summer it became so very lively that most of the men preferred sleeping during the fine weather under the spruce trees in the vicinity. It could hardly be expected that either harmony or good order prevailed in two rooms occupied by 80 or 90 men under such conditions where all were upon equal terms and free from restraint. Brawling and fighting seemed to be the order. (Martell 1980: 52)

Most of these large boarding houses, following from this early cook-room model, now exist only in the memories of individuals who grew up in Cape Breton mining and steel towns.

Fig. 14 – Floorplan of boarding house, 1906. Plan 552-Y. Beaton Institute, Cape Breton University.

Type 4

Type 4 houses are locally called "shacks"—small, one-storey, temporary structures built for single men and situated close to the mine sites (see figure 15). Few of these houses still exist, having been torn down, modified, moved or renovated to suit new purposes.[6] Accounts describe these units as minimal, consisting of one or two rooms. The moniker "shacks" was also applied to these houses because they were constructed using discarded materials ranging from tarpaper to shingles. The term "shacks" is applied to these houses in Bell Island and in other frontier mining communities (MacKinnon 1982a).

In New Waterford, the term "company shacks" is also given to one-storey rows of four units built close to the mine sites. Each unit had one large multi-functional space—a combined kitchen/parlour— and two small bedrooms. Known in the local vernacular as "[No.]12 shacks," "[No.]14 shacks" and "[No.]16 shacks," each row was built close to the respective mine site. The row closest to the No. 12 colliery was also known as the "red row." These rows no longer exist in the town; however, oral accounts suggest that some parts of these buildings have been re-used in the construction of private homes in areas near mine sites.[7]

Fig. 15 – Shacks near Franklin Mine Florence, 1946. Photographer unknown. 96-1021-27715. 1946. Beaton Institute, Cape Breton University.

Type 5

There are two management houses remaining in New Waterford, one on Ellsworth Avenue, across from the former No. 12 colliery, and one on Smith Street that is now a doctor's office.

Sydney

The pattern of Sydney's company housing is similar to that found in New Waterford, with single-family dwellings, duplexes and boarding houses in the Ashby and Whitney Pier districts of the city.

While New Waterford's housing was constructed for coal miners, much of Sydney's housing was built for steel workers. With the construction of the Sydney steel plant by Dominion Iron and Steel Corporation (DISCO) commencing in 1899, and the concomitant economic boom in Sydney, construction of workers' housing began in earnest. Sydney's population grew from 3,200 in 1899 to 9,900 in 1901, and to 22,000 in 1913 (Black [n.d.]: 1). As Crawley (1990: 145) wrote:

> The establishment of the Sydney Steel industry at the turn of the century came on the heels of the vast expansion in the Cape Breton coal industry. A syndicate of Canadian and American capitalists, headed by Henry Melville Whitney of Boston, formed the Dominion Coal Company in 1893 and obtained a 99 year lease of the unworked resources of the Sydney coal fields.

Rapid industrialization brought about many changes to Sydney. With this transformation, the small, independent producer was displaced by the wage earner; "Sydney had become predominantly a community of wage labourers" (150). There were many problems facing the city during this period, including a lack of proper sanitation and housing, and the working classes had a difficult life. Crawley wrote:

> The working life of a Sydney steelworker in the early twentieth century consisted of low wages and poor working conditions. He usually worked a thirteen hour night-shift or an eleven hour day-shift, six days a week, with no extra pay for overtime, Sundays and holidays. Most steelworkers at Sydney earned between $1.35 and $1.75 per day, the lowest rate usually paid to the unskilled immigrant workers, the highest to the Anglo-Saxon skilled workers. (Crawley 1990: 154)

In addressing a meeting of the Canadian Political Science Association in 1913, Bryce Stewart described Sydney's company housing. In essence, he said there were too few houses in the city to meet the needs of the burgeoning population. In 1909, DISCO owned 142 houses, yet there were 303 applications for housing on file with the company (Stewart 1913: 13). He points out that there were various ethnic groups living in the company-owned housing around the steel plant and coke ovens. These included Austrians, Russians, Poles, Italians, West Indians from Barbados, Newfoundlanders and native Cape Bretoners.

Stewart closely examined one block enclosed by Tupper Street, Lingan Road and Laurier Street in the area of Sydney known as Whitney Pier. There were twenty-seven families with seventy children, four widows and 130 male boarders living in this block, for a total of 257 residents. Of these, there were 172 Italians, twenty-two Austrians, twenty-two Poles, fifteen Canadians, eleven Hungarians, eight black people (the source does not identify their nationality), four Spaniards and three Russians. The average rent on the block was $11.94 per month. His survey indicates there were five different types of houses in this neighbourhood: double houses, three family houses, five family houses, one family house (shack) and one family house with store. Eleven houses had inside toilets and all had water connection. The average number of people in each house was 13.5 (Stewart 1913: 13).

On another block, between Victoria Road and Tupper Street, there were twenty-one families with forty-seven male boarders. The ethnic makeup of this block included fifty-eight British, twenty-three black people, twenty-two Italians, seventeen Austrians, eleven Russians, three Assyrians and two Germans, for a total population of 136 (the Austro-Hungarian and Russian empires encompassed multiple nationalities). He indicates that about half these houses had electricity and a bath and toilet. The rental houses in this neighbourhood were old and small, and the average monthly rent was $10.30. On average, there were eight people in each house in this neighbourhood. According to Stewart, many of the yards were strewn with rubbish.

A third block examined was bounded by Robert, Bryan and Ferris Streets and the steel works. Of the thirty-eight families in this neighbourhood, there were ninety-one children and 165 boarders. There were nineteen single-, two-, three- and four-family houses. The ethnic makeup of this neighbourhood was listed as 201 Poles and 130 "Russians" (Stewart 1913: 15). There was no sewer system in this district, which Stewart said had created a grave problem for the city's health officials. The rent was, on average, $4 per family and $8 per house. The wages of married men averaged $1.61 per day (16).

One type of house was a four-room, one-storey, single-family dwelling. Built in the early 1920s, this form had a 5 x 4 ft. (1.5 x 1.2 m) porch, a kitchen, pantry and living room, and two small bedrooms on the ground floor.

As in New Waterford, boarding houses, or so-called hotels, were the first buildings constructed in this area to provide shelter for temporary construction workers (see type 3). "Hotel Breton," as it was colloquially known, was constructed adjacent to the coke ovens. It accommodated the roughly one thousand construction workers who built the Sydney steel plant (Black [n.d.]: 3). A telephone directory referred to the address as the "Coke Ovens Hotel."[8] The building was sold in January 1901; the sale listing directed interested parties to contact the "Boarding House Department" of DISCO (*Sydney Daily Record*, January 18, 1901: 1). An ad appearing in May of that year indicates that the hotel was dismantled, divided into sections, and the sections were converted into dwelling houses and relocated to the Ferris Street area of Whitney Pier (*Sydney Daily Post*, May 23, 1901). In 1903 there were more than thirty-eight hotels listed in business directories for Sydney (Black [n.d.]: 10).[9] A plan, dated February 26, 1906, of what we think was one boarding house, the location of which is uncertain, shows a building of twelve rooms with a kitchen, pantry, dining room, sitting room, washroom, parlour and a bedroom on the ground floor. There are six bedrooms in the upper storey. The building is approximately two-and-a-half storeys in height and rests on a concrete foundation.

Row housing in Sydney used forms similar to those found in New Waterford (see type 2.2). Adjacent to the coke-ovens section of the steel plant, approximately thirty-five company houses were constructed in 1903 on Victoria Road (figure 16). These duplexes make use of a central dormer, hinting at the Gothic Revival architectural fashion. They are 24 x 24 ft. (7 x 7 m) in size. They have a front room with a fireplace, a dining room and a kitchen on the ground floor, with four small bedrooms on the second floor. They were built without foundations and had an outhouse and coal shed outside the rear of the dwelling. Plumbing was installed in many of these houses by 1920.

One resident, Mike McCormack, remembered that

> these houses were drafty, and frequently during winter we arose to find the water frozen and kids were compelled to huddle around the fireplace until the pipes were thawed. Fires were usually banked but morning found us rising to cold kitchens, cold furniture and bread that had lost all courage to rise. Even after the plumbing and hot water burners were installed it was not uncommon to find that the hot water front in the old coal stove had frozen solid during the night. (McCormack [n.d.])

A sense of some of the activities inside Victoria Road company houses is provided by McCormack in his narrative about growing up in one of these houses:

> But growing up on Victoria Road wasn't all bad. I made my friends I still cherish 60 years later. Only the very affluent had telephones and radio was in its infancy. Gramophones were quite the thing and television had not even been contemplated (Oh happy day!). We got to be pretty good 45 players and in the neighborhood regular games were played for groceries and small cash prizes. Some of us couldn't carry a tune in a bucket but those with musical inclinations were forever exchanging the words and music of popular songs.... As for sports, we had no proper equipment but we managed to field a pretty fair baseball team playing a series every year with the boys from the Coke

Fig. 16 – Victoria Road company houses, 1912. Photographer unknown. 91-637-22598. Beaton Institute, Cape Breton University.

Oven district. (McCormack [n.d.]: 2)

Two other versions of company-house duplexes were also constructed on Park Street in 1903 and on Richmond Street in 1912 (*Sydney Daily Post*, December 17, 1903; January 1, 1913).

Type 2.5 – Park Street

Company duplexes on Park Street were larger than the Victoria Road houses (figure 17). Located farther from the steel plant, these houses are almost a full two storeys in height. When they were constructed in 1903, rents were expensive. As a Sydney newspaper then reported,

> People are beginning to move into the new houses, erected by the Steel Company, on Park Street. Notwithstanding the number of families moving into the company houses, there are many who cannot secure desirable locations in Sydney. High rents still rule, and apartments on Commonwealth Avenue in Boston, are cheap compared to houses on side alleys in town. (qtd. in Black [n.d.]: 14)

The Park Street homes had a typical ground floor plan of a front room, dining room and kitchen, with four bedrooms in the upstairs.

Type 2.6 – Richmond Street

Twenty duplexes were constructed on Richmond Street in 1913 (figure 18). The common plan of each half of the duplex included a front room (15 ft. 9 in. x 11 ft. 3 in. [4.8 x 3.3 m]) with a coal-burning fireplace, a small dining room (10 x 12 ft. 9 in. [3 x 4 m]) and a kitchen (12 ft. 9 in.

[4 m] square) to the rear. The upstairs contained four small bedrooms, two being 11 ft. 4.5 in. x 11 ft. 3 in. (3.5 x 3.4 m) and two being 11 ft. 4.5 in. x 9 ft. 6 in. (3.5 x 2.9 m) in size. A veranda (6 x 20 ft. [1.8 x 6 m]) was built at the time the houses were constructed. Each kitchen contained a sink and a trap door leading to the unfinished cellar along with a built-in corner cupboard that resembled the ubiquitous British Isles "sideboard," so common in the old-world communities of Scots, English and Irish settlers (Fenton and Walker 1981). John Mannion (1974) points out that large wooden dressers with bottom drawers and shelving on top were the most outstanding feature of Irish peasant furniture. This built-in corner cupboard had two enclosed lower cupboards and four exposed upper shelves, and was roughly 4 ft. x 8 ft. high (1.2 x 2.4 m). The lower cupboards were 3 x 3 ft. wide (90 x 90 cm); the upper shelves were spaced 15 in. (38 cm) apart and were 15 in. wide. Sigurd Erixon (1938) points out that this form of kitchen furniture had descended in Europe from the court sideboards of an earlier aristocracy. Each front room had a coal fireplace 19 3/4 in. wide x 26 in. high (50 x 66 cm). The fireplace had a Number 12 iron fender in front. The fireplace sat on a concrete foundation and employed both firebrick and red brick in its construction. A concrete wall provided the foundation on the front and rear; a concrete pier provided support in the centre of the house. The joists were 2 x 8 in. (5 x 20 cm), in 5-foot lengths (1.5 m). The upright studs were 2 x 4 in. (5 x 10 cm) in size; a 1 x 6 in. (2.5 x 15 cm) wall plate separated the ground floor wall from the upper-storey wall. Joined at the peak were 2 x 6 in. rafters, supported by a 2 x 4 in. tie beam. Rough sheathing (1-in. board [2.5 cm]) covered the entire structure. On the roof there were two layers of tarpaper covered with wooden shingles. The rest of the wall had one layer of wallpaper followed by 1 in. sheathing and a layer of wooden shingles. The yard was fenced in by the owner and contained an outhouse and a coal shed. In floor plan, these houses are similar to the Victoria Road forms; however, the roof isn't as steeply pitched and the facade possesses a small porch or veranda.

Fig. 17 – Company houses on Park Street, Sydney, 1998. Photo by Richard MacKinnon.

These houses are located on one side of Richmond Street. Until the 1940s there were no houses across the road; instead, there was an open field where residents kept cattle and planted gardens. According to a lifelong resident of this row, everyone kept a small kitchen garden, a cow and a few hens to supply fresh produce, milk and eggs for the family.

A lot of men who worked in the heavy mills of the steel plant— including the blooming mill, the bar mill, the nail mill and the plate mill—resided in the Richmond Street workers' houses. In contrast, many who lived in the Victoria Street houses worked in the coke-ovens and open-hearth sections of the plant. One resident said his house was purchased from DOSCO on July 6, 1948, for $1,775 (Ray Muise, personal communication, May 21, 1992).

A crew of company carpenters looked after the company houses. The houses were reportedly spray painted with oil and oakum every ten years. The houses were not built with cellars; residents often dug their own after a few years' tenure. The front and rear walls were supported by a small concrete wall. The end wall did not have concrete support. Two-foot concrete pillars were placed close to the centre of the building for support.

Fig. 18 – Company houses on Richmond Street, Sydney, 1998. Photo by Richard MacKinnon.

A coal fireplace heated the front room, and a cast-iron stove, locally referred to as a "Quebec heater," warmed the small hallway in the downstairs. This stove regularly used coke, while the large kitchen stove used coal for fuel. In some houses, a small coke heater was also used upstairs. In the 1940s, hot-air coal furnaces began to appear and, by the 1950s, Warm Morning-brand coal stoves became commonly used throughout Cape Breton Island. In the late 1940s and early 1950s, oil furnaces also began to appear on Richmond Street. One source remembers that oil furnaces started showing up after a strike at the plant in 1947.

Garbage and ashes were thrown into an alley behind the row of houses. Once a year, in the spring, the company would send workers to clean out the alleys. Each house originally had a coal shed and an outhouse in the back yard. In the early 1940s, shortly before selling the properties, the company built small garages in the back yards of most homes because many workers had begun to purchase cars.

The interior walls of the houses were surfaced with plaster and lath. Today, most are covered with layers of wallpaper. Originally the houses had no insulation; at present, most have insulation and are covered by vinyl or aluminum siding on the exterior.

Type 2.7
Another form of duplex built by companies was the one-storey, six-room duplex. Found in Whitney Pier, and built in 1922, this form followed a minimal unit floor plan. Nineteen feet by eighteen feet (5.8 x 5.5 m), each half house contained one large multi-purpose room and a combined kitchen and living room, approximately 18 x 11 ft. in size (5.5 x 3.4 m). A small pantry was situated in the corner of that room. Two small bedrooms, approximately 9 x 8 ft. (2.74 x 2.4 m) each, were located off this main room. A small vestibule was placed at the entry of the house. This duplex sat on six concrete pillars.

Sydney Mines
The General Mining Association, the English company cited earlier, arrived on Cape Breton Island in 1827, having a monopoly on Nova Scotia mining rights. They were based in Glace Bay, Lingan, Sydney Mines and in Albion Mines (now the town of Stellarton) on mainland Nova Scotia. The company transplanted to Nova Scotia housing types already used by developers of the English coal fields. Rows of small

cottages and rows of two-storey cottages were constructed by General Mining Association throughout the 19th century. In Sydney Mines, one General Mining row still exists; other rows can be seen in the communities of Dominion and Glace Bay on Cape Breton.

Type 6.1

This company-house type has its origins in the British Isles coal fields (figure 19, 20). The red row of Sydney Mines has twelve units, with a front room/parlour at the front of the unit and a kitchen at the rear. Originally, an open hearth was used for cooking; a back kitchen was added at the turn of the 20th century. In plan, these rows are very similar to types 1.2 and 2.4 buildings in New Waterford. The upstairs contained two bedrooms.

Type 6.2

Historical photographs suggest that two-storey stone rows were also built in Sydney Mines (Holdsworth 1984: 6). Deryck Holdsworth quotes a mining engineer who mentions the British flavour of Sydney Mines in 1870.

> The Sydney Mines, located on the North side of the Sydney River. This establishment is probably more like an English colliery than any other of the Cape Breton mines. Owned by the General Mining Association of London, a wealthy English corporation, the whole of the equipment of this colliery are purely English. A stranger arriving at Sydney Bar from England after a long sea voyage, and seeing the old-fashioned chaldron, or 53 cwt coal wagons on the [General Mining] wharves, would fancy he was near one of the Newcastle collieries. (Ibid.)

By the mid-19th century, GMA had constructed a series of cottage rows in Sydney Mines as well as at their other works at Albion Mines. Holdsworth states:

> Adjacent to the Foord Pit and Crushed Mines, were clusters of three and six cottage rows, along Cricket Row and Leahy's Row. Rows of four pairs of cottages along Cunard and Mount Pleasant Terraces, served the Dalhousie and Cage Pits. A second variant of the connected cottages and there were 25 of them along Victoria and Pleasant Rows, utilized a party-wall chimney between two units. This represented a 60 foot [18 m] frontage along the street. About fifty tiny detached cottages complete

the housing stock (Two churches, a school, and a store rounded out the non-mining buildings in the community). (Holdsworth 1984: 4-5)

Sydney Mines also contains detached company-built houses on Fraser Avenue, identical to those found next to the No. 16 mine in New Waterford (Type 1.1). Moreover, the town has single-family units comparable to the Type 1.2 houses constructed in New Waterford.

Conditions

Reports indicate that after construction, company housing was not well maintained by the companies. The 1925 royal commission on the coal industry in Nova Scotia interviewed a number of miners on the conditions of their housing. One miner living near the No. 6 mine in Glace Bay reported that "Housing conditions are not good.... Sanitary conditions are bad.... They [the houses] are cold, drafty, most of them are leaky" (Royal Commission on Coal 1925: 82). The miner told the commission that the house is heated with heaters supplied by the miner, but that "it is almost impossible to keep these houses warm" (83). He described drafty windows and loosely hung doors which permitted the cold. He told the commissioner that the miners often complained about the conditions of the houses: "it is a habitual complaint" (ibid.). The miners paid $7.50 per month in rent for a six-room house, with three rooms upstairs and three rooms on the ground floor. The miner said his rent would be considered reasonable if the house was kept in good repair and if the sanitary conditions were different (84). He also indicated that the houses were recently wired for electricity, and although the miners had paid for the wiring themselves, their rent had increased.

Another miner interviewed by the commission explained that his house in Caledonia had recently been purchased from the company.

> In May 1924 I received a notice from Mr. Simpson to say that the company was selling the house and that there were some buyers after mine and I better come down and—well either buy or get out, I supposed. That is the way I take it. So after considering the thing over I thought I would want just as large a place as what I was in, and anyway I was paying $4.50 a month rent to the company before they sold me the house. (121)

Fig. 19 – General Mining Association Red Rows, Sydney Mines. Photo by Richard MacKinnon, 2016.

Fig. 20 – Interior, General Mining Association Red Rows, Sydney Mines. Photo by Richard MacKinnon, 2016.

Pressed by the commissioner, the miner acknowledged that he was forced into purchasing the house. He described the interior:

> There was three rooms downstairs: kitchen, dining room and front room. Upstairs there was two bedrooms, but there is other two holes in the wall, I would not exactly like to call them bedrooms, they are too small, one you cannot get a bed in at all unless you saw it off. (Ibid.)

He was paying $4.50 per month in rent when the company owned the building. The house was sold to him for $950 over ten years, making the total outlay $1,470. There was no connected sewer; instead, there was a "dry closet" or outhouse on a nearby hill. The commission concluded:

> Many families occupy houses that are much too small for their needs.... Where water is piped into the house, there is an almost total absence of bathrooms or water closets, due, we are informed, to the lack of sewers. There is much complaint of the leaky conditions of the roof, of ill-fitting doors and windows, of floors that are rotted or badly worn, and of walls on which paper and plaster are in shreds and patches. (Latremouille 1988: 61)

The same miner provides an insight into the kind of building activity in boom-town environments by explaining that the house, as far as he knew, was built in Port Morien in 1860, but was "torn down at Port Morien and taken over and rebuilt at Caledonia, which made it much colder" (Royal Commission on Coal 1925: 121). The dismantling and moving of houses seems to have been a fairly common activity in company towns. When mining activity ceased in Port Hood, Cape Breton, many of the houses were moved great distances throughout Inverness County. And as we have seen, Black's study of company housing in Whitney Pier refers to a hotel being dismantled and sections of it re-used for workers' housing (Black [n.d.]: 3-5). There is actually an extensive literature on the moving and dismantling of buildings in rural and urban settlements.[10]

Another miner testified to the poor conditions:

> The rain comes through every window in the house. Last Saturday morning, when I come down to go to work at half past five, I stepped in four inches of water in the dining room.... It [water] comes in just like turning a tap on. We have to stay

there with slop pails, mopping it up as fast as it comes in. (Royal Commission on Coal 1925: 758)

Roy Wolvin,[11] known throughout Cape Breton by the nickname "Roy the Wolf," answered questions to the commission and provided a description of some of the "shacks" (see Type 4) in the Glace Bay area:

> Mr. Cronyn, might I say something about the shacks. These shacks were built for construction purposes, for housing a great number of Newfoundlanders who came over here in connection with construction work, and when they left, the shacks were left, and we have had people move into them without the company's permission, and we simply cannot get them out. We would like to remove or simply destroy all those shacks, tear them down, because they were not originally built for houses, and are not fit for people to live in. (Royal Commission on Coal 1925: 363-64)

Shacks were often re-used, moved and modified into permanent dwellings near mine sites. The housing shortage in the industrial region, combined with the boom environment, meant that boarders were common in workers' houses. Richard Uniacke (1903) observed:

> All private houses were chock full of boarders. Some six room houses contained as many as twenty people. Glace Bay, being the centre of all the collieries and the headquarters of the railroad and mechanical work, was more crowded than any of the villages. Men were living everywhere. In some cases where boarders were working on alternate shifts, the night men jumped into the beds at 6:30 in the morning when the day men jumped out. The beds were never cold.

Taking in boarders provided extra income for the household, whose affairs—financial and otherwise—were usually managed by the woman of the household (Frank 1971).

Conclusion

This typology outlines some of the more common patterns of company-house architecture that were once common throughout the Cape Breton industrial region. These buildings as cultural artifacts reveal much about the attitudes of companies toward workers and demonstrate clearly how class is manifest in the built landscape. Mining and steel companies built smaller, rudimentary homes for their workers: shacks, boarding houses, single-family homes and duplexes. In contrast, large, commodious, fashionable homes were constructed for upper management. A clear example of this would be the construction of Moxham Castle, King's Road, Sydney, located a distance away from the smells and sound of the working steel plant located in Whitney Pier (figure 21). Rich-

Fig. 21 – Moxham Castle, 1936. Photo by Norman McLeod. 79-1164-4144. Beaton Institute, Cape Breton University.

ard Brown's house, far away from the mines in Sydney Mines, and the Petersfield home in Westmount, on a point overlooking Sydney Harbour, are other examples of ornate, ostentatious houses built for upper company management. These should be also considered as a particular type of company housing.

More research clearly needs to be done on the material culture of working-class families in the former coal and steel towns of Cape Breton. Interior studies showing what kinds of artwork, furnishings and cosmetics—paints, wallpapers and decorative arts—were to be found, for example, might reveal new insights into working-class culture. Many questions come to mind. For example, what kinds of furniture were being purchased, and from where? Were there small-scale local furniture factories in the Maritime region meeting the demand at this boom period of mining and steel construction? What might these interior studies reveal about working-class aesthetics and taste? Clearly, having a typology provides us with a broad pattern of the built landscape. More detailed micro-studies of other mining and steel districts in Atlantic Canada to fully understand the working-class culture of regional mining and steel communities would be welcomed.

Notes

1. *Sydney Daily Post*, July 26, 1917.

2. Allan Noble (1984: 106), following from Glassie, argues that this form grew in popularity because it allowed owners to build dwellings on narrower and less-expensive lots.

3. See Latremouille (1988: 30), Maitland (1984), Fredericton Heritage Trust (1982: 10-11), and Hamlin (1964 [1944]).

4. Fifty Years (Glace Bay, NS: Town of Glace Bay, 1950).

5. Many New Waterford streets and avenues are named after some of the early Irish settlers of the town: Duggan Avenue, Clogham Avenue, Heelan Street and Mahon Street, for example. The names of mine-company managers were also used, such as for one of the main streets, Plummer Avenue, named after J. E. H. Plummer, general manager of DOSCO in 1913, the date the town was incorporated.

6. As Upton and Vlach (1986) state:

> It is tempting to people steeped in the rapidly shifting fashions of modern popular culture to think of vernacular architecture, particularly in its traditional forms, as changeless. An emphasis on the enduring as indicative of deeply held values leads us at times to ignore change, or to treat it as unimportant.

For more on the crucial issue of change, see Glassie (1969) and Hubka (1979). See also Hugil (1980), Lowenthal (1980) and Hubka (1985).

7. This issue of re-use and modification is an important yet under-studied phenomenon in most vernacular regions. See, for example, the special 1987 issue of an American journal devoted to re-use and renovation, Material Culture 19 (2-3), 63-141; see also McIlwraith (1983) and MacKinnon (1995).

8. Record Guide Book and Business Directory for Sydney, 1901 (Beaton Institute, Cape Breton University), 57.

9. McAlpines Directory, 1903 (Beaton Institute, Cape Breton University).

10. See Tizzard (1979: 214-17) and Cape Breton's Magazine (1981, 1984). For a discussion of a late-18th-century house that was stolen and moved, see Herman (1987); for an analysis of house moving by an anthropologist, see Rodman (1985).

11. Roy M. Wolvin was president of the British Empire Steel Corporation (BESCO), in the 1920s.

References

PERIODICALS

Sydney Daily Post

Sydney Post Record

PUBLISHED SOURCES

Berger, Stefan, Andy Croll and Norman LaPorte, eds. 2005. *Towards a Comparative History of Coalfield Societies*. Aldershot, U.K.: Ashgate.

Black, Joe [n.d.]. Hunkey Town: The Immigrant Family and its Company Home. Unpublished paper, Beaton Institute, Cape Breton University.

Boone, Glen. 1990. Early Twentieth Century Company Housing in New Waterford. Unpublished paper, Department of Geography, Mount Allison University.

Boutilier, Ted. 1963. *The New Waterford Story, 1913-1963: A Souvenir of New Waterford's Golden Jubilee, August 4-8, 1963*. New Waterford, NS: Privately printed.

———. 1988. *New Waterford: Three Generations, 1913-1988*. New Waterford, NS: Town of New Waterford.

Byers, Mary and Margaret McBurney. 1994. *Atlantic Hearth: Early Homes and Families of Nova Scotia*. Toronto: University of Toronto Press.

Cape Breton's Magazine. 1981. A Visit With Mary and William Crowdis. No. 30:1, 31-35.

———. 1984. Dan Alex MacLeod: "I Moved Houses." No. 35:13-19.

Comiter, Alvin and Elizabeth Pacey. 1988. *Historic Halifax*. Willowdale, ON: Hounslow.

Crawley, Ron. 1990. Class Conflict and the Establishment of the Sydney Steel Industry, 1899-1904. In *The Island: New Perspectives on Cape Breton History, 1713-1990*, ed. Ken Donovan. Sydney, NS: University College of Cape Breton Press.

Ennals, Peter and Deryck Holdsworth. 1981. Vernacular Architecture and the Cultural Landscape of the Maritime Provinces: A Reconnaisance. *Acadiensis* 10 (2): 86-102.

———. 1998. *Homeplace: The making of the Canadian Dwelling Over Three Centuries*. Toronto: University of Toronto Press.

Erixon, Sigurd. 1938. West European Connections and Culture Relations. *Folkliv* 2:137-72.

Fenton, Alexander and Bruce Walker. 1981. *The Rural Architecture of Scotland*. Edinburgh, UK: John Donald.

Frank, David. 1971. Coal Masters and Coal Miners: Strikes and Roots of Class Conflict in the Cape Breton Coal Industry. MA thesis, Dalhousie University.

———. 1983. The Miner's Financier: Women in the Cape Breton Coal Towns, 1917. *Atlantis* 8 (2): 137-43.

———. 1986. The Industrial Folksong in Cape Breton. *Canadian Folklore Canadien* 8 (1-2): 21-42.

———. 1999. *J. B. McLachlan: A Biography*. Toronto: James Lorimer Press.

Fredericton Heritage Trust. 1982. *Heritage Handbook*. Fredericton, NB: Fredericton Heritage Trust.

Glassie, Henry. 1969. *Pattern in the Material Folk Culture of the Eastern United States*. Philadelphia: University of Pennsylvania Press.

———. 1972. Eighteenth-Century Cultural Process in Delaware Valley Folk Building. *Winterthur Portfolio* 7:29-57.

———. 1975. *Folk Housing in Middle Virginia: A Structural Analysis of Historic Artifacts*. Knoxville: University of Tennessee Press.

———. 1982. *Passing the Time in Ballymenone: Culture and History of an Ulster Community*. Philadelphia: University of Pennsylvania Press.

———. 1986. Eighteenth Century Cultural Process in Delaware Valley Folk Building. In *Common Places: Readings in American Vernacular Architecture*, eds. Dell Upton and John Michael Vlach, 400-404. Athens: University of Georgia Press.

———. 1999. *Material Culture*. Bloomington, IN: Indiana University Press.

———. 2000. *Vernacular Architecture*. Bloomington, IN: Indiana University Press.

Gold, Sara M. 1925. A Social Worker Visits Cape Breton. Beaton Institute Archives, Cape Breton University.

Hamlin, Talbot. 1964 [1944]. *Greek Revival Architecture in America*. Reprint, New York: Dover.

Herman, Bernard L. 1987. Architectural Renewal and the Maintenance of Customary Relationships. *Material Culture* 19 (2-3): 85-99.

Holdsworth, Deryck. 1984. Housing the Industrial Worker. Paper presented at a conference on the history of industrial housing, Ironbridge, UK, November 9.

Hornsby, Stephen. 1989. Staple Trades, Subsistence Agriculture, and Nineteenth-Century Cape Breton Island. *Annals of the Association of American Geographers* 79 (3): 411-34. http://www.jstor.org/stable/2563726.

Hornsby, Stephen. 1992. *Nineteenth Century Cape Breton: A Historical Geography*. Montreal: McGill-Queen's University Press.

Hubka, Thomas. 1979. Just Folks Designing: Vernacular Designers and the Generation of Form. *Journal of Architectural Education*, vol. 32 (3): 27-29

———. 1985. *Big House, Little House, Back House Barn: The Connected Farm Buildings of New England*. Hanover, NH: University Press of New England.

Hugil, Peter J. 1980. Houses in Cazenovia: The Effects of Time and Class. *Landscape* 24 (2): 10-15.

Hyde, Susan and Michael Bird. 1995. *Hallowed Timbers: The Wooden Churches of Cape Breton*. Erin, ON: Boston Mills Press.

Jackson, John Brinckerhoff. 1984. *Discovering the Vernacular Landscape*. New Haven, CT: Yale University Press.

———. 1980. *The Necessity for Ruins, and Other Topics*. Amherst: University of Massachusetts Press.

———. 1994. *A Sense of Place, A Sense of Time*. New Haven, CT: Yale University Press.

Jackson, John Brinckerhoff, and Ervin H. Zube. 1970. *Landscapes: Selected Writings of J. B. Jackson*. Amherst: University of Massachusetts Press.

Katers, Nicholas. 2010. Company Town. In *Daily Life through History*. ABC-CLIO, 2010-. http://dailylife.abc-clio.com/ (accessed May 10, 2013).

Kniffen, Fred. 1965. Folk Housing: Key to Diffusion. *Annals of the Association of American Geographers*, 55 (4): 549-77.

Kniffen, Fred. 1986. Folk Housing: Key to Diffusion. In *Common Places: Readings in American Vernacular Architecture*, eds. Dell Upton and John Vlach, 4-10. Athens: University of Georgia Press.

Latremouille, Joann. 1988. *Pride of Home : The Working Class Housing Tradition in Nova Scotia, 1749-1949*. Hantsport, NS: Lancelot Press.

MacGillivray, Donald. 1974. Military Aid to the Civil Power: The Cape Breton Experience in the 1920s. *Acadiensis* 3 (1): 45-64.

———. 1991. Work Poetry/Poésie de Travail: The Industrial Verse of Slim Mcinnis. *Labour/Le Travail* 28:271-84.

MacKinnon, Richard. 1982a. Company Housing in Wabana Bell Island, Newfoundland. *Material History Bulletin* 14:67-71.

———. 1982b. The Regional Architectural Forms of the Margaree Valley, Cape Breton Island. *Society for the Study of Architecture Selected Papers*. Ottawa: Society for the Study of Architecture in Canada.

———. 1995. House Movings and Alterations: Stability and Change in the Codroy Valley Landscape. *Canadian Folklore Canadien* 17 (2): 31-50.

———. 1998. Research Report: Making a House a Home: Company Housing in Cape Breton Island. *Material History Review* 47:46-56.

———. 1996. Tompkinsville, Cape Breton Island: Cooperativism and Vernacular Architecture. *Material History Review* 44:45-63.

MacLeod, Mary K., and James O. St. Clair. 1992. *No Place Like Home: The Life and Times of Cape Breton Heritage Houses*. Sydney, NS: University College of Cape Breton Press.

———. 1994. *Pride of Place : The Life and Times of Heritage Homes in Cape Breton*. Sydney, NS: University College of Cape Breton Press.

Maitland, Leslie. 1984. *Neoclassical Architecture in Canada,* Studies in Archaeology, Architecture and History. Ottawa: National Historic Parks and Site Branches Parks Canada, Environment Canada.

Mannion, John J. 1974. *Irish Settlements in Eastern Canada: A Study in Cultural Transfer and Adaptation.* University of Toronto Department of Geography Research Publications, No. 12. Toronto: University of Toronto Press.

Martell, J. S. 1980. Early Coal Mining in Nova Scotia, in *Cape Breton Historical Essays.* eds. Don MacGillivray and Brian Tennyson. Sydney, NS: University College of Cape Breton Press.

McCormack, Mike. [n.d.]. Reminiscences of Life in the Company Houses on Victoria Road. Beaton Institute, Cape Breton University.

McIlwraith, Thomas F. 1983. Altered Buildings: Another Way of Looking at the Ontario Landscape. *Ontario History* 75:110-34.

McKay, Ian. 1986. "By Wisdom, Wile or War:" The Provincial Workmen's Association and the Struggle for Working-Class Independence in Nova Scotia, 1879-97. *Labour/Le Travail* 18:12-62.

Meinig, Donald W. and John Brinckerhoff Jackson, eds. 1979. *The Interpretation of Ordinary Landscapes: Geographical Essays.* New York: Oxford University Press.

Mellin, Robert. 2003. *Tilting : House Launching, Slide Hauling, Potato Trenching, and Other Tales from a Newfoundland Fishing Village.* 1st ed. New York: Princeton Architectural Press.

———. 2011. *Newfoundland Modern : Architecture in the Smallwood Years, 1949-1972.* Montreal: McGill-Queen's University Press.

Mills, David B. 1977. The Development of Folk Architecture in Trinity Bay, Newfoundland. In *The Peopling of Newfoundland: Essays in Historical Geography,* ed. John J. Mannion, 77-101. St. John's, NL; Institute of Social and Economic Research, Memorial University.

Muise, Del. 1980. The Making of an Industrial Community: Cape Breton Coal Towns, 1867-1900. In *Cape Breton Historical Essays,* eds. Don MacGillivray and Brian Tennyson, 76-94. Sydney, NS: College of Cape Breton Press.

Noble, Alan. 1984. *Wood, Brick and Stone: The North American Settlement Landscape.* Amherst: University of Massachusetts Press.

Pacey, Elizabeth, and Alvin Comiter. 1994. *Landmarks: Historic Buildings of Nova Scotia.* Halifax, NS: Nimbus.

Pacey, Elizabeth, George Rogers and Allan F. Duffus. 1983. *More Stately Mansions: Churches of Nova Scotia, 1830-1910.* Hantsport, NS: Lancelot Press.

Palmer, Marilyn, and Peter Neaverson. 1998. *Industrial Archaeology: Principles and Practice.* London: Routledge.

Penny, Alan. 1989. *Houses of Nova Scotia.* Halifax: Formac and the Nova Scotia Museum.

Pocius, Gerald. 1991. *A Place to Belong: Community Order and Everyday Space in Calvert Newfoundland.* Athens and Montreal: University of Georgia Press and McGill-Queen's University Press..

Polard, S. 1964. The Factory Village in the Industrial Revolution. *English Historical Review.* 79:516-19.

Relph, Edward. 1976. *Place and Placelessness.* London: Pion.

———. 2000. Author's Response: *Place and Placelessness* in a New Context [Classics in Human Geography Revisited, *Place and Placelessness*]. *Progress in Human Geography* 24 (4): 613-19.

Rodman, Margaret C. 1985. Moving Houses: Residential Mobility and the Mobility of Residences in Longana, Vanuatu. *American Anthropologist* 87:56-72.

Royal Commission on Coal, 1925. Provincial Archives of Nova Scotia, Halifax. Micro N 93, 1925, reels 1-3.

Soloman, Nancy. 1985. Folk Housing in a Company Town: The Case of Kitzmiller, Maryland. MA thesis, George Washington University.

Stewart, Bryce. 1913. Social Survey of Sydney. Paper presented at First Annual Conference of the Canadian Political Science Association, Ottawa, September 4-6, 1913. Beaton Institute Archives, Cape Breton University.

Story, George M, William J. Kirwin and J. D. A. Widdowson, eds. 1982. *Dictionary of Newfoundland English.* Toronto: University of Toronto Press.

Tizzard, Aubrey. 1979. *On Sloping Ground: Reminiscences of Outport Life in Notre Dame Bay, Newfoundland.* Memorial University of Newfoundland Folklore and Language Publications, Community Studies No. 2, ed. John D. A. Widdowson. St. John's, NL: Memorial University.

Trinder, Barrie. 1996. *The Industrial Archaeology of Shropshire.* Chichester, U.K.: Phillimore and Co.

Tuan, Yi Fu. 1974. *Topophilia: A Study of Environmental Perception, Attitudes, and Values.* Englewood Cliffs, NJ: Prentice-Hall.

―――. 1977. *Space and Place: The Perspective of Experience.* Minneapolis: University of Minnesota Press.

―――. 2004. *Place, Art, and Self.* Chicago, Il: Center for American Places, Columbia College.

Uniacke, Richard J. 1903. *Sketches of Cape Breton.* Toronto: Nation Publishing Company.

Upton, Dell and John Vlach, eds. 1986. *Common Places: Readings in American Vernacular Architecture.* Athens: University of Georgia Press.

Chapter Two

Alex Forbes

A Patriarch's Company Town:
Boss Gibson and the Marysville Legacy

C ompany towns are the result of economic, social and technical forces being brought together for industrial purposes. When a town's dominant industry fails and the local economy suffers, it often falls into decline and eventual abandonment. There are prominent exceptions, however. Located on the Nashwaak River, near the confluence of the Nashwaak and Saint John River systems, lies the nationally recognized historic community of Marysville, New Brunswick.

This former 19th-century industrial town has retained many of its features, making it one of most intact company towns in Canada. The credit for such an accomplishment can be traced directly back to the leadership, vision and style of its patriarchal founder, Alexander "Boss" Gibson. For without Gibson's financial and cultural support throughout its early development, Marysville would never have been more than a short-lived "boom and bust" company town. Instead, the former town (it was amalgamated with Fredericton in 1973) was bequeathed with an endowed patrimony—a rich architectural legacy of company houses and a former cotton mill centrepiece that would be successfully re-purposed as part of a late-20th-century community-revitalization effort.

The people behind the revitalization effort were inspired by Gibson's stubborn, unwavering commitment to his town, a commitment that would cost him personally as well as financially. The decision to build the cotton mill created a rift between Gibson and his eldest son John, who was expected to carry on the Gibson legacy. This tension resulted in the son walking away from his father's industrial enterprises, never to return; the two were estranged until John's premature death. Despite such costs, Marysville would achieve the longevity that Gibson so desired for the community.

Marysville's architectural legacy has been significant enough to receive national recognition, beginning in 1986 when the Historic Sites and Monuments Board of Canada (HSMBC) designated the cotton mill as a National Historic Site. In 1993, Marysville itself became a National Historic District, and Gibson would subsequently be recognized as a "Person of National Historic Significance" by the HSMBC in 2007. Fresh honours were bestowed in 2012, when a statue of Gibson was put up along with relevant interpretive panels in order to explain his importance to the community. All levels of government contributed to this project and had representatives present to commemorate the event.

Who was Boss Gibson, and what contributions did he make to a company town to be so nationally recognized and commemorated? What made Marysville unique in terms of its planned development? Are there important heritage conservation lessons that other postindustrial company towns can learn from Marysville? This chapter will focus on answering these questions. Clearly, Gibson wanted Marysville to become more than a boom-and-bust company town. His risky decision to finance and establish a new industry in Marysville is a testament to that commitment, a testament that gave the community a century of social stability and inspired other community leaders to follow suit, so that much of Marysville's architectural legacy would be preserved.

Boss Gibson and the Founding of Marysville

The area that would later become Marysville was dammed and a lumber mill established in the early 19th century. Several operators had unsuccessfully tried to take advantage of the lumbering opportunities on the Nashwaak River system. Then Gibson came along. Originally a lumberman from Lepreau, New Brunswick, he had started out as a lath sawyer in nearby Milltown (now St. Stephen) before quickly coming to own his own lumber mill at Lepreau (Young 1998: 400). Milltown was the most industrialized landscape in New Brunswick at the time, and Gibson was able to master the operation of water-powered sawmills. He sold his interest in the Lepreau lumber mill and invested in one on the Nashwaak River, near Fredericton. The previous owners of that lumber mill had made significant improvements to the operation, but then allowed it to deteriorate to the point where it was offered for sale (Rosevear 1986: 11). In 1862, Gibson purchased the mills, buildings, land and the rights-of-way for the river-driving and rafting of timber for $28,000. A valuation on the assets and holdings that Gibson purchased in 1862 was close to $130,000.

From the moment Gibson arrived on the Nashwaak, he exercised the knowledge of water-powered sawmills that he acquired in Milltown, and the cutting capacity of the existing mills was increased six-fold. Rivers and streams were cleared out and dams were built on the Nashwaak River, so that logs could be transported to the mill over more months of the year. Due to Gibson's innovation in sorting and ranking logs by size and quality, costs were reduced and profits

Fig. 1 – Lumber mill in foreground and cotton mill across the river, ca. 1890. Source unknown.

increased (Rosevear 1986: 11). After his first year in operation, he was able to pay off his promissory notes and transformed the lumber mills on the Nashwaak into some of the busiest and most productive lumber mills in the province. While there were a number of markets, most of Gibson's cut lumber was bulk-shipped to England, an enterprise that became so significant during Gibson's career that he was offered a knighthood by Queen Victoria (Grey 1923: 5). He who could have been "Lord Nashwaak" declined the aristocratic title, preferring to be recognized for his philanthropy.

Fig. 2 – Alexander "Boss" Gibson, 1871. McCord Museum, Montreal, I-62589.1.

The revenue generated from the lumber operations was transferred into other area businesses. Wooden boats and larger vessels were built, and an investment was made in the newly developing railway industry in the province (Young 1998: 401). These new railway lines opened up the interior of New Brunswick to timber stands in forests that were previously inaccessible for shipping purposes. After becoming a founding member of the New Brunswick Railway Company, Gibson partially financed a project to develop a line from Devon (north side of Fredericton) to Fort Fairfield, Maine (ibid.). He went on to become the company president in 1872. This association proved financially fruitful. In 1880, Gibson sold his interest in this line for $800,000. This capital provided the means for Gibson to pursue the most ambitious and bold project of his life—the construction in 1885 of a large cotton mill in Marysville.

Questions have been raised about why Gibson would venture into such a new business endeavour. He did not have previous experience or any great knowledge of the industry. The raw material for the mill—the cotton—had to be shipped in from some distance, from the southern United States. He was sixty-four. There was also some family conflict. He quarrelled on this matter with his oldest son, John Thomas, who preferred building a pulp-and-paper mill because of their existing knowledge of the lumber industry. Gibson's reply was telling: "And what of all this?" he said in reference to Marysville. Concerned about what would happen to the town when the timber supplying his lumber mills was exhausted, Gibson felt a paternalistic duty to create new industry (Rosevear 1986: 13). The desire to move forward with a cotton mill resulted in him and his eldest son parting ways. They were estranged until John's premature death at age 38.

The senior Gibson foresaw the decline in the timber supply more clearly than others, including his son. As historian Murray Young states:

> If Boss Gibson had followed the principles of the business developers of today, he would never have spent his money on building a cotton mill in such an unlikely place. If his family had come first in his thoughts, he would certainly not have done it. It must have been the spirit of Christian charity that fired his spirit. (Young 1997)

Even though Gibson had little knowledge of cotton production, there were some benefits to setting up the cotton mill: Marysville had some of the attributes of a typical New England mill town. There was an existing supply of labour, sufficient land to enlarge the operations and access to water power. This new venture would also benefit from the protectionist National Policy of the Canadian government, which established trade tariffs to protect Canadian manufacturers from American competition.

Most importantly, Gibson's knowledge of the railway business gave him an advantage over his competitors. He understood the critical role the railway could play in bringing raw cotton to the mill. He used this information initially to cross-subsidize his own rail lines. Over time, he became part owner and eventually sole owner of Canada Eastern Railway, which ran from the north side of Fredericton through Marysville to the Miramichi region, in northern New Brunswick. The extension of the Canada Eastern line to Miramichi was necessary to justify the construction costs of building a railway bridge over the Saint John River to obtain access to the cotton mill on the north side of the river. Gibson needed this line to bring raw cotton up from the United States and to send the finished product back toward Fredericton to connect with the main railway lines to Upper Canada. Trains at that time burned wood as fuel, and Gibson's control over various rail lines and his access to a steady supply of wood helped defray the costs associated with transporting raw cotton to the mill's more isolated location.

Gibson's need for trains to move his raw materials to and from the cotton and lumber mills helped these enterprises financially, but the rail line also provided access for the residents of Marysville to nearby Fredericton. As early as 1893, a shuttle service, known as the Suburban, operated six round trips per day between Marysville and Fredericton (Squires 1980: 75). This level of daily service of public transportation was exceptional for its time and was not replicated until the early 1970s when the City of Fredericton began to provide bus service to Marysville.

The new cotton mill was one of the largest textile mills in Canada at the time. Gibson travelled to Boston, New York and the southern United States to inspect mill operations. Inspectors were also sent to report on the mill operation at St. Croix, New Brunswick, on the Canada-U.S. border (Rosevear 1986: 36). Careful thought was given to the labour component

Fig. 3 – Photo of Boss Gibson. New Brunswick Provincial Archives P5-373.

that would become part of a planned industrial community (Pelletier and Coghlan 1975: 10). At that time, there were two types of production in cotton mills that required different configurations for labour. Gibson chose the type of production that could provide employment for an entire family (11). This model relied on a labour force that was primarily female, and men were secondarily employed to work in the picking and initial carding processes, in the repair shop, and they filled supervisory positions. Women were employed drawing, speeding, spinning, weaving and dressing. A typical room in a mill employed eighty women, with two men overseeing and two boys assisting them (Dublin 1975: 106). Therefore, a married couple could be employed as well as their children. The style of company housing built in Marysville (tenements and single-family dwellings) would reflect this choice.

Gibson's Planned Community

Marysville's successful architectural preservation is based on a number of factors. These factors include the quality of the building materials that were used, the sense of community that Gibson helped foster (albeit along management-labour class lines) and Marysville's location on the periphery of Fredericton, where development pressure was not significant. And unlike the hastily thrown-up buildings in a typical company town, careful thought went into Marysville's architectural layout.

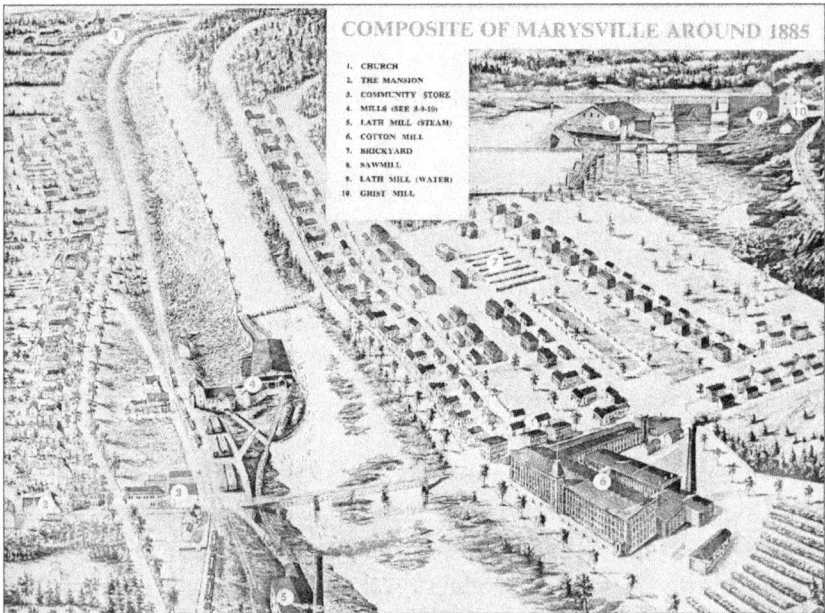

Fig. 4 – Bird's-eye view of Marysville, ca. 1885. New Brunswick Provincial Archives P102-1B.

Prior to Gibson's arrival, a number of wooden tenement houses had been constructed for area lumber-mill workers. However, the majority of the cotton-mill buildings, including houses, were to be made of brick. Gibson built the community from brick to avoid the loss and devastation that occurred as a result of fire, as was later seen in the great fire of Saint John, in 1877. This fire-resistant material would assist in the preservation of more than a hundred buildings in Marysville. Most of the brick buildings exist today, whereas a number of wooden company houses have been lost through the years. Any structure fires that occurred in brick buildings were readily contained on site. By contrast, wooden buildings that caught fire in many instances ignited adjacent wooden structures, often destroying entire neighbourhoods. As a result, Gibson wanted architecture that would last; a considerable amount of time was spent in choosing the appropriate designs for the town development. In 1864, the lumber mill operation and the company housing were built on the east side of the Nashwaak River. Gibson's family and his managers were housed on the west side. Most other non-industrial buildings would also be located on the west side. These buildings included one of the finest provincial schoolhouses of the time, as well as a public hall, library and general store.

After some deliberation, Gibson settled on the firm of Lockwood and Green from Rhode Island to provide the plans and technical expertise to build the new mill and company housing. Unlike other maritime entrepreneurs who financed their new operations by selling bonds or shares to multiple owners, Gibson chose to finance the cotton mill by himself (Rosevear 1986: 36). This sole-proprietor approach would create significant financial problems later. The cotton mill cost an estimated $1 million by the time it was made operational, then generating 10,000 yards (9,100 m) of cotton daily (McIntyre 1983: 19).

The cotton mill has been described by A. J. H. Richardson as being "architecturally more than just a very huge building for its day ...

Fig. 5: Early photograph of the cotton mill. New Brunswick Provincial Archives P5-319.

something that seems to have been very new in industrial design, part of a new direction from the horizontally-stressed other great mills that had just preceded it" (qtd. in Young 1998: 401). It is also interesting to note that the plans for the cotton mill, the mill manager's house and a couple of brick tenements are in the archives of the Smithsonian Institution in Washington, DC.[1]

In order to reduce overall expenses, a brickyard was opened to aid the building of the mill along with the brick tenements for mill workers. Even after the building boom of the 1880s, the brickyard continued to produce for the local market until the 1930s, when it was purchased by a larger competitor.

Gibson had a modest house built on the west side of the river, which was used until his permanent home was completed in 1866. The latter was designed by Saint John architect Matthew Stead, who was regarded as one of the finest architects of his time. Gibson's home was known in the community as "the mansion." The main house and large coach house exhibited elaborate exterior Gothic detail, and the grounds were extensively landscaped with a terraced lawn and three-tier water fountain adorned with cherubim in the front yard. This stunning example of two-and-a-half storey Gothic design put all on notice as they entered Marysville about where the centre of the social hierarchy was located.

Gibson was a Methodist whose religious convictions and beliefs were central to his identity. So much so that he felt that these values needed to be shared, and, in 1873, he committed $68,000 of his own money to have a Methodist church built for the community. Gibson retained Matthew Stead to design the Marysville Methodist Church, then regarded as one of the finest examples of Gothic architecture east of Montreal. A correspondent for the Toronto *Globe* even wrote that the church was "probably as fine a specimen of pure Gothic as can be found in America, and it is as chaste in ornamentation as it is beautiful in design" (qtd. in Young 1998: 401). Gibson also donated the

Fig. 6 – The Gibson mansion with an ornate wooden fence around it. Source unknown.

land in the community for the Anglican church and provided funding to the Olivet Baptist Church (Philips 1946: 12).

In 1866, Boss Gibson built a home for his brother near his own house on Canada Street. In that same year, Gibson built homes for his three sons. His oldest son, John, lived on the southern end of the street, near his father. Sons Sandy and James lived on the northern end of the row, beside the new church. The row of housing from the Gibson mansion to the Methodist church came to be known locally as "Nob Hill."

Once Gibson moved forward with his plans to build the cotton mill, he placed the mill and workers in brick tenements on the east side of the river. On the west side, he built nine overseers' (cotton-mill managers') houses along Nob Hill. The mill manager's house was located in the middle of Nob Hill, between the mansion and the church. Gibson's daughter married the first manager of the cotton mill. This marriage ensured that Gibson's daughter and future grandchildren had an economic future in Marysville. Gibson strategically placed people along the row of houses on Canada Street in such a manner that he and his sons anchored each end of the row, with his daughter located in the centre. This arrangement allowed Gibson to keep a close eye on the comings and goings of the mill managers, who were dispersed between the various Gibson family members. The commer-

Fig. 7 – The Methodist Church with James Gibson house in foreground and Marysville schoolhouse behind. New Brunswick Provincial Archives P37-488-4.

COMPANY HOUSES, COMPANY TOWNS

cial area was located just below Nob Hill, on Mill Street. Mill Street contained the town's general store, butcher shop, railway station, post office and hotel.

On the east side of the river, the lumber-mill workers lived along River Street in wooden tenements. There were originally twenty-four duplex houses in this row, but a number were removed to make way for the cotton mill. Of the original twenty-four constructed, only seven remained standing in 2015. Behind River Street were fifty-three brick houses that consisted of thirty-nine duplexes and fourteen single dwellings for the cotton-mill workers. All of the fifty-three brick tenements have survived.

Gibson constructed a three-storey brick hotel near the cotton mill in 1886 to accommodate young rural women who came to Marysville seeking employment in the cotton mill. Typically, these single women eventually married and moved into one of the brick tenements built to accommodate the cotton-mill employees. Women went to work in textile factories for many reasons, but often they were escaping overcrowding at home and seeking to earn wages before getting married.

Changing Economic Conditions

Eventually, Gibson's sole ownership of a number of large-scale business operations made him vulnerable to changing market conditions and outside economic forces. Canada Eastern was sold to the federal government in 1904 for $800,000 (Rosevear 1986: 70). The railway had been losing money and the sale was an attempt to lessen the financial losses on his enterprises. He lost control of the lumber-mill operation in 1908, which stopped operating in 1920 when it burned to the ground. Competition from Upper Canadian cotton mills and a glut of Maritime cotton product forced Gibson to sell the cotton mill, to David Maurice and Sons from Montreal, also in 1908. McIntyre (1983: 10) indicates that in that same year Boss Gibson retired, at age 89, with a pension of $5,000 a year, a considerable amount at the time. He died in 1913 at the age of 94 at his residence on Canada Street. The house burned to the ground in 1914.

Canadian Coloured Cotton Mills successfully ran the operation until 1954. The reason cited for the mill closure was competition from the United States. Marysville, it would turn out, fared better than places like Lowell, Massachusetts, where cotton mills were decimated in the 1920s and during the Depression, and were closed down shortly after the Second World War. New England mills that had previously been able to take advantage of water power and other natural features were replaced by ones producing cotton product where the cotton was grown, thereby eliminating expensive transportation costs. Cotton mills in the southern United States were also much cheaper to heat in the winter months than their northern competitors. The British textile industry suffered a similar fate and was eventually undermined

Fig. 8 – Gibson mansion in disrepair, ca. 1914. Courtesy of Frank Hicks.

by textiles from India. It is therefore significant that the cotton mill at Marysville was reopened in 1956, and Hamilton Cottons ran it until 1973 (Pond 1983: 32). Another large cotton manufacturer then

Fig. 9 – Cotton mill in disrepair. Courtesy of R. Lyons.

operated the mill for two more years, until 1975. The mill never fully reopened and eventually ceased operation permanently in 1980.

The cotton mill was initiated by Gibson to give the people of Marysville a future. It operated relatively uninterrupted for ninety years and continued sixty-two years beyond his death. The most vulnerable period in Marysville was the period from the mill closure in 1975 until the province intervened in 1982 with a plan to convert the mill into government offices. This decision was not an easy one. The construction estimates were quite high because the building had to be completely gutted and the equipment removed. The former mayor of Fredericton, Les Hull, who was the minister of social services in the provincial government at the time, recounts that then-Premier Richard Hatfield was wavering about whether the province should develop the buildings for government offices. Ed Allen, the minister of supply and services in the Hatfield government, was the local member of the legislative assembly (MLA) for the Marysville area. Allen told the premier that both he and Hull would resign from cabinet if the plan was not approved. Hull recounts that he had no intention of resigning, but he also did not want to disappoint his cabinet colleague by not supporting him (personal interview, May 15, 2003). Eventually, Hatfield agreed to renovate the mill and it was completed in 1985 at a cost of $20 million.

The renovation of the cotton mill resulted in a new wave of enthusiasm and confidence for the residents of Marysville. At the commemoration of the HSMBC plaque, Dr. Murray Young, a historian from the University of New Brunswick, spoke about the significance of the mill, but also about Boss Gibson and his contribution to the area and to the province. It seems that the renovation of the cotton mill and the recognition by the federal government reinforced the legacy that Gibson had left the community. As a result, there was also renewed outside interest in Marysville. A successful local artist, Catherine Karnes Munn, purchased an original overseer's house on Nob Hill and established Nob Hill Gallery. A municipal councillor, Walter Brown, was elected in 1989 on a platform of improving the public infrastructure in Marysville, which was already in serious need at the time of amalgamation with Fredericton in 1973. Over the next twenty years, he worked systematically to ensure that these upgrades occurred.

In 1992, the City of Fredericton undertook an extensive study of the history and architecture of Marysville in anticipation of designating the area a municipal heritage district. It was determined that the area clearly met the historical and technical requirements for such designation, but residents preferred promoting heritage through education, and less so through heritage rules and requirements established by municipal bylaws. After public discussion of a municipal heritage bylaw, some high-profile demolitions took place that concerned neighbours as well as the wider community. As a result, the Marysville Heritage Committee was created to ensure that the public was aware of how these buildings should and could be preserved into the future.

In order to more fully recognize Gibson's influence in the community, local officials and organizations decided to locate a marble statue and a number of interpretative panels in the neighbourhood of Devon (formerly Gibson), at the north end of the Bill Thorpe Walking Bridge over the Saint John River. There were numerous reasons why this location was appropriate. It is near one of Gibson's former railway roundhouses that serviced the Canada Eastern line and near the railway bridge that he and other prominent businessmen in the community built in 1888. Moreover, it is at the intersection of the Nashwaak and Saint John Rivers, where deals from the Marysville lumber mill were floated and placed on barges. This project was completed in the fall of 2012, and all three levels of government were present to commemorate the event.

Fig. 10 – HSMBC plaque in Devon. Photo courtesy the author.

The Marysville Heritage Committee continues to collect information to build upon the unique industrial-heritage resource that exists in Marysville. Sometimes, this information serves as a renovator's resource. For example, in 2011 one of the extant fifty-three brick tenements was painted by the owner, the type of small individual action by one property owner

Fig. 11 – After restoration. Photo courtesy the author.

that concerns residents about the future of this area. The Marysville Heritage Committee also continues with an effort of public education on how to best preserve and maintain these buildings.

Boss Gibson's Leadership Style

For a man who bestowed such an incredible architectural legacy to Marysville, the Boss actually left few written records. Gibson was self-educated and could read and write, but seemed compelled to leave it to others to transcribe his achievements. Besides his actions and deeds, Gibson's personality and character are largely revealed through the stories and anecdotes of others. If you review a number of these stories, a pattern of his leadership style, character and personality emerges. Indeed, Gibson seems to exhibit what some regard as the characteristic traits of a classic entrepreneur who is driven by vision, innovation, personal motivation and an autocratic leadership style.

Gibson was a complicated individual and it is not known what truly motivated him to be such a highly successful businessperson. Manfred F. R. Kets de Vries wrote an article in the *Harvard Business Review* in 1985, "The Dark Side of Entrepreneurship." Kets de Vries' research focused on whether there were common patterns, traits and personality characteristics that defined entrepreneurs in general. His research revealed that there are such patterns and in many cases these traits are deep-seated in the psyche of overly ambitious and successful businesspeople. Kets de Vries suggests that the drive of many entrepreneurs is related to the relationship between father and son.

The article is applicable to numerous business personalities, but Kets de Vries seems to capture the essence of what motivated Gibson. In particular, entrepreneurs have a need for control, a distrust of others, a desire for recognition and the inherent personality defence mechanisms that entrepreneurs use to cope in the world (Kets de Vries 1985).

Kets de Vries (1985: 161) points out that the desire for control affects both the entrepreneur's ability to take direction and to give it. For example, when a business becomes very large the need for the entrepreneur to control everything paralyzes operations. An account of this behaviour is related by Young (1998), who points out that Gibson was reliant on the banks for working capital, operated the businesses like a patriarch but was contemptuous of banking rules and regulations. More particularly, Young points out that Gibson was "given to arbitrary decisions which made it impossible for the bookkeepers to keep track of his affairs" (Young 1998: 403). Another account of Gibson's inability to give up control touches on when (in 1901) Lord Beaverbrook (Sir Max Aitken) went to see Gibson at his home in Marysville to undertake an audit in order to recapitalize the company. In the end, Gibson would not take Beaverbrook's advice regarding reorganization because he would have to relinquish authority (Aitken 1965: 131). Gibson would not agree to someone else's terms and the banks later foreclosed. He was eighty-two years old at the time, and would remain in charge of the company until he was forced to retire seven years later.

Gibson not only distrusted the banks; he wasn't confident in the judgment of his business partners. In order to raise the capital to purchase the lumber mill in Marysville, Gibson had to buy out his brother-in-law John Robinson from their joint venture in Milltown. He gave Robinson an ultimatum that he would either buy Robinson out of his $10,000 share of their joint lumber business, or vice versa. There would be no middle ground with Gibson and he got his way when his brother-in-law purchased his financial interest in the business. Pelletier and Coghlan (1975: 4) state, "In all probability, Gibson's personality and innate desire to be 'Boss' plus a desire to use his enormous energy to better advantage, led him to sell his half of the business to his bother-in-law in 1862." After the New Brunswick Railway Company was sold to Montreal interests in 1880, Gibson, a founding member, retained his shares but eventually sold them for $800,000 because of a disagreement with stockholders over a rail gauge. An account in *The Capital* (Fredericton newspaper) noted that Gibson's departure from the company "has occasioned a great deal of talk on the streets, Mr. Gibson and the railway having been identified in the minds of most people. His indomitable courage and extensive means alone made the construction of the line possible" (qtd. in Rosevear 1986: 22). Gibson showed the same traits when he entered into a business venture with a rival lumber baron, Senator Jabez Bunting Snowball, from the Miramichi. The two men were partners in Canada Eastern. In 1889, Senator Snowball was elected by the board of directors as the president of the company and, as a result, Gibson boycotted using the line for over a year. He eventually made a buy-or-sell offer to Snowball that was similar to the one he made to his brother-in-law in Milltown in 1862. According to an account, "The rivals were aboard a Canada Eastern train when the proposition was put, and before they alighted in Chatham, Senator Snowball was merely a passenger on one of Gibson's trains" (Philips 1946: 12).

It is not clear from the literature review that Gibson had recognition-seeking personality traits or a "desire for applause." Kets de Vries suggests that most of the cases he studied stem from "the common heroic myth that begins with the hero's humble birth, his rapid rise to prominence and power, his conquest over the forces of evil, his vulnerability to the sin of pride and finally his fall through betrayal or heroic sacrifice" (Kets de Vries 1985: 163). His description of entrepreneurs in general fits Gibson's personality. Even the account of Lord Beaverbrook trying to help Gibson sort out his financial problems shows Gibson unwilling to yield, even to save himself and his family from financial ruin. Beaverbrook states that the last thing that Gibson told him at their meeting was if the banks were to move in on him, it would be better if it happened sooner than later. What Gibson was really conveying to Beaverbrook was likely "I am eighty-two years old and I am not going to give up on the community I built up as a legacy, to see it sold into various pieces to outside interests." Gibson knew it would happen, but he did not want to show that he had a hand in it.

Therefore, he is the heroic figure standing between the community he built and the various outside forces that he had to rely on for financing.

Kets de Vries (1985: 9) also states that many entrepreneurs have a deep-seated desire for this need for recognition that manifests itself, "in building monuments as symbols of their achievements." Clearly, Gibson left the community with a number of monuments that rivalled buildings in the Fredericton area at the time. As mentioned earlier, his home, church, school and cotton mill were some of the finest architectural examples of their time. Boss Gibson also took care of his employees by providing them with amenities like the libraries, recreational areas and general store that also existed in nearby Fredericton and, in some cases, creating amenities that could only be found in Marysville. For example, the first covered rink in the Fredericton area was built in Marysville (1878). Gibson also provided a baseball field in a prominent location on a pine bluff adjacent to the workers' houses. The first recorded baseball game in Marysville was played in 1895, ten years after the cotton mill opened. To this day, Baseball Hill

Fig. 12 – *Skating rink, ca. 1885. From* Marysville New Brunswick, 1889, *in* Our Dominion.

Interior James Gibson's Skating Rink, Marysville.

and the team called the Royals—a legacy established by the Boss—are known in baseball circles throughout New Brunswick. Gibson also constructed a racetrack to rival one in Fredericton, though his horse track was shorter-lived.

It is interesting that with all of the known research on Gibson there are very few photographs of him or quotes attributed to him in period news accounts. He seemed content to show to the world his vision as expressed by the labour of others in his employ and by his owns deeds. He was thought to be the first person to respond to the request for aid from Saint John after the devastating fire of 1877. He sent down a train car load of flour but did it with his customary lack of public announcement. Notwithstanding, he could also be very prescriptive when it came to moral issues. He made it known, for example, that no liquor was to be sold in his community.

Kets de Vries's "last entrepreneur trait" is that personalities are largely determined by the way an individual views the world. He suggests that a personality consists of enduring, pervasive behaviour patterns that are functions of complex, deeply embedded psychological characteristics. Quite a few entrepreneurs whom Kets de Vries interviewed were inclined to turn introspection into an active or action-based agenda, a characteristic that relates to their difficulty controlling their impulses and managing anxiety and depression. Such entrepreneurs defend against anxiety (evidenced by their restlessness and irritability) by turning to action as an antidote.

Historians suggest that Gibson went through a considerable personal transformation between 1880 and 1881, as the result of personal setbacks, not the least of which were the loss of his father, his eldest son, his daughter Mary and his grandson, named after him—deaths that spanned four generations of a family in little more than a year. Gibson did not think he had the strength to carry on. Edward Blake, the leader of the Liberal Party of Canada (and a former premier of Ontario), consoled Gibson in his Marysville garden and told him to direct his attention to those in need in his community: "For as you minister to those people your burden will be lessened and gradually disappear, it was the Master's way" (Young 1997: 4). It appears that these personal setbacks became the motivating force behind the decision to build the cotton mill and provide the people of Marysville with a future. Young points out that this change in Gibson's personality was recognized by Martin Butler, the Fredericton-based socialist editor and poet, who wrote, "There has never been a case of necessity or a calamity, brought to his notice in which Mr. Gibson did not ... go down deep into his pockets to alleviate: and were the capitalists of the United States as considerate for the welfare of their employees ... there would not be the strikes, strife, and bloodshed that is now happening" (Young 1998: 403).

Gibson had the benefit of building his cotton mill at a time when the Industrial Revolution had matured, and labour relations, working conditions and wages were improving. At the start of the Industrial Revolution, working conditions were so bad in the English mill towns that William Blake, in his 1804 epic poem *Jerusalem*, referred to them as "those dark satanic mills." Blake was alluding to the injustice of these places if Jerusalem (i.e., heaven on earth) were ever to be truly realized. There were also a number of social reformers in the early 19th century, such as Robert Owen of New Lanark in Scotland, who were trying to respond to the plight of cotton-mill workers by ensuring that they experienced much better working conditions. Owen and the other social reformers knew that taking care of your employees resulted in higher production and less social unrest. Owen's son, Robert Dale Owen, moved to the United States and also promoted his father's philosophy of social reform in the context of industrial productivity and design.

The United States did not take long to adopt the English model of industrialization. Early in the 19th century cotton manufacturing on a large scale was set up in Lowell, Massachusetts. This area quickly grew to become the centre of the textile industry in the United States. Lowell went through the transformation of employing thousands of female workers to manufacture cotton products on an industrial scale never seen before in the country. By 1840, the Lowell textile mills employed almost 8,000 workers, with the majority being women between the ages of sixteen and thirty-five (Dublin 1975: 106). The human capital required to drive these mills was greatly exploited, and labour strikes by women employees started to break out. In 1836 factory women protested against the labour conditions and formed the Factory Girls' Association and organized a strike (Robinson 1883). A popular protest song during the 1836 strike went:

> Oh! Isn't it a pity, such a pretty girl as I
> Should be sent to the factory to pine away and die?

Oh! I cannot be a slave, I will not be a slave

For I'm so fond of liberty.

That I cannot be a slave. (Lavender 1998)

The Lowell mill factory workers felt that their conditions could be likened to wage slavery because the labour movement at that time was not accustomed to working for a wage paid by an owner. The Mill Girls leadership were quoted as saying during the strike that: "Those who work in the mills ought to own them, not have the status of machines ruled by private despots who are entrenching monarchic principles on democratic soil as they drive downward freedom and rights, civilization, health, morals and intellectuality in the new commercial feudalism" (qtd. in Chomsky 2002: 29). The women workers eventually realized that the pursuit of a fair wage was the only way they could be fairly compensated as well as retain their human rights and dignity.

So, by the time Gibson entered cotton manufacturing in 1885, the industry on both sides of the Atlantic had matured. However, labour strife and tension still existed, and employees sought to assert themselves by organizing. In fact, most of the bosses hired to run Gibson's mill came from Lowell, so they were acquainted with the different approaches to working conditions. Gibson ran his cotton-mill operation with the same monarchic principles as his counterparts in the United States, with the exception that he personally had high moral convictions, which he also expected from his employees. Gibson was also concerned for the health and well-being of his employees, and he did not exploit the position he held over them by charging higher prices than necessary for goods in the company store or higher rents for housing. He was also interested in the spiritual well-being of his employees, demonstrated in his generous contributions to various religious faiths. This interest in the health and spiritual well-being of employees prevented labour from successfully organizing in his cotton mill during his ownership. In 1900, a provincial publication indicates that: "English experts recently declared that this mill surpassed in its equipment the vast majority of English cotton mill factories" (Province of New Brunswick 1900: 587).

In 1888, the federal government established the Royal Commission on the Relations of Capital and Labour in Canada. Gibson testified that 425 people were employed at the cotton mill and most of them were women. Wages varied because of piece work, but the average wage in the spinning department was 75 cents to 80 cents a day for women and $1.50 for men. Employees worked from 6:45 a.m. until 6:00 p.m., with one hour for lunch. It was reported that child labour was common, and children as young as twelve years old were employed for 30 cents a day. Employees lived in the company houses and paid $4.00 to $7.00 dollars a month and purchased what they needed from the company store. The rent and bill from the store was deducted from their wages.

It was also reported by the royal commission that the superintendent of the Marysville Cotton Mill testified that: "This is the most quiet place I ever worked in, so far as dissatisfaction among employees is concerned." But there were contrary voices in the community that were trying to raise the profile of worker issues. Martin Butler, who was referred to as a "self-styled obscure socialist editor with no education to boast of, a certain sense of right and justice and a little experience mixed with a certain amount of horse sense," established a monthly newspaper called *Butler's Journal* (B. Pond, *Daily Gleaner* 1976). He was focused on social reform and published the first edition of his paper in Fredericton in July of 1890. He advocated for workers' rights and published articles such as "The Factory Girl's Last Day," a poem from 1832 about the death of a ten-year-old girl who died while working in a Derbyshire cotton mill. Although Butler respected the way Gibson treated his employees, he was not averse to portraying what he considered to be unfair labour practices in the Fredericton area, including Marysville.

There is no doubt that Boss Gibson was generous to the people of Marysville. He paid for the salary of the minister and stipend of the choir at Marysville Methodist Church. He gave land or materials to other churches in Marysville. He allowed people to take as much wood as they could physically carry from his lumber operations to either build a house or to use as firewood. Gibson was known to load up a train and take his employees on a picnic along the Nashwaak River. He paid for a brass band that graced various community events over the years. In 1885, to celebrate the opening of the cotton mill, he seated one thousand of his employees and their families for a turkey dinner (Pond 1983: 150). Alex Gibson was also known to burn the ledger accounts of workers who purchased items from his store on credit when he was having a particularly good financial year.

Like most entrepreneurs, Gibson was a complicated person. It would seem that his desire to build a cotton mill and a Methodist church that would rival any in the province or elsewhere is indicative of his competitive character and desire to be recognized. There is no doubt that Gibson was committed to work. This was clear when Sir John A. Macdonald and his wife were in Fredericton to lay a cornerstone for a new railway bridge across the Saint John River. Gibson was not present because he was in Saint John for business, so the Macdonalds came to visit him at his home in Marysville the following day. This account seems to convey that business was indeed more important than social etiquette.

Since he left so few accounts from his own life, it is sometimes difficult to determine what exactly defined Gibson's personality. Charles Henry Lugrin, in his obituary of Gibson, gave the following summary of his character: "A very shy man ... [he] appeared to live in a world apart from others.... Some men loved him: many men esteemed him; more men feared him; no man understood him. He probably did not even understand himself" (qtd. in Pond 1983: 36).

Gibson's Legacy

When the Methodist church burned in 1911, the congregants no longer had the Boss to cover expenses and maintenance. The members decided to rebuild the church in 1913 and have maintained it ever since. They have shown their continued commitment to their faith as well as to their founder; Gibson is frequently referenced during services, and members of the congregation have taken it upon themselves to maintain the gravestones in the Gibson family plot. It seems that the congregation realizes the debt that is owed to Gibson for all of the things he did for the community.

It would appear that Gibson put considerable effort into ensuring that the town of Marysville had a future after his death in 1913. In that same year, Canadian Cottons Limited from Montreal sent down a twenty-six-year-old manager to run the mill. Joseph Dolphin treated the workers in much the same way as Boss Gibson had. According to Pond, Dolphin tended to generally emulate Gibson in part by determining a need in the community and taking care of it (Pond 1983: 31). He was instrumental in having the recreational centre in Marysville constructed (Dawson Centre) and supported the residents in their pursuits to improve their company homes. He also supported baseball and allowed people to cut wood on company land at reasonable rates. After thirty-one years as the mill manager, he was transferred back to Montreal and retired shortly after when he saw what the owners of the company wanted from their workforce. Dolphin is quoted as saying "I never saw men so obsessed with money and yet so unconcerned about their mills and who cared less for their employees" (ibid.). After Dolphin's departure, the mill had four managers between 1944 and 1954.

An article appeared in *Maclean's* magazine when the mill closed for the first time in 1954. The article focused on how manufacturing in the country was under increasing pressure from foreign competition and profiled Marysville as an example of how hundreds of employees were being forced out of work for the first time in their lives. The economic shock was somewhat lessened by the introduction of unemployment insurance, which was a relatively new tool to offset hardship. The mill workers were at a loss as to how to find new work. Notwithstanding this, the mill re-opened two years later, under new management, and continued to operate for nearly twenty more years.

After the 1973 mill closure, people were still talking about Boss Gibson and speculating on what he would do if he were still alive to show them the way. An anonymous resident submitted a poem in Fredericton's *Daily Gleaner* newspaper following the closure that summed up the sentiment of many Marysville residents. The first stanza went like this, "I dreamed last night the Boss came back; Alexander was his name. He strolled around the town he built, And muttered 'What a shame'" (qtd. in Pelletier and Coghlan 1975: 13). The poem goes on to suggest that there is something wrong with the present generation because they could not figure out how to keep people employed at the mill. The poem seemingly gives voice to a community looking for guidance on how to move forward, perhaps still looking for the Boss to lead, sixty years after his death. A similar account of this occurred when Mac Campbell, the minister of Boss Gibson's former church, was telling a story about Gibson to a new member of the community. The newcomer responded to the minister by asking if Gibson was still alive. The minister replied: "Yes indeed, his spirit is still very much alive" (personal interview, Malcolm Campbell, May 2004).

According to Pelletier and Coghlan (1975: 12), Boss Gibson's "patriarchal munificence had a stultifying effect on individual initiative that continued on until present day." There is a history in Marysville of looking to local politicians, whether municipal or provincial, to ensure that issues and concerns are addressed. Ed Allen, the MLA, was the go-to person for many years, and a local councillor, Walter Brown, later fulfilled this role.

The renovation of the closed cotton mill resulted in a new wave of enthusiasm and confidence for the residents of Marysville. In 1986, the mill was designated a National Historic Site. It seems that the renovation of the cotton mill and the recognition of the federal government reinforced in the community the venerable legacy that Gibson had left them.

The other lasting component of Gibson's legacy was the school and churches in the area. The original schoolhouse was built by Gibson in 1864. It was replaced in 1927, when the Alexander Gibson Memorial School was built and became a cornerstone of the community. In 2001, the school hosted a reunion and more than 2,000 people returned and participated in various events. Historian Murray Young addressed the children at the school and recounted his experience as a student there many years earlier. "With a stable workforce, solid buildings and the tradition of Boss Gibson to inspire it, there was a happy and generous spirit in Marysville. I remember it from the many hours I spent there on the playground of Alexander Gibson Memorial School." In 2012, the school, in conjunction with the 150th anniversary of the founding of Marysville, hosted another celebration to recognize the school's relocation. After considerable debate, Gibson's name remained on the school.

In 2002, the former Marysville Hotel, built by Gibson on Mill Street in 1886, caught fire and the interior of the building was a total loss. The building was so compromised by the fire that the fire department had called for machinery to tear the structure down. City staff met with the fire chief on site to determine if the building absolutely had to be razed. The chief eventually deferred to the advice of a structural engineer that the building could remain standing without additional bracing. City of Fredericton staff worked to find a developer willing to take this building on as a project. A local non-profit affordable-housing group came forward in 2004 with a rezoning proposal to redevelop the building. The proposal was accepted by the City of Fredericton and the building was renovated into eight residential units. This project was able to show how two different interest groups could come together to preserve an important historical landmark, as well as provide needed affordable housing. The hotel was a unique brick building in a very high-profile location, and its removal would have been a significant loss. The community recognized the value of this building to the overall integrity of the former mill town and were prepared to work to preserve it.

In 2011, the community participated in a great neighbourhood contest sponsored by Royal LePage (realtors). The submission consisted of a lengthy YouTube clip containing numerous historical photographs of Marysville. This entry came in third out of 540 from across the country and had 15,000 views. In 2012, the community took part in a similar program sponsored by the Canadian Institute of Planners, and this entry received approximately 3,000 votes. These recent examples of community competitions clearly illustrate that Marysville is proud of the community and the people who have been a part of it.

It is not particularly surprising that Gibson's legacy endured. Some insight into how well regarded Gibson was in Marysville begins to appear in the local Fredericton newspaper the day after his death. Writers were already commenting on his contribution to the town he had created and to the province as a whole. The obituary states:

> With all of those with whom he came into contact throughout the Province of New Brunswick, Mr. Gibson has been looked up to with universal respect and admiration. In the eyes of his friends and neighbours he has been regarded as combining all of the good points of Rockefeller and Carnegie with none of their defects. He made Marysville an important point on the map commercially and a place of happy homes socially, in which dwell a contented prosperous people. To his energy and activity much of the industry and prosperity of the whole Province has been due. (*The Daily Gleaner*, August 14, 1913)

Another local newspaper commented that the story of his life read like a romance and the founder of Marysville "established therein industries which have made employment for hundreds and who for nearly half a century held the enviable position of New Brunswick's foremost citizen and greatest captain of industry" (*Semi-Weekly Mail*,

August 15, 1913). One might suggest that it is an accomplishment to have such complimentary sentiments shared about you days after your death, but it is extraordinary to have these same sentiments shared about you 100 years after your death.

Conclusion

When people discuss the legacy of Alexander Boss Gibson it seems to be with a mixed message. Due to a number of economic pressures beyond Gibson's control, his larger enterprises faltered at the end of the 19th century. Local folklore suggests that Gibson died a pauper, but it is well known that he had a $5,000 per year pension and remained in his mansion on Canada Street until his death.

Today, there are more than a hundred buildings in the community that are related to the various commercial developments of Boss Gibson. Most observers would agree that of the five communities amalgamated into Fredericton, Marysville has retained the strongest pre-amalgamation identity. The reason for this is twofold: physically, Marysville is unique because of the company houses and the renovated former cotton mill that still exist at its centre. Moreover, the older residents of Marysville and their children remember a time when the community had its own industry that employed much of the citizenry. As a result, this was a community that worked together, played sports together and worshipped together. The tight-knit community that once existed is no longer, and those who have moved to Marysville recently will never have the opportunity to interact so closely. Mill towns created a unique economic opportunity, but they also created a unique social environment that is hard to replicate.

People who have recently moved into Marysville certainly do realize that the town had an industrial history. However, they will not be able to experience the culture that once existed there. As the older generation passes and is replaced by residents with no direct ties to the industrial legacy of the community, it is important to ensure that the architectural integrity of the community remains intact. In this, the historic designations have enhanced awareness and appreciation.

Industrial towns emerge, prosper and decline for a number of reasons. Marysville has witnessed all three of these periods, but presently seems stable, and some of this stability has to be attributed to the founder himself. Some recent leaders have indeed recognized the vision that Gibson had for his community, and they have tapped into community sentiment by trying to protect, enhance and celebrate the boss's considerable legacy.

The economic seeds Gibson sowed over a century ago took root in Marysville and have survived challenging times. A number of Gibson's peers did well at the end of the 19th century and left a substantial endowment to their families. Gibson, on the other hand, was not able to provide a large endowment to his children. But maybe he realized that personal wealth is more temporal than the wealth that is created when a community believes in itself.

Note

1. Lockwood and Green donated a number of plans for industrial buildings they had constructed for clients in the United States to the Smithsonian. It was subsequently discovered that the plans for the Marysville cotton mill were included within this collection.

References

Acheson, T. W. 1972. The National Policy and Industrialization of the Maritimes, 1880-1910. *Acadiensis* 1 (2): 3-28.

Aitken, Maxwell. 1965. *Lord Beaverbrook: My Early Life*. Fredericton, NB: Brunswick Press.

Chomsky, Noam and C. P. Otero, eds. 2002. *Chomsky on Democracy and Education (Social Theory, Education and Cultural Change)*. New York: Routledge.

Daily Gleaner [Fredericton, NB]. 1913. Death Closes Remarkable Life of Alexander Gibson. August 14.

Daily Gleaner [Fredericton, NB]. 1975. Bonny Pond, History of Mill Dominates Marysville, June 5.

Dublin, Thomas. 1975. Women, Work, and Protest in the Early Lowell Mills: "The Oppressing Hand of Avarice Would Enslave Us." *Journal of Labor History* 16 (1) 1975: 99-116.

Grey, W. H. 1923. *The History of Marysville and the Nashwaak, 1923*.

Johnson, Dana. 1993. Historic Marysville [District]. Fredericton, New Brunswick. Historic Sites and Monuments Board of Canada Agenda Paper. November 1993-47. Ottawa: Parks Canada.

Kets de Vries, Manfred F. R. 1985. The Dark Side of Entrepreneurship. *The Harvard Business Review* 63 (6): 160-67.

Lavender, Catherine. 1998. 1834 *Boston Transcript* reports on the Strike. *"Liberty Rhetoric" and Nineteenth-Century American Women.* http://csivc.csi. cuny.edu/americanstudies/files/lavender/lowetext.html#transcript (accessed May 18, 2015).

Marysville New Brunswick. 1889. In *Our Dominion: Historical Toronto.* Historical Publication Company of Canada.

McIntyre, Glen. 1983. "And What Of All This?" Alexander Gibson's Marysville: A Walking Tour. Fredericton, NB: Fredericton Historical Research Project.

Pelletier, Francine and Coghlan, Ruth. 1975. A Study of Alexander Gibson's Influence on its Architectural and Social Development, University of New Brunswick Essay.

Philips, Fred. 1946. Boss Gibson Came to Marysville. *The Maritime Atlantic Advocate and Busy East.*

Pond, Douglas D. 1983. *The History of Marysville, New Brunswick.* Fredericton, NB: Centennial Print and Litho.

Province of New Brunswick. 1900. Alexander Gibson. In *Biographical Review.* Boston: Biographical Review and Publishing Company.

Robinson, Harriet. 1883. Harriet Hanson Robinson: Lowell Mill Girls. *Internet Modern History Sourcebook*, August 1997. https://legacy.fordham.edu/ halsall/mod/robinson-lowell.asp (accessed May 17, 2015).

Rosevear, Susan G. 1986. Alexander "Boss" Gibson: Portrait of a Nineteenth Century New Brunswick Entrepreneur. MA thesis, University of Maine, Orono.

Semi-Weekly Mail, [Fredericton, NB]. 1913. Alexander Gibson Sr. Terminated Long and Useful Life Early This Morning, After an Illness of Several Weeks – Was New Brunswick's Greatest Captain of Industry, August 14.

Squires, Austin W. 1980. *History of Fredericton, The Last 200 Years.* Fredericton, NB: Centennial Print and Litho.

Young, D. Murray. 1988. Slabtown: What's in a Name? *The Officers Quarterly* 4 (1): 3-6.

———. 1990. Our Industrial Heritage: The Marysville Cotton Mill. Address, at Marysville Place, on the occasion of the Marysville Cotton Mill being recognized as a National Historic Site by the Historic Sites and Monuments Board of Canada.

———. 1997. Industry in Marysville. Address, at the Alexander Gibson Memorial School, on the occasion of Marysville being recognized as a National Historic District by the Historic Sites and Monuments Board of Canada, 6.

———. 1998. Alexander "Boss" Gibson. In *Dictionary of Canadian Biography: Volume XIV, 1911-1920*, eds. Ramsay Cook and Jean Hamelin. Toronto: University of Toronto Press.

Chapter Three

Gail Weir

Company Housing at Wabana Iron-Ore Mines, Bell Island, Newfoundland

Prologue

Mines start up and shut down; miners and their families arrive and leave; their stories are part of the history of the company houses in which they lived. My grandmother Emeline's story is one of these. In the spring of 1908, the iron-pyrites mine at Pilley's Island, Newfoundland, closed down. Some of the laid-off miners travelled to Cape Breton each of the next few springs to work in coal mines, such as those at New Aberdeen and Caledonia, returning home in the fall to work in lumber camps. One of them was Stewart Luffman, whose wife, the former Emeline Rideout, had given birth to their third child that same month that the Pilley's Island mine closed. During this time, Wabana mines at Bell Island, which supplied the iron ore used in the Sydney steel plant, were increasing productivity. The two companies that owned these mines were each building houses to entice permanent employees, and they had agents recruiting labour throughout Newfoundland. Many men from Pilley's Island heeded the call and the companies were pleased to get these experienced miners.

Stewart, his two brothers and father were among them, as were three of Emeline's brothers and their families. They arrived at Bell

Island seeking a more settled life with good prospects for future prosperity. Stewart and Emeline had four small children when they came to Bell Island, in about 1911, and moved into their brand-new company house on Scotia Ridge. After so much economic uncertainty and the long train trip through the wilderness of Newfoundland, the permanency of the situation must have seemed a godsend to them.

Stewart was a driller and quickly became a drill foreman with the Scotia Company, driving the new submarine slope for the No. 3 mine. The family settled in and two more sons were born in the next few years. Stewart and his men worked the night shift, blasting the ore ahead of the muckers, who came down on the morning shift to shovel it into ore cars. Stewart was generally expected home for breakfast on work days at 7:30 a.m. Emeline had awoken one such morning earlier than usual, feeling there was something wrong. She came downstairs with her six-month-old baby to light the fire and start preparing breakfast. Her uneasy feeling was intensified when her oldest boy, Ned, came down and said he had just met his father on the stairs and wondered why he had not spoken to him. Emeline believed that this was an omen of death, and it sent a chill down her spine. When a knock came on the door a few minutes later, she opened it to the mine captain and the Salvation Army officer, and knew before they spoke why they were there. Just earlier, at 6:30 a.m., August 22, 1916, thirty-five-year-old Stewart was killed in a mine explosion, along with three of his men.

The two older boys, aged thirteen and eleven, were taken on by the company to run errands and do other work suitable for their ages. This supplemented the family income and allowed the family to remain in their company house. Emeline received a paltry widow's allowance of $8 a year from the Newfoundland government. From the company, she received compensation of $25 a month, which would be discontinued after five years. To make ends meet, she took in boarders, one of whom was John Dawe, a miner who was ten years her junior. A few years later, they married and went on to have four more children. The family continued to live in the company house on Fourth Street until about 1933. Emeline's five sons all grew up to be miners of Wabana iron ore, and her daughters, including my mother, married miners.

The company houses are a tangible reminder of the strength and fortitude of the men and women who came to Bell Island in those early years of mining: the men to perform the back-breaking, and sometimes deadly, work of extracting the iron ore that built the great steel industry of Nova Scotia, and the women to nurture and sustain them and their children. Before the Nova Scotia companies came to exploit the iron-ore riches of Bell Island, nobody lived on the island's north side, where the landscape was mostly forest and rock, but this is where most of the houses, both private and company-built, are located today. None of these houses would be there now if it had not been for mining. No one would have come from former mining towns such as Pilley's Island, Tilt Cove and Little Bay, from fishing communities around Conception Bay, Trinity Bay, the south coast, nor from the capital city of St. John's and other parts of Newfoundland. Nor would they have come from Nova Scotia, or Great Britain, Syria, Lebanon, Germany, Russia, Bulgaria, Lithuania, China or anywhere else to settle on Bell Island, following a dream of finding steady work that would sustain them and their families, if it had not been for the iron ore.

These houses represent the hopes and aspirations, hard work and determination of several generations of people of diverse cultural backgrounds. It is important to study and preserve these houses to understand who these people were and why they were here, from the beginnings of the Canadian steel industry, through two world wars, the Great Depression and beyond. They made enormous sacrifices just to get here and they accomplished extraordinary things in difficult circumstances. Houses that were provided for them by the mining companies eased their burdens and helped create a community of people with one goal: to live a better life. These houses should be recognized and celebrated. In doing so, we will recognize and celebrate the brave, hard-working people who lived in them.

Introduction

Bell Island, Newfoundland, is the home of the Wabana iron-ore mines, which were worked continuously from 1895 to 1966. They were developed by two companies based in Nova Scotia to supply steel mills there, so it is not surprising that the Wabana company houses are similar in style to those found in Cape Breton. Company employees were either "staff" or miners. The term "staff" was commonly used when speaking of the supervisory personnel, engineers, surveyors and clerical people who worked in and from the company's main office. They were fewer in number and their housing was generally of better quality than that provided to the miners. The miners were the "labouring class," the men who worked directly with the ore, extracting it first from open pits, but soon going underground, and then three miles (4.8 km) out under the ocean floor. Many commuting (weekday-resident) miners lived in either shacks or bunkhouses, while commuting staff lived in staff boarding houses. Company houses for resident miners were smaller and had fewer amenities than those for resident staff.

When the mines shut down in the 1960s, a dark cloud of economic depression settled over the area and a large portion of the population headed west to find new employment. Of those who stayed behind, some were close to retirement age, perhaps with little formal education or training, and did not care to uproot at this stage in their lives. Still others had large families of young children, making relocation a difficult prospect. Because of Bell Island's proximity to the province's capital city, some who remained found work as labourers and custodians with the provincial government as well as with private businesses in and around St. John's. Improved ferry services allowed them to commute daily and continue to live on Bell Island. Some who could not find regular work got by with government make-work projects and social assistance.

Within a year after the last mine closed, the population had dropped by about 50 per cent from its 1961 high of 12,281, then by about 20 per cent in each of the last three decades of the 20th century. Falling another 13 per cent between 2001 and 2011, it was down to fewer than 2,700 people in the 2011 census. As young people complete high school, many move away to study and work elsewhere. For 2012 and 2013, there were forty births and eighty-five deaths, a net loss of forty-five people, and the student population dropped by thirteen, reflecting the problem many rural communities face: an aging demographic and decreasing birth rate. In spite of the nearness of St. John's and the much cheaper housing on Bell Island, the ferry commute has been a deterrent to population growth.

It is mainly the descendants of the last generation of miners who have championed the heritage movement on Bell Island. They focused their attention on opening one of the mines for tours and building a miners' museum, both of which were enormous tasks considering the circumstances. This focus on the mining site was the most obvious and has proven to be a good choice, but it only showcases the work life of the area, overlooking the miners' home lives and the company houses as historic monuments. The house is the centre of family life, a place of refuge, sustenance and comfort after a hard day's work. Yet older houses are often taken for granted, as has happened here. This, coupled with the declining population, has resulted in a decline in the number of company houses and a lack of recognition of those that remain. Attention needs to be paid to these houses before their stories and what can be learned from them about the miners' home lives is lost forever.

The following is an inquiry into the history of the company housing at Wabana that, in the absence of official documentation, is based on published and personal accounts, as well as archival photographs.

Early Mining History

The first operator of the Wabana mines was the New Glasgow Iron, Coal and Railway Company (subsequently the Nova Scotia Steel and Coal Company, referred to hereafter as the Scotia Company). It sent its chief ore and quarries engineer, Robert E. Chambers, to Bell Island in 1893 in search of a good supply of iron ore for its Ferrona steel mill, near New Glasgow, on mainland Nova Scotia. That province had coal for the manufacture of steel, but attempts to obtain a reliable local source of iron ore had proved futile (Cameron 1960; McCann 1981). By coincidence, just as the Scotia Company was in need of iron ore, some amateur prospectors, by the family name of Butler, had taken out claims on what they believed to be a rich source of iron ore at Bell Island. They lacked the finances to exploit their discovery, and Newfoundland, which was not then part of Canada, lacked the coal needed to start a steel industry, so the Butlers engaged an agent to seek an enterprise interested in purchasing their claims (RPANL PBF, P6/B/62; Fay 1956: 217-18). Chambers arrived in June 1893 and immediately realized that the property had value, finding the iron ore that was needed just 412 miles (663 km) from Nova Scotia and directly on the marine track of North Atlantic shipping. With little fanfare, the stage was set for launching the steel industry of Nova Scotia, and the fate of a small Newfoundland island on the easternmost coast of the North American continent was sealed.

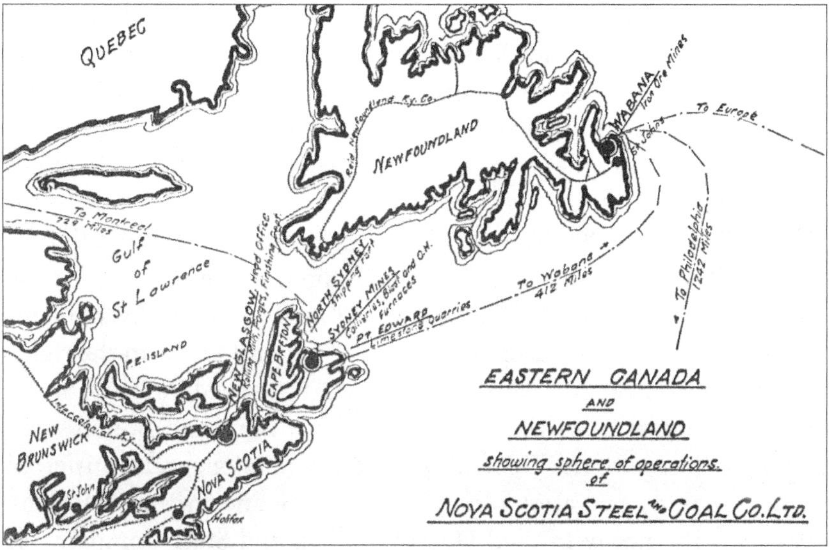

Fig. 1 – *The Scotia Company's "sphere of operations" in 1912, including the shipping route to Wabana and beyond (Nova Scotia Steel and Coal 1912: 3).*

On that first visit, Chambers found a tranquil, pastoral setting. The majority of the local population of 709 were farmer-fisher families of English and Irish descent, living mainly in the two natural landing spots on the south side of an island that was otherwise a fortress of steep cliffs. The iron-ore deposits were located on the uninhabited north side of the island, which was "heavily timbered with fir trees, and to find one's way it was necessary to make use of a compass; the south side was dotted at intervals by primitive farms" (Chambers and Chambers 1909: 139). Chambers returned with company officials a year later and began "locating the exact landing place of a line of railway and laying plans generally" (Bown 1957 [1894]: 2).[1]

When Thomas Cantley, then secretary of the Scotia Company, visited Bell Island in September 1895, Chambers had already begun work on the building of the pier and tramway, and 160 miners, mostly native Bell Islanders, were employed in the surface pits. For this new mining enterprise, Cantley chose the Abenaki word *wabana* meaning "the place where daylight first appears," a fitting name for the continent's easternmost mine site (Bown 1957 [1895]: 3; Cantley 1911: 274). By December 1895, 2,500 tons of ore were ready for the first shipment to Ferrona. In 1896, surplus ore was being shipped to the United

States, and a year later to Europe. Wabana's location was ideal for the company's purposes, and Chambers proclaimed that "The quiet peace of the silent forest has given place to the noise and bustle incidental to the operation of a great industry; while the nearly untenanted wilderness has become a populated centre of activity" (Chambers and Chambers 1909: 139).

By February 1899, the American entrepreneur Henry Whitney had consolidated coal mines in Cape Breton into the Dominion Coal Company (also known as DOMCO) and now looked to Wabana for iron ore for steel production. The Scotia Company sold him the rights to its lower iron-ore bed while retaining the upper bed for itself. Scotia used the money from this sale to purchase the Cape Breton coal-mining holdings of the General Mining Association, and transferred its steel-making operations from Ferrona to Sydney Mines (McCann 1981: 52). The newly formed Dominion Iron and Steel Company (or DISCO, referred to here as the Dominion Company) began constructing its iron and steel plant in Sydney that same year. Both companies used Wabana iron ore, and it was the sole source of ore for the Sydney steel plant blast-furnace until the 1950s (Anson 1951: 601).

Fig. 2 – Map of Bell Island showing the position of the submarine mines in 1951 (Anson 1951: 597).

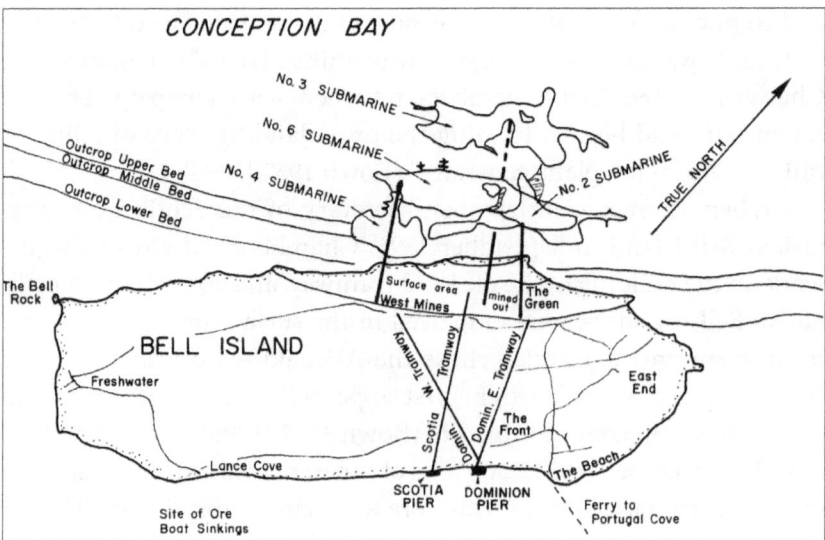

82

Early Company Housing

The first company housing on Bell Island was built for the original Scotia staff, including for Chambers, who planned and managed the mining operations, an accountant and a few other supervisory staff, all recruited from head office in New Glasgow. They arrived each spring to administer activities for the mining season and went back to Nova Scotia when shipping ceased for the winter. When supplies had begun arriving at St. John's for the mine in July 1895, included was a large quantity of dressed lumber for the construction of buildings. No doubt this was for the staff housing and office space at the pier.

There was no local newspaper in the early days of the mining community. Published details of developments on Bell Island were dependent on sporadic visits by journalists and those monitoring the comings and goings through the port of St. John's and via sittings of the Newfoundland legislature. Generally, visitors seemed to be so in awe of the magnificent structure of the pier, the cross-island ore-car tramway and the blasting and excavation that they did not make note of things as mundane as where or how incoming workers were living. The few early accounts that do exist do not mention the building of staff or miners' housing. Most information about housing in that period appeared after the fact. It was reported, for example, in January 1931 in the St. John's *Daily News* that

> One of the Island's landmarks, and a link with its early history, disappeared when the old Scotia [Company] staff house was torn down. It was one of the first buildings erected by the pioneer company, Nova Scotia Steel and Coal, when mining operations began. (Bown 1957 [1931]: 37)

The staff house, as it was commonly called, was a combination boarding house and private hotel that accommodated mining-season Nova Scotians, visiting company officials and special guests who were there for the short term. It was not long before the mining was year-round and staff from Nova Scotia started moving permanently to Bell Island, bringing their families with them.

Arthur House, who would become DISCO's local assistant manager in 1907, arrived at Bell Island in June 1899, shortly after his employer acquired the original Scotia Pier. Here is his description of the pier area, and of some early Dominion housing, when he arrived:

Standing at the house in which Mr. Chambers lived, only three other houses were to be seen over the whole panorama of the Dominion Iron and Steel Company's property, in fact there were no more there to see. The old Mine House under the hill, Doctor Freebairn's Surgery, which was originally a blacksmith's forge, and our office. Mr. Chambers moved out of the house he had originally built for himself to a new house at the [new] Scotia Pier and, two years after, I moved in the house he had vacated. We built three official residences and ten miners' houses which were known as "Ten Commandments," a Staff House at Gully Pond Ridge [West Mines], a staff [boarding] house at the Pier, a residence for Warehouse man, a residence for Mechanical Foreman and the Doctor, a General Warehouse, and enlarged the old office. (House 1939)[2]

Fig. 3 – Map of Bell Island showing the locations of company housing and offices (author illustration).

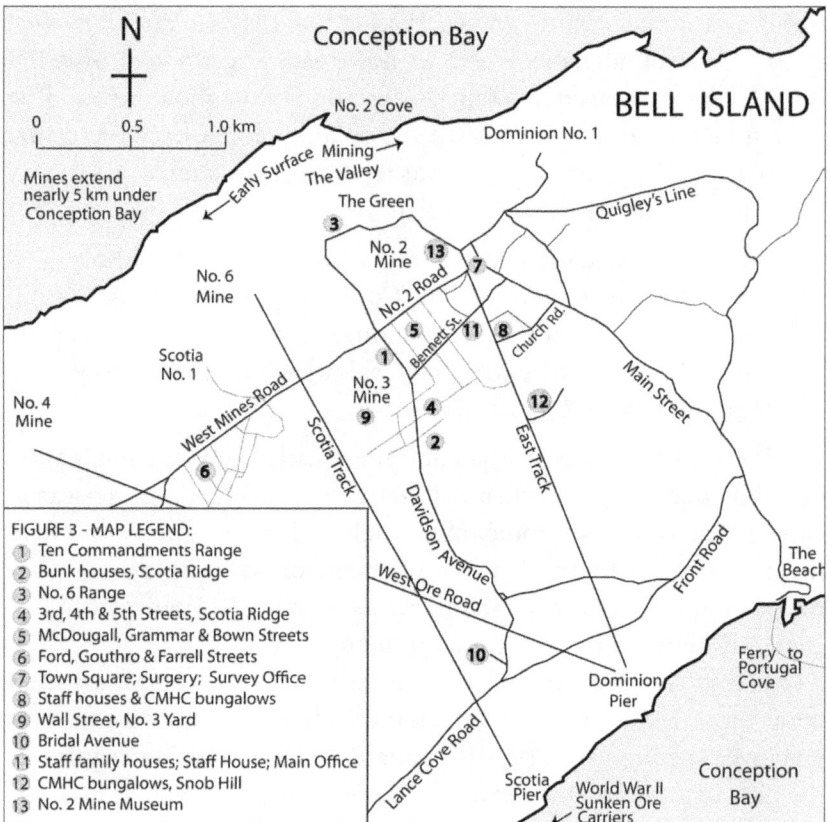

Staff housing will be dealt with in more detail later, but first a look at how the miners were accommodated. Most of the earliest miners were Bell Islanders. In January 1897, Rev. W. R. Smith of Portugal Cove stated that the Bell Island Beach, one of the two original settlements, "had been deserted since October 1896, all the former residents having moved up on the Island after the start of mining so as to be nearer their farms and the mine" (Bown 1957 vol. 1: 6). Presumably, these were the owners of the "large number of new houses being built by young men in the eastern section of the island," as reported in the *Daily News* in August 1896 (Bown 1957 [1896]: 5).[3] One old-timer lamented that "the sound of the steam whistle told of a new order of things," as the native families were abandoning their traditional livelihoods of agriculture and the fishery, selling their boats, neglecting their lands and disposing of their cattle to seek employment in the mines (Bown 1957, vol. 1: 8; Morris 1906).

Men from other areas were also obtaining employment on Bell Island. Of the two hundred men on day and night shifts in the summer of 1896, sixty or seventy were from Portugal Cove, the nearest community on the mainland of Newfoundland (Bown 1957 vol. 1: 5). These men would arrive by small sailing vessels on Sunday evening and, weather permitting, they would return home to their families the following Saturday evening. On Bell Island, these weekly commuters were called "mainlandsmen." They continued to find work at Wabana, along with others who were being recruited by the company as business increased. Mining was all done on the surface at this time; by 1898 ore shipments were expected to more than double those of the previous year, so more men were needed. Some of these mainlandsmen may have boarded with residents, but most probably lived in shacks.

The "Shack Method" of Housing Men

With two companies now operating mines at Wabana, and the plans of both to build steel plants in Cape Breton, mining activity moved into high gear. Along with the resident miners, men from small fishing communities from all around Conception Bay, as well as from St. John's, found work. There were 1,300 employed by 1899, and visiting journalist I. C. Morris (1899) commented that "many miners were living in rough shacks constructed of inch board and covered with roofing felt." This was the first reference in the contemporary press to how the mainlandsmen were living. In a later article, Morris (1906: n.p.) recalled that when he had visited in 1900, "labourers were living in temporary shacks along the line and around the mine."[4]

By 1900, the two companies employed 1,600 men between them. Wabana experienced its first serious labour strike that year. When it was settled, almost six weeks later, it was observed that "soon after daybreak the next morning, the surface of Conception Bay was black with boats bringing men from all parts of the Bay back to the Island to resume work" (Bown 1957, vol. 1: 13). Many of these men would have been living in shacks during the tenure. When they arrived for work each week, they brought their week's supply of food in cardboard boxes tied up with string. They would carry their clean clothing and loaves of homemade bread in white flour sacks.

A survey of the literature on housing for miners in North America reveals little consideration of the use of shacks. Where they are discussed, not much attention is paid to their construction or design,

Fig. 4 – Miners, ca. 1930, arriving at the wharf on The Beach at Bell Island in small open motor boats from their homes around Conception Bay on a Sunday evening. The man standing in the foreground is holding a cardboard box that contains his week's food (ASC BIPC C-202: 1.12.030).

or whether they were built by the miners, or if the mining companies employed carpenters to build them to particular specifications (MacKinnon 2009: 120, 141; Queen's University 1953: 27-28). One thing is certain: amenities were sparse; there was no running water or electricity. Wabana's miners' shacks were single-room, containing no more than a small wood/coal stove for heat and cooking, and as many as six bunks.

Frederick Jardine came to Bell Island in 1907 as a DISCO clerk and frequently contributed accounts of local history and lore to newspapers. In a 1938 report he wrote,

> In the initial days of mining on Bell Island, mining life was rough and hard, mostly an out of doors life, in dirt and grime. It was no place for the weakling, or fastidious. Living conditions were poor, the pay small.... [The miner] had to fend for himself, if he could not rough it he suffered. Fending for one's self was mostly the cause why a shack town sprang into being, with unsightly lodgings of every description. (Jardine 1938)

Jardine was referring here to the area known as "The Green." By the end of 1899, Bell Island's permanent population had doubled from when mining began. For an election held that autumn, two polling booths were added, both in "The Mines" neighbourhood. This was the area on the north side that included The Green, and that had previously been unoccupied forest. Since the start of mining, it had become home not only to the mines themselves, but to the growing business district, and to miners and their families moving in from other areas. The No. 2 mine ran beneath The Green, "where many of the miners were living in shacks" (Bown 1957, vol. 1: 23).[5] While there were only 325 registered voters on the island in the spring of 1904,

> it should be remembered that it consisted of resident voters only. There was quite a large population but the majority were miners belonging to other districts who did not claim Bell Island as their permanent home, and did not vote there on polling day. (Bown 1957, vol. 1: 18)

With so many men living away from their homes and families, and fending for themselves in overcrowded shacks, The Green garnered a lot of notoriety in the first half of the 20th century. Much of its bad reputation came from drinking on payday and the fights that resulted. It was an important neighbourhood in the life of the Wabana mines, and deserves special attention to uncover its rich and colourful history.

Accounts of the living and working conditions of the miners were rare and only appeared in the St. John's newspapers when there was death or destruction, such as the following story. A severe snowstorm was raging on March 4, 1904, when

> Constable Greene, while patrolling the mines area during the night, noticed the door of a shack half open. On investigating, he found a man, who was living alone there, in a dying condition. Rev. Booth was called, also a doctor. The patient died during the night and death attributed to hunger and exposure. Deceased was sixty-eight years old and belonged to Cornwall, England. He had been working in the mines. (Bown 1957, vol. 1: 17)

Then, in May 1905, seven men from Upper Island Cove, Conception Bay, narrowly avoided death. "They had retired at ten o'clock, tired after their day's work in the mine, leaving a fire burning in their stove. Four hours later, one of them awoke and found the place in flames. They barely escaped with their lives" (Bown 1957, vol. 1: 19).

Output rose to more than 800,000 tons by 1905. A new deck head was started for Dominion's No. 2 mine. Scotia's surface ore was depleted in June and it became necessary to start driving a slope under the waters of the bay. The mines were now closing for the Christmas season only, staying open in the wintertime. Scotia's labour agent was in St. John's early in 1907 on a recruiting drive to engage five hundred men for the winter. They were being offered $1.35 a day, less $0.20 for lodging, which was provided by the company. The Scotia Company had 160 shacks, each housing six men. Six hundred men were already employed in 1907 (Bown 1957 [1907]: 21). Some of these shacks may be the "rough shacks" as described by Morris.

An indication of the common use of shacks is found in a November 24, 1920, letter from a company accountant to the prime minister of the Dominion of Newfoundland during the turmoil in the industry that accompanied the merger of the Dominion Coal Company, DISCO and the Scotia Company into the British Empire Steel Corporation (BESCO), which resulted in a large number of layoffs: "Many of the men own their homes on Bell Island and are not shackmen, so distress will be great" (ASC SRSC, C-250: 7.02.014). By January 1922, a serious situation had developed on Bell Island, when the creation of BESCO was finalized. There were stockpiles of ore on the surface sufficient for two years and the mines had to be closed owing to lack of markets.

Following a mass meeting of miners, a committee was formed to meet with government officials and mine managers. An arrangement was worked out whereby mining resumed for three days a week, reducing miners to half-time pay of $8 per week. Four hundred laid-off miners from communities around Conception Bay were called back to work but were unable to reach Bell Island due to ice in the bay. When they did arrive, they quit work again after a short time, claiming they could not live on $6.25 a week, which was the net amount of their earnings after paying for lodging. BESCO pointed out that it did not need the ore and was only staffing the mines as a relief measure. The government attempted to relieve the burden on the commuting miners by requesting of the company "the free use of Shacks for destitute miners." The manager of the Wabana mines, C. B. Archibald, responded, "During late years the Company has given up the Shack method of housing men, and now we do not own any Shacks which could be used for the purpose required" (Bown 1957 [1922]: 66; ASC SRSC, C-250: 7.02.030).

Despite this statement, shacks were still being used years later. Matthew Smith, a commuting miner, said that when he first went to Bell Island to work, in 1938, there were not many houses on The Green; there were mostly shacks, which were owned by a local merchant who rented them out for $1 per month (personal communication, August 1, 1991). While no documentation has been found stating that these were the original company shacks, it is likely that the company sold its shacks to a private business owner who rented them to commuting miners. If that was indeed the case, it was a win-win situation for the company. Not only had it divested itself of these "temporary" shacks that it was now replacing with bunkhouses, over which it would have more control, but the fact that another business was continuing the "shack method" of housing miners meant that the company did not need to provide as much housing as it might have if these shacks were no longer available.

Though the company may no longer have owned shacks, there is a suggestion that management felt some responsibility for them. In May 1933, the Depression was hitting hard and the mines were worked only two days a week. The first to be laid off were the mainlandsmen. As a result, the miners' shacks on The Green would have been empty until things improved. Eighty-five resident families were receiving relief at that time and the government introduced a policy requiring work in return. The local health officer was instructed to put able-bodied men to work, "for the benefit of the community," to clean up The Green. The company contributed horses for hauling away rubbish, paint for hydrants, lime for fences and implements such as shovels and rakes. It was the first thorough clean-up of the area. In praise of the effort and the amazing transformation that had taken place, a song was written in parody of the popular song "Twenty-One Years":

> He put on the dole crowd to clean up The Green,
> And in twenty-one hours a change could be seen.
> A big job he tackled, so give him three cheers,
> It hadn't been cleaned up for twenty-one years.
> He used Company horses and plenty of lime,
> For twenty-one years, boys, is a mighty long time.
> A new place you'll see, boys, if you b'lieve all you hears,
> There won't be a shack left in twenty-one years. (Bown 1957, vol. 2, 51)

Mess Houses/Bunkhouses

In response to the Newfoundland government's 1922 request for the free use of shacks for commuting miners, Archibald wrote, "In place of the Shack system, the Companies have built Mess and Bunk Houses, of which we have enough to handle 500 men; these we will arrange to let the men have, rent free, but they will have to pay their own cooks" (ASC SRSC, C-250: 7.02.030). Whereas, with the shack method of housing, the men paid for the use of the shack but had to provide everything else and took turns with the cooking and dishwashing, for the men in the bunkhouses, at least in later years, the company provided the house and bunks and paid the cooks. The men had to bring their own mattresses and pay for their food (personal communication with Hubert Rose, July 2, 1991).

The first record of company bunkhouses was in early 1908, when it was announced that the Dominion Company was building ten mess houses for two hundred men (Bown 1957 [1908]: 24).[6] Eventually there were bunkhouses near most of the mines (Clayton King, personal communication, February 7, 2006; Patrick Mansfield, personal communication, July 4, 1991). When, in November 1937, "A large shed used for storing hay near Dominion No. 1 was burned down with its contents which consisted of forty tons of hay," it was pointed out that "it had been used in earlier days as a mess house for mainland workmen" (Bown 1957 [1937]: 67).

James Case was reported to be "building a mess house" in 1928. Case was a builder and general merchant who also sold building supplies. His business was in the Scotia Ridge area of Davidson Avenue, and it is likely that the "mess house" he was building was one of the company's four one-storey mess and open-dormer-style bunkhouses that were quite near his store. We know they were there in 1933, as they were mentioned in a news item about a rock crusher that "went into operation on the Scotia Ridge opposite the mess houses" (Bown 1957 [1928]: 23, 1957 [1933]: 53).

Hubert Rose started working in the mines in the early 1940s and lodged at one of the Scotia Ridge bunkhouses. He recalled that there was a mess house with a cook and "cookie" (assistant cook) and three bunkhouses, each accommodating thirty-two men. On payday, the cook would take his food order to one of the merchants. The food would be delivered and money would be collected from each man for his share.

> There were no facilities or hot water or anything like that, just cold water. They had two or three 200-pound pork barrels, and they had a pump outside with the water running all the time. And these barrels had to be filled up every day for cooking and for washing. They used to cook a 200-pound barrel of salt meat for one meal for 100 men. Every day they used to mix up a 100-pound bag of flour to make bread. The company wouldn't supply a mattress. All they supplied was the wooden bunks, so you had to buy the mattress. We've taken the mattress out by the door, held open the rolled edges and swept the bedbugs out with a broom. They'd be so thick that it'd be right full. That's where they'd be, in the rolled edges. Every weekend practically, the mess houses would have to be smoked out. When the men would all

Fig. 5 – Photo taken in July 1926 at Bell Island of two unidentified buildings that appear to be bunkhouses. Elements of these buildings are similar to the bunkhouse described by MacKinnon in 1982 as being the last example of a Wabana bunkhouse, except that these buildings seem to be at least twice as large. The photographer, Alphonsus Lawton, titled the photo "Building a Boat," but unfortunately did not mention the buildings (ASC ATLPA, C-354: 1.03.004).

> leave Friday or Saturday evening, there'd be somebody go in and light this sulfur to smoke out the bed bugs. (Hubert Rose, personal communication, July 2, 1991)

In 1980, when Richard MacKinnon, who was then a Memorial University graduate student, did a study of Wabana's company housing, only one example of a bunkhouse remained, but the interior had sustained fire damage and was inaccessible. The building was "near Scotia No. 1, the earliest mine site in Wabana, and was two storeys high, two rooms wide and one room deep" (MacKinnon 1982a: 67). It no longer exists.

It should be noted that when all four mines were working, not all commuting miners could be accommodated in the company's shacks and bunkhouses. At those times, some men rented backyard sheds on company or private property. Others boarded with families, as John Dawe did when the newly widowed Emeline Luffman had to take boarders to help feed her children. While technically these men were often living on company property, it was the lady of the house who cooked for them, and their rent money went to her.

Company Houses for Resident Miners with Families

All the company houses built for families at Wabana were detached single-family units. While the Scotia and Dominion companies built many double houses for their workers in Cape Breton, they also built some detached houses there. In company towns such as Sydney Mines, Sydney, New Waterford, Glace Bay and area, there are streets of company houses similar in style to those at Wabana. No records have been uncovered specifically stating who designed the Wabana company houses or even who built them, but it seems obvious that they were constructed from the same plans as the detached company houses in Cape Breton, where the Rhodes and Curry Company built hundreds of miners' houses (Tye and Latta 1989: 32). The 1913 directory for Bell Island lists 47 carpenters, and it seems likely that these local men were employed in the building of the company houses (Newfoundland Directory 1913: 459-84).

None of the companies' miners' houses had bathrooms, running water or electricity when they were built, and not for many years afterward. This was common for houses all over North America in that era, not just miners' houses. Many house-plan books from the first decade of the 20th century feature houses without bathrooms. The company drilled wells for community taps in central areas, and householders had to fetch water in buckets from these taps. Each house had a privy in the backyard. The company employed men who came at night to remove what was politely termed "night soil." A horse pulled a so-called honey cart from outhouse to outhouse through service lanes behind the houses. While electricity became available in the late 1920s, many of the company houses did not get indoor plumbing and bathrooms until they were purchased, in the 1950s and 1960s, by their occupants or by others after the mines ceased operation (Canadian-British Engineering Consultants 1958: 10-11). Attached to the outhouse was a coal shed. Coal from Cape Breton was used in the kitchen stove, the sole source of heat for the house. Further, as a 1927 news report observed, "Company tenements, which hitherto had been painted a uniform colour, red, blossomed out in light shades, with each house having a different colour" (Bown 1957 [1927]: 19).

By 1931, the Depression had arrived and miners resultantly worked only two ten-hour shifts a week, giving them $21.60 a month. From this came many payroll deductions: rent $5.00, coal $4.00, doctor $0.30, cartage (of outhouse waste) $0.80 (down from $1.00) and electricity $1.40. Total deductions were $11.50, leaving families $10.10 per month for food and clothing (Bown 1957 [1931]: 39).

As with the shacks and bunkhouses, references to the building of the family houses are sparse. House said in his 1939 article that by 1903, "A great many houses had been built at the mine by private parties and along the road," the only road to the mining district at that time being the one that connected it to the Beach (House 1939; Canadian-British Engineering Consultants 1958: 5).[7] Morris reported that when he had visited in 1900, "dwellings were limited to residents of the place and the staff quarters were small," but, by 1906, "new homesteads were taking the place of the shacks" (Morris 1906).

Fig. 6 – A Scotia Company one-and-a-half-storey, one-room wide, two-rooms deep, front-gabled miner's house on the north side of No. 6 Range (The Green), built ca. 1906 (author photograph, January 4, 2013).

Scotia Company Miners' Family Houses

It was not until 1907 that it was reported in the *Daily News* that the Scotia Company had fifty dwellings, the first documentation that either of the companies had built family houses. These may have been the "new homesteads" that Morris mentioned. His article gave no indication where these dwellings were located, but Jardine remembered that when he arrived in 1907, "the Scotia Company had a whole street of houses at what is now called No. 6 [Range]" (Bown 1957 [1907]: 21; Jardine, 1938).[8] This was just east of No. 6 mine in the northwestern section of The Green. There were about a dozen one-and-a-half-storey front-gabled houses on this street. The ones remaining today on the north side of the street are one-room wide and two-rooms deep, while the ones on the south side were built taller and are three-rooms deep. Some on the south side have since been converted to bungalows; a few were destroyed by fire. One of these houses has been occupied over the past 100 years by four generations of the Nathan Picco family, from Portugal Cove. Picco moved his family into the house in about 1915. The present owner, Nathan's granddaughter, grew up in the house and raised her own family there. Family tradition has it that the house was built in 1897 (George Picco, personal communication, November 11, 1984; Annette Hurley, personal communication, December 22, 2010, May 16, 2012).

The 1954 Wabana insurance plan (Insurers' Advisory Organization 1954: 1) shows the service lane to the south of No. 6 Range as "First Street," even though it had no houses fronting it in 1954. The remainder of Scotia Company's "fifty dwellings" may have included small bungalows that were built close by, in The Valley, The Green and along the No. 2 Road, which ran along the southern boundary of The Green. Originally, this road had been the tramway track from the No. 2 mine to the Scotia tramway track, but this mine ceased operations in 1950 and the tracks were removed. The insurance plan shows this road labelled as "Second Street," perhaps through a misinterpretation of "2" as "Second." There are still a few one-storey company houses along the north side of this road. MacKinnon said of them,

> These houses do not appear to be Company houses upon first viewing, but according to oral tradition, the Companies did construct a number of [one-storey] houses along "The [Scotia] Ridge," on "The Green" and in "The Valley." Few remain in each

of these areas. They are similar in size, built in rows, and are prevalent in areas adjacent to the open-pit mines. They resemble the ubiquitous bungalow found throughout North America. It is difficult to pinpoint the original location of these houses because many were moved after being constructed. Only a few remain near the former mine sites ... these houses are similar in floor plan and size. (MacKinnon 1982a: 68; see also MacKinnon 1982b: 10, 22)

The company bungalows contained only four rooms: a living room, kitchen and two bedrooms (Jessie Dawe-Hussey, personal communication, December 1, 2010). While it is fairly easy to spot the bungalows that were built by the Scotia Company in the Scotia Ridge neighbourhood, there are quite a few bungalows on The Green, in The Valley, and in the Scotia No. 1 and Dominion No. 1 areas that may or may not have been company-built. Only a detailed heritage inventory of all houses would uncover their origins.

Third Street, Fourth Street and Fifth Street, immediately south and southeast of Scotia's No. 3 mine yard, make up the neighbourhood of Scotia Ridge. As Jardine related, "In 1911, the Scotia Company selected the Scotia Ridge for their new houses, all were of a different pattern, from the bungalow type to the two-storey saddle roof, and two-storey square cottage, all painted in different bright colours. The street after street of houses presented a gay appearance" (Jardine 1938). In 1924, Jessie Dawe was born in the company house on Fourth Street into which her mother, Emeline, had moved with her first husband about thirteen years earlier. She was not aware her street had a name, only that she lived on Scotia Ridge. When the Wabana insurance plan was created in 1954, there were no street markers and few streets had official names. The map creators assigned numbers to unnamed streets, and these numbers are shown inside brackets on the map. The Scotia Company streets from First to Fifth are not placed in brackets, suggesting the mapmakers possibly had access to company documents in which engineers had given them these numerical designations. It may have just been coincidence that the No. 2 (mine) Road happened to be the company's second "street" of houses.

Dominion Company Miners' Family Houses

DISCO's mines at Bell Island were in full swing in February 1907, with 640 men employed. At a meeting in Sydney on September 6, 1907, the company's directors decided to branch out (as the Scotia Company had done) and sell their ore on the open market. Until then, it had all been absorbed by the Sydney steel plant. DISCO was reputed to have an inexhaustible ore supply at Wabana, enough to last three hundred years. Among other mining construction that fall, the company was building twenty-one new houses for their workmen. In October, there was a windstorm during which many fences were blown down and windows broken. The greatest damage was done in the "Ten Commandments" Range, the ten miners' houses Arthur House spoke of in his list of buildings DISCO constructed shortly after start-up. It is likely the name was being used here to specifically pinpoint the houses being built on the new streets that would become known collectively as Dominion Range. By 1908, the company had 1,350 men in its employ and was building twenty-five more miners' houses. These were being erected on three streets to the east of Ten Commandments, named McDougall, Grammar and Bown after three managers who served at Wabana in the first decade of the century. Bown became manager in 1908, and that street was the furthest from Ten Commandments, so was probably among those being developed that year (Bown 1957 [1907-1908]: 23-24; House 1939; Canadian-British Engineering Consultants 1958: 5).

Jardine stated that, around 1907, "the Dominion Company had built, and were building, whole new streets of miners' houses. A new townlet sprung up at the West Mines" (Jardine 1938). This "townlet" consisted of another three streets: Ford, named for a civil engineer and short-term manager; Farrell, named for one of the company's first foremen at Wabana; and Gouthro, who was a company doctor. Jardine went on to say that, "the Dominion houses were all of one pattern, painted red and green and, when viewed from a distance, looked like a penal settlement."

Because Dominion built most of their miners' family houses in one pattern, and Scotia also built many on Scotia Ridge in that same pattern, it is the most easily recognized style of company house at Wabana. It is one-and-a-half storeys high with an intersecting gabled roof, which locals refer to as a "saddle roof." The roof is side-gabled at the front where the house is two rooms wide, and end-gabled at the

Fig. 7 – Two "saddle-roof" houses at Dominion No. 1, built ca. 1907. They are one-and-a-half storeys high with side-gabled roof at the front, where the house is two-rooms wide, and end-gabled at the back, where it is one-room wide. The house in the foreground shows the front with the central added porch. The one in the background shows the rear kitchen end of the house with the side porch and back door that was used as the main entry. In 2005, these were the only two remaining of six identical back-to-back houses originally in this area. By 2013, the house in the foreground had been demolished (author photograph, November 20, 2005).

back where it is one-room wide. It is two-rooms deep. The facade is symmetrical with a central doorway separating two windows. Many of the houses in Dominion Range have a small front porch between the two windows, while those at West Mines and Scotia Ridge do not.[9] This is how Jessie Dawe-Hussey described her family's company house, which is of this design, on Scotia Ridge, where she lived from 1924 to 1934:

> There was no front porch and the front door was never used. The parlour was on the right side of the front, with a "sleeping room," that could also be a dining room, on the left side. The kitchen was at the back of the house and had a pantry and porch on the right side.[10] As you came in the back door through the porch and entered the kitchen, you were facing the chimney and stove. Just to the left of the chimney, mid-way along that wall, was the door to the stairs. The upstairs contained two bedrooms on the front and the main bedroom at the back. Heat was provided by

the coal/wood kitchen stove, with a vent above the stove to heat the upper floor. There was no electricity, so kerosene lamps were used for light. There was no basement, no bathroom and no running water. A laneway on the east side of the house, between it and the next identical house, allowed people from Fifth Street to access the public well across the street. (Jessie Dawe-Hussey, personal communication, July 13, 2005)

While many of the saddle-roof houses remain structurally the same today as when they were built, several on Grammar Street have been converted to double apartments. The 1954 insurance plan shows there were originally fifty-four company houses in the Dominion Range (Canadian-British Engineering Consultants 1958: 5). Only twenty-eight, just more than half, were still standing in 2014. An inventory of all the Wabana company houses would probably show a similar decrease in other neighbourhoods. Such a study is needed, not only to ascertain how many of the houses have been lost, but also to reveal scattered company houses that were built in less obvious areas or that no longer stand out as being company houses.

Company Housing for Staff

The location of miners' housing was determined by the location of the mines. There were no buses and few cars, so the miners had to be within walking distance of work. For the same reason, most staff housing was close to the companies' main offices. The first staff housing was at the piers because that is where the offices were. Arthur House (1939) said that when DISCO took over the first Scotia Pier in 1899, one of the buildings there was "our office," presumably the original Scotia Company's and, thus, the first main office. He noted that they soon enlarged that office and built a staff house at the pier and another at West Mines (Gully Pond Ridge). It was not long before they moved their main office to the mining district: As a newspaper article from 1954 stated, "A fire ... destroyed the old main office of Dominion Iron and Steel Company.... The building, which was one of the oldest on the island, has been used since the merger of Dominion and Scotia Companies in 1922 to store electrical equipment and part as a record office" (*Daily News* 1954). The article went on to say that it was situated at the east end of the No. 2 Road, next to the company surgery.[11] This office may have been constructed around 1908, as there were four Dominion staff family houses built that year, probably ones a five-minute walk away, which will be discussed in the next section. The company also had plans for a new boarding house for staff to replace the one at the Dominion Pier that was now too far from its office. The staff boarding house was completed in 1912 and was located on what was then called the Dominion East Tramway Road at the corner of Church Road. It remained in use until 1957 (Bown 1957 [1908]: 24, 1957 [1912]: 40).[12] It was large, three storeys high and had a gambrel roof that gave it a barn-like appearance. Herbert Dickey, who lodged there for a time when he first came in 1953 as the new general manager, described it as "a barn that shook with the wind." He said that the matron did a good job of making it an attractive and pleasant place to live and eat, but added, "It was never more really than a place to spend a night and to do your eating" (Herbert Dickey, personal communication, May 11, 1992). There was no reference to a company main office in the *Daily News* until 1927. The subject came up while describing a new bridge being constructed just east of it over the Dominion East Tramway Road (Bown 1957 [1927]: 21). It is likely that this main office, the one that served the purpose until the mines closed, was built in 1922 after the two companies merged as BESCO. It was within a minute's walk of the "new" staff boarding house (of 1912).

The clientele of the staff boarding house were mainly single male staff members, most from Nova Scotia. They lodged there for varying lengths of time until they married, or until their families moved to Bell Island, at which time they moved into staff family houses. Some were there on short-term business and only stayed for a night or two. When rooms were vacant, people such as travelling salesmen and other non-company businessmen would stay there as well. The staff boarding house employed a matron and three female domestics, who cooked and cleaned. The 1935 census also lists four lodgers. These would have been permanent residents for whom Bell Island was now "home." At least one, a mechanical superintendent, spent his entire working career at Wabana and lived at the staff boarding house, where he died in retirement. On occasion, special guests and visiting sports teams were entertained there. In February 1916, the "bachelors at the Dominion Staff House gave an 'At Home' when they were hosts to a number of lady friends" (Bown 1957 [1916]: 50). The company manager's wife acted as chaperone. Life in the staff boarding house was certainly a world apart from life in the miners' bunkhouses, where the men basically fended for themselves, slept two to each bunk, and often shared that bunk with bed bugs.

Staff Family Houses

While most staff family houses were built in a style similar to the miners' family houses, in that they had the same sharply pitched gable roofs, with a half storey on the upper floor, they differed in their proportions and in such things as extra windows and added porches and sunrooms. Some had a second chimney, bay windows, attic dormers and verandas. At least one was a full two storeys with hipped roof and attic dormer, while a few were two-and-a-half storeys high. The staff family houses constructed early in the century did not have indoor plumbing when built, but the company installed it later (Sydney Bown, personal communication, March 18, 1991). The company performed yearly interior decorating and exterior painting on staff family houses, while the miners' houses were painted inside and out every three years or so (Charles Somerton, personal communication, November 15, 2004; Jessie Dawe-Hussey, personal communication, June 5, 2012). All staff paid rent, generally in the range of $6 to $8 a month, although the monthly rent for the manager's large house at Scotia Pier was $25 (Census 1935).[13] That was the house built for Robert Chambers at the new Scotia Pier location around 1899. It became the residence of C. B. Archibald when he took over as manager of Scotia Company around 1918, and remained so after he became manager of the merged companies under BESCO in 1922. He served as manager and lived in the house until returning to Nova Scotia in 1948 (*Submarine Miner* 1954a). Herbert Dickey recalled that when he arrived in 1953, his predecessor, W. L. Stuewe, was living in the house at Scotia Pier. It was a large house, which he described as "quite a beautiful home." It was divided into two apartments in the mid-1950s. The company was investing a great deal of money at that time to improve efficiency and ore quality, so there were many experts arriving who needed accommodations (Herbert Dickey, personal communication, May 11, 1992; Sydney Bown, personal communication, March 18, 1991). It is no longer standing.

Dickey and the managers who succeeded him lived in a staff family house on the corner of East Track and Bennett Street, just east of the main office. Prior to it becoming the manager's home, it had been occupied by Reid Proudfoot, who came from New Glasgow in 1908 as a Scotia accountant. As part of his duties, Proudfoot was in charge of all the company housing. He rose through the ranks to become general superintendent until retirement in 1954, at which time his house became the manager's residence (*Submarine Miner* 1954b). This house, like the Scotia houses at No. 6 Range, has the gable end to the street. Unlike the miners' houses, it originally had two chimneys. It also has an intersecting side extension with roof gable to the side. The side extension has been extended several times in the past twenty years to allow the house to be used as a restaurant, pool hall, bar and, most recently, a boutique hotel.

As seen earlier, a few houses for staff had been built at the pier in the early stages of mining. It was not until 1908 that housing for staff was first mentioned in the press, with the announcement in the *Daily News* that "the Dominion Company had four staff dwellings under construction" (Bown 1957 [1908]: 24). These may have included the three large staff family houses that were built on the east side of the Dominion East Tramway in the same block and just to the north of where the new Dominion staff boarding house was built four years later. They were on a side street now called Greenwood Avenue. Like the Dominion miners' houses, these staff family houses had a side-gabled roof. Two of them had an intersecting roof gabled at the back. There the resemblance to the miners' houses ended as these were much larger, two-and-a-half storeys high with two chimneys, bay and dormer windows, front veranda and a certain attention to detail, with window casings, soffits, friezes and corner boards. There was another large staff family-use house at the corner of Bennett and Bown Streets. This was a square two-storey house with hipped roof, attic dormer, bay window, front veranda and trim details similar to the other three houses.

No mention was made in the press of five Scotia staff family houses built in a row literally in the No. 3 mine yard in 1911. These houses were separated from the Scotia Company's miners' houses on Scotia Ridge by a field on which a skating arena was built a year later, and onto which the houses then backed. It is hard to imagine a less hospitable site for family homes. Jean Alcock, who grew up in one of those houses, was the daughter of William Lindsay, who came from Scotland in 1910 to install the equipment for the No. 3 mine hoist. Alcock surmised that the residents of these houses facetiously dubbed their street "Wall Street" as an ironic nod to New York's financial district, "probably because nobody had any money" (Jean Alcock, personal communication, February 13, 1996). Meanwhile, it was reported in the *Daily News* in September 1911 that "Construction of a range of houses at the Front was begun by the Scotia Company." Bown commented that this street was labelled "Bridal Avenue" because the houses were subsequently occupied by five newly wedded staff couples (Bown 1957 [1911]: 37)—once again, a bit of whimsy bestowed by the residents of the street. Like the Proudfoot house, the houses on both these "staff" streets were of the gable-to-the-street style. Most had side extensions with an intersecting side-gabled roof. They had front porches with covered verandas. Another three similarly styled staff family houses were built on the north side of Bennett Street, and a fourth was a stand-alone at the north end of Town Square behind the company surgery. These latter four all had small front porches like the miners' houses in Dominion Range. All the staff family houses were close to where the occupants worked, including the Bridal Avenue houses. They were not far from the old Scotia main office, located near the pier when they were built.

The Depression Years

Except for the mess houses built on Scotia Ridge in 1928, there are no accounts of company-house construction for the next forty-five years. Wabana suffered a depression leading up to and during the First World War, due mainly to the temporary loss of the German market. The slump continued into the 1920s with the upheaval caused by the merger of the two companies into BESCO. Ore shipments for 1921 were the lowest since 1899, indicative of the depressed condition of the industry. Despite this, the 1921 Newfoundland census showed that Bell Island, with a permanent population of 4,357, was now the second-largest centre in Newfoundland, next to St. John's. The Wabana mines were the largest iron-ore mines "in the British Empire and fourth on the world's list" (Bown 1957 [1921]: 66; 1957 [1924]: 1).

In the 1920s, there were two attempts by the Newfoundland

government to extract royalty payments from BESCO, both of which failed because the company threatened job losses. The government attempted to mitigate the threat by stipulating that the corporation provide houses near the mines for its resident workmen on a twenty-year purchase plan "when requested so to do by the Governor-in-Council," and also "the provision of suitable lodgings for mainland miners" (Bown 1957 [1925]: 12;).[14] But there is no evidence of any houses being built as a result of these stipulations. BESCO was replaced by DOSCO (Dominion Steel and Coal Corporation) in 1928 and, although things improved somewhat, it is unlikely any company houses were built in the Depression years of the 1930s or during the Second World War.

Boom to Bust

Between 1950 and 1956, DOSCO invested $22 million into an expansion and modernization program of the Wabana site. These were boom years and optimism was high for a bright future. The sons of miners were leaving school early to take jobs with the company, marrying daughters of miners and building houses of their own to raise their baby-boom families. Private houses were going up in all parts of Bell Island. Meanwhile, professional mining people were arriving for short-term projects, while new equipment was being installed and new procedures introduced. In 1957, a twenty-room, one-storey staff boarding house was built on Bennett Street immediately west of the main office to replace the old 1912 building. Four new one-and-a-half-storey staff family houses were erected, two on the 1912 site and two around the corner, just off Church Road. Two modern bungalows were built a few years later to replace the large staff family house on the corner of Greenwood Avenue on that same block. All were constructed from plans provided by the Central Mortgage and Housing Corporation, a federal agency created to support affordable housing in Canada. The company chose a lonely piece of boggy woodland a quarter-mile south on the East Track for another five staff family houses, all modern-style bungalows from the same plan book (*Small House Designs* 1957). Built to house some of the experts coming in, they were prefabricated in Montreal and were the last company houses erected at Wabana (MacKinnon 1982a: 68).

At the same time that DOSCO was investing in upgrading

Wabana ore, new iron-ore deposits that were cheaper to excavate and contained fewer impurities were coming on the market. Steel manufacturers began adopting new methods for using the less expensive ore and Wabana's markets started to disappear. A. V. Roe Limited acquired the majority of DOSCO shares in 1957, bringing a change in ownership that would spell the end of the Wabana mines (Martin 1983: 59). In May 1959, the closure of No. 6 mine resulted in the layoff of 573 men. This huge loss of jobs coincided with the building of those last staff family houses. This bred resentment, which resulted in that street being dubbed "Snob Hill" (Queen's University 1953: 100, 142).[15] A sign bearing that moniker marked it for a number of years, but it has since been changed to "DOSCO Hill." Oddly, ore shipments reached an all-time high in 1960 and the population peaked, at 12,281, in 1961.

After such a large investment in improvements, residents were confused when the No. 4 mine closed in 1962, and were shocked at the closure of No. 3, the final mine, on June 30, 1966. Two years earlier, surrounded by her children and grandchildren, Emeline Dawe had died at age eighty. She had lived a relatively secure and settled life at Wabana, after the upheaval of moving from northern Newfoundland with her young family, followed closely by the death of her first husband. In the same way that she and Stewart Luffman had had to leave Pilley's Island to travel to an unknown place for work, her sons and daughters and many others now packed up their families and left Bell Island for employment elsewhere. Most found it in factories in southern Ontario and mines across Canada.

Unlike many mining towns, Wabana did not become a ghost town, due to its proximity to the provincial capital. The arrival of a modern car ferry in 1961 facilitated daily commuting to jobs on the local mainland. A place that workers once commuted to thus became a dormitory town for people who commute to jobs elsewhere. Today, two car ferries serve Bell Island as part of the Portugal Cove run, making twenty-one trips each way throughout the day and evening. Commuters begin lining up at the ferry terminal weekday mornings at about five o'clock. They often have to wait in the ferry line for an hour or more to get back home in the evenings, making their workday even longer than what their grandfathers endured in the early days of mining. Mechanical breakdowns and weather delays are frequent occurrences. Still other workers commute to jobs in far-off Alberta, flying out for several weeks at a time, and returning home for a week or so before going back again. Each day, many other residents cross on the ferry to attend to various bits of business in the capital region, where they have access to colleges, hospitals, medical specialists, banks, big-box stores, cultural and sporting facilities, and other services not available on Bell Island, or simply to visit friends and relatives.

During the 1950s, the company had offered to sell its houses to the occupants, and many took them up on that offer in what amounted to a "rent-to-own" plan. One informant recalled that the small miners' bungalows sold for about $600, while a staff member bought his older-model staff house for $1,500 (Sydney Bown, personal communication, March 18, 1991; Charles Somerton personal communication, April 11, 2005). Not all of the houses were sold, as a 1967 news item stated, "When DOSCO pulled out of Bell Island last June the Newfoundland Government purchased all mining equipment and property owned by DOSCO, including twenty-four homes and the Staff [boarding] House, for $100,000" (*Evening Telegram* 1967). A 1971 executive-council memorandum pointed out that five houses in the Railroad Street area were to be offered for sale to the occupants, while six other DOSCO houses were to be retained as rental units. "With respect to the rest of the housing, which is generally of a poorer character ... these units [should] be conveyed to the present occupants for a purely nominal consideration" (RPANL, PDMA, PRC12/4/7/2/2).

Around the time the Wabana mines closed down, the provincial government brought in a scheme whereby people wishing to move from an economically depressed area could sell their house to the government for a fixed price of $1,500, no matter its age or condition. The seller was then given the option of buying it back for $1, with the stipulation that it be dismantled. They could use the materials to rebuild in another community. If they did not pursue this option, the province would either offer it for sale for $1 to be torn down, or it would be retained as social housing (Harold Kitchen, personal communication, June 21, 1984).

In the time since DOSCO left, some of the company houses have been demolished and, in several areas, have been replaced by government-funded housing, usually duplex-style. At Wabana today, many of the houses constructed by the mining companies over a century ago are still standing, and almost all are occupied, some by former miners, some by descendants of the original occupants. Most seem to be well maintained. In many cases, vinyl siding has replaced or covered the original clapboard, horizontal vinyl sliders have taken the place of traditional wooden vertical windows, and exterior doors are now steel instead of wooden. Aside from these superficial changes, and perhaps the addition of a patio deck off the back door, most remain structurally the same as when they were built. The company houses that have seen the most change are some of the larger staff family houses. A few of these have been remodelled beyond recognition, such as one at the corner of Bennett and Bown Streets that has been divided into several apartments. Its front veranda has been enclosed, windows and doors have been changed, and clapboard has been replaced by vinyl siding. The former Proudfoot/manager's house, as mentioned earlier, has been renovated as a small hotel. One staff family house at the north end of Town Square received provincial heritage status, but later sustained fire damage. It was in the process of being rebuilt with some exterior alterations when it was struck by vandalism. It has been boarded up for the past few years. One of the Bridal Avenue houses was renovated and operated as a bed and breakfast for a time, but is now a private residence again.

While it might be expected that the high cost of housing in the nearby St. John's region in recent years would have resulted in an increased demand for the lower-cost housing of Wabana, this has not been the case simply because of the inconvenience of ferry travel, especially during the stormy winter months. A continued steady drop in population has been the combined result of a falling birth rate, due to young people moving away for study and/or work, coinciding with an increasing death rate in the aging demographic. Extrapolating from the 2011 Canadian census count of 2,690, which saw a loss of about twenty people per year from the 2006 Canadian census, there will likely be fewer than 2,600 residents by 2017. While approximately 500 people commute to work off the island every day, another 855 residents reported receiving income support assistance in 2013.[16]

Remembering and Celebrating Wabana's History

After the mines were shut down in 1966, most of the mining infrastructure was dismantled and sold to companies in other parts of the world, leaving little physical evidence of the once-prosperous industry that had been the beating heart of this little island for such a long time. Today, only those who know where to look can discern the few extant structures that had been integral to the day-to-day functioning of the mines. Some are being reused by the town council and community groups. For example, the original No. 3 hoist house is now a council garage. The Wabana Boys' and Girls' Club building was once DOSCO's carpenter shop. The company survey office has been used as the town-council office and is now a centre for persons with special needs, the only hint of its former use being depictions of mining carved by local sculptor Brian Burke on the exterior west wall. The entrance to the No. 4 mine is still intact and was used briefly as the stage for a Shakespearean production. Crumbling concrete retaining walls and odd pieces of mangled steel are all that remain of the two loading piers.

As Wabana's glory days have faded into the past, there has been an increasing interest in celebrating its history. The first manifestations of this were in film, books and other writings. In 1974, a film entitled *Wabana* employed archival footage and photographs to tell the story of the mining days (Harvey 1974). Books on the island's history soon followed, including volumes of personal reminiscences and an account of enemy attacks in Conception Bay during the Second World War (Bell Island Lancers 1985; Coxworthy 1993, 1996; Hammond 1978, 1982; Neary 1994). *The Miners of Wabana*, a study of the miners' work life, was published in 1989 (Weir 2006). The 1990s saw further preservation of Wabana's heritage through art when large murals of mining scenes were painted on town buildings, including No. 3 hoist house. These attempts to record the mining history were no doubt partly a response to the loss of visual clues to that history. Another response was the erection of monuments to commemorate significant events from Bell Island's past. The Historic Sites and Monuments Board of Canada declared the Wabana mines a National Historic Site in 1988, with the plaque outlining the significance unveiled just east of the post office on the No. 2 Road in 1991. The Seamen's Memorial Monument at Lance Cove was unveiled in 1994 in memory of the sixty-nine sailors lost in 1942 when German U-boats sank four ore carriers anchored near the island. A monument was unveiled at The Beach in 1995 in remembrance of the twenty-two people, mostly commuting miners, who drowned when two ferries collided in November 1940.

The murals project did much to promote cultural tourism on Bell

Island, but the biggest draw by far is the mine itself. Throughout the 1980s and 1990s, the Bell Island Heritage Society, made up of a small but energetic group of volunteers, worked tirelessly to establish a miners' museum, featuring a mine tour. With the momentum created by the 1995 centennial-year celebrations, a year of events marking one hundred years since the mining started, their hard work came to partial fruition with the opening of a temporary museum. This was followed by the opening of the No. 2 mine for tours in 1998, almost fifty years after it ceased production. This was the first submarine mine tunnel at Bell Island, begun on land in 1902 by the Scotia Company. Its submarine holdings were reached in 1909, having been dug out under the waters of Conception Bay by men using drills, dynamite, picks and shovels. The submarine slopes would eventually extend three miles out under the ocean floor. Of the three thousand people who visited that first season, more than 90 per cent were non-residents, an indicator of tourism potential.

Inspired by all this activity, and the historical events and miners' own personal experience stories portrayed in the book *The Miners of Wabana* (Weir 2006), a group of young performers developed a theatrical production, "Place of First Light: The Bell Island Experience," which ran throughout the summers of 1997 to 1999. This half-day show wove together live theatre and sightseeing, including scenes enacted on the ferry from Portugal Cove and at the monuments. The show culminated in a tour of No. 2 mine, in which the audience played the roles of novice miners and historical figures were played by actors. The show received rave reviews and was proclaimed a theatrical landmark event by the Professional Association of Canadian Theatres. The final showing was a special command performance for the vice-regal visit of Governor General Adrienne Clarkson in 2000, as she was especially interested in seeing how Bell Island was preserving the memory of its mining heritage through art.

A new museum building attached to No. 2 mine was opened in 2000 and is operated daily during the tourist season by the Bell Island Heritage Society. The Heritage Foundation of Newfoundland and Labrador, established in 1984 by the provincial government with a mandate to preserve the architectural heritage of the province, designates buildings and other structures as "registered structures" and assists with grants for preservation. In 2008, the foundation designated No. 2 mine a registered heritage structure, the only underground and the first engineering structure recognized for its importance to the people of the province. Each summer, enthusiastic tour guides—sons and daughters of former miners—lead tourists into the No. 2 mine. They have immersed themselves in the mining history and now they relay to others the story of the work that went on three miles out under the ocean, keeping those memories alive. Visitor statistics range from 10,000 to 12,000 annually, making it one of the most popular tourist destinations in the province. While much has been accomplished, there is still much to do in showcasing what remains above ground of Wabana's glorious past. No storyboards relate the history of the few mining-related structures still standing. Similarly, no plaques or signage denote the company houses or delineate the mining districts.

Conclusion: A Future for the Past

Iron ore was mined at Wabana, Bell Island, Newfoundland, for seventy-one years, beginning in 1895, and was the sole supply for the steel plant at Sydney, Nova Scotia, for most of that time. The two Nova Scotia companies that developed the mines provided housing in the form of shacks and bunkhouses for commuting miners, single-family houses for resident miners and "staff," and boarding houses for commuting or short-term staff. The family houses were similar in style to the detached company houses in Cape Breton. Many are still in use after a hundred years.

The small group of volunteers involved with the Bell Island Heritage Society have done tremendous work in showcasing the history of the mining operation, but the home life of the miner and his family has not received the attention it deserves. Thus far, no organized attempt has been made to preserve or celebrate the history of the company houses or the neighbourhoods in which they are located. Other than MacKinnon's 1982 paper, there has been no study done of the Wabana company houses until this present historical review. The Heritage Foundation of Newfoundland and Labrador made its first attempt at documenting built heritage in Newfoundland in 1995 with an inventory of the Bonavista Peninsula. To date, it is the only inventory of its kind for the province. Nothing has yet been done to catalogue the Wabana company houses, whose numbers are declining with each passing year. While government grants have been made available to low-income families for house repairs, these are not specifically for company houses. Neither is there any municipal policy to encourage owners to retain the heritage features of their homes. A declining population and poor economic conditions make this a difficult task, but it is precisely because of these circumstances that it is so important to preserve what remains before it is too late. The heritage society, town council and tourism committee all agree that company houses should be preserved and their historical significance commemorated (Clayton King, personal communication, October 4, 2012; Gary Gosine, personal communication, October 10, 2012). The heritage society is hoping to include company housing in a new interpretive plan that is being developed for the museum site, while one of the ideas under consideration is having a company house on display near the museum (Teresita McCarthy, personal communication, November 16, 2014).

Housing was, and is, extremely important for miners and their families. It is a topic that is often overlooked in the discussion of mining operations, yet these operations could not function efficiently without it. The family houses that the mining companies provided at Wabana were well built and many are still occupied today. They are the last vestiges of the massive operation that once flourished here and provided economic benefit to many people, and not just in Newfoundland and Nova Scotia. The economic spinoffs were felt throughout the world where Wabana iron ore was used in steel plants, and from there in the many manufacturing industries that used that steel to make ships, railway tracks, rail cars, bridges and so much more. The distinctive company houses and their neighbourhoods are monuments to what once existed. The houses should be showcased and celebrated to help us visualize their place in relation to all the mine structures that once loomed over them and that no longer exist. Yes, it is important to study and commemorate the mines, but the same should be done for the housing that played a major role in supporting the men and women who built and maintained the mining operation and the community as a whole.[17]

Notes

1. In the 1950s, Addison Bown gleaned all references to Bell Island between 1894 and 1939 from the pages of the St. John's *Daily News*. Bown annotated these news items and then, between 1957 and 1960, published them as a series in *The Daily News* under the heading "Newspaper History of Bell Island." This series was then compiled and bound into two unpublished volumes that are held at the Queen Elizabeth II Library, Memorial University of Newfoundland.

2. Four of the original ten miners' houses on Ten Commandments Range are still standing. They are one-and-a-half storeys, front-gabled, one room wide and two rooms deep.

3. The 1935 census of Newfoundland, in which home owners are distinguished from renters, shows that in the eastern section of Bell Island most of the family names were of the pre-mining era and that most of the homes were owned, not rented, so this was not company housing.

4. The "line" referred to here was Scotia's first ore tram track between the mines and its first pier, which was now owned by DISCO. (See note 12 below for the names this line was known by over the years.) Conditions on the north side of the island were unsuitable for docking ships, hence the location of the piers on the south side.

5. "The Green" was originally a green, grassy area where the pre-mining farming families pastured their cattle and sheep each summer. Once mining got underway, it soon looked more like a shanty town of the old American west than the traditional English village green that the name implies.

6. The terms "mess house" and "bunkhouse" were used interchangeably at Wabana.

7. This road was eventually named Main Street.

8. These houses are the same design as those at Ten Commandments Range, which Arthur House said Dominion built shortly after they began operation on the island.

9. Photographic evidence shows that small, enclosed front porches were added to Bown Street houses sometime in the 1950s, before the company sold them. Why they were added is a mystery, as the front door was only used on special occasions, such as weddings and funerals.

10. The back porch was an essential room that served as the main entry to the house and separated the cold, dirty outside world from the warm, clean kitchen. Such things as the slop bucket, wood splits, overshoes and the miner's work clothes and boots were stored there.

11. This "record office" fire may be the reason for the dearth of historical information about the houses.

12. The 1912 staff boarding house was referred to locally as "the staff house," but will be referred to here as the "staff boarding house" to avoid confusion

with staff family houses. At the time it was built, tramway tracks for the ore cars going from No. 2 mine to Dominion Pier ran past it. This was Dominion East Tramway, shortened by locals to "East Track," or simply "The Track" in conversation. The tramway tracks were removed when the ore cars were replaced by Euclid trucks in the early 1950s. Sometime around 1970, a new street sign identified it as "Railroad Street." It was renamed "Steve Neary Boulevard" in 1996.

13. The 1935 Tenth Census of Newfoundland and Labrador gives details such as monthly rent paid by each family.

14. As Newfoundland was not part of Canada until 1949, in 1910 the Newfoundland Government negotiated with the two Canadian companies operating the Wabana mines to pay a royalty of 7 ½ cents per ton on all ore shipped over the next 10 years. The agreement ended just as BESCO was taking over. The 1920s saw much turmoil in the industry, and each time the government tried for a new royalty agreement, BESCO threatened to shut down the mines. When DOSCO took over from BESCO, the government refused to allow the impasse to continue. The first ore ship to arrive from Nova Scotia in 1929 was seized and "held hostage" until DOSCO put up a bond and agreed to resume royalty payments.

15. This survey of company towns found that "Snob Hill" was a common term for areas housing managerial and technical staff; in some towns, the company hotel was referred to as the "snob centre."

16. Bell Island population profiles are from "Newfoundland and Labrador Statistics Agency. Profiles, Local Area 12: Bell Island. Newfoundland and Labrador Community Accounts, 2015," online at nl.communityaccounts.ca (accessed May 21, 2015).

17. The writer is currently constructing a web site (www.historic-wabana.com) dedicated to the history of the Wabana Mines, with plans for an initial focus on the company housing and the structures of the mining district.

References

Primary Sources

ASC (Archives and Special Collections). Alphonsus Thomas Lawton Photograph Album (ATLPA), 1910-1956. Queen Elizabeth II Library, Memorial University of Newfoundland, St. John's, NL.

ASC (Archives and Special Collections). Bell Island Photograph Collection (BIPC), ca. 1895-1995. Queen Elizabeth II Library, Memorial University of Newfoundland, St. John's, NL.

ASC (Archives and Special Collections) Sir Richard Squires Collection

(SRSC), 1855-1957. Queen Elizabeth II Library, Memorial University of Newfoundland, St. John's, NL.

Census of Newfoundland and Labrador, 1921. St. John's, NL: Colonial Secretary's Office. 1923.

RPANL PBF (The Rooms Provincial Archives of Newfoundland and Labrador. Papers of the Butler Family). 1804-1963.

RPANL PDMA (The Rooms Provincial Archives of Newfoundland and Labrador. Papers of the Department of Municipal Affairs). 1971. Disposal of DOSCO Buildings. Government of Newfoundland and Labrador.

Tenth Census of Newfoundland and Labrador, 1935. St. John's, NL: Dept. of Public Health and Welfare. 1937.

PUBLISHED SOURCES
Anson, C. M. 1951. The Wabana Iron Ore Properties of the Dominion Steel and Coal Corporation, Limited. *Canadian Mining and Metallurgical Bulletin* 473: 597-602.

Bell Island Lancers. 1985. *Memories of an Island.* St. John's, NL: Jesperson Press.

Bown, Addison, comp. *Newspaper History of Bell Island, 1894-1939.* 2 vols. St. John's: *Daily News*, 1957-1960. [Queen Elizabeth II Library, Memorial University of Newfoundland, St. John's, NL.]

Cameron, James M. 1960. *Industrial History of the New Glasgow District.* New Glasgow, NS: Hector.

Canadian-British Engineering Consultants. 1958. Wabana, Bell Island: report on the municipal plan. January 1958. [Queen Elizabeth II Library, Memorial University of Newfoundland, St. John's, NL.]

Cantley, Thomas. 1911. The Wabana Iron Mines of the Nova Scotia Steel and Coal Company Limited. *Journal of the Canadian Mining Institute* 14: 274-99.

Chambers, R. E. and A. R. Chambers. 1909. The Sinking of the Wabana Submarine Slopes. *Journal of the Canadian Mining Institute* 12: 139-48.

Coxworthy, Kay. 1993. *Tales From Across the Tickle.* Bell Island, NL: Scott Publications.

———. 1996. *The Cross on the Rib.* Bell Island, NL: Kay Coxworthy, self-published.

Daily News [St. John's, NL]. 1894. Mining Begins at Belle Isle, September 12.

———. 1898. Native Families Seek Employment in the Mines, July 29.

———. 1954. Fire Destroys Record Office, April 3, 1.

Evening Telegram [St. John's, NL]. 1967. Company Making Inventory of

Equipment on Bell Island," May 23, 3.

Fay, C. R. 1956. *Life and Labour in Newfoundland.* Toronto: University of Toronto Press.

Hammond, John W. 1978. *The Beautiful Isles: A history of Bell Island from 1611-1896.* St. John's, NL: self-published.

Hammond, John W. 1982. *Wabana: A history of Bell Island from 1893-1940.* Grand Manan, NB: self-published.

Harvey, Joe, dir. 1974. *Wabana*, film. St. John's, NL: Memorial University of Newfoundland, Extension Services.

Heritage Inventories. *Heritage Foundation of Newfoundland & Labrador*, 2015. www.heritagefoundation.ca/reports/inventories.aspx (accessed May 21, 2015).

House, Arthur. 1939. Early History of Bell Island Mines. *Daily News* [St. John's, NL], March 1, 4.

Insurers' Advisory Organization of Canada. 1954. *Insurance Plan of Wabana, Nfld., Bell Island.* Toronto, ON: Underwriters' Survey Bureau.

Jardine, Frederick F. 1938. Forty-Fourth Anniversary of Wabana Mines. *Evening Telegram* [St. John's, NL], December 24, 12.

MacKinnon, Richard. 1982a. Company Housing in Wabana, Bell Island, Newfoundland. *Material History Bulletin* 14: 67-71.

―――. 1982b. Bell Island Housing. Unpublished research paper, Memorial University of Newfoundland Folklore and Language Archive, St. John's, NL, 1982.

―――. 2009. *Discovering Cape Breton Folklore.* Sydney, NS: Cape Breton University Press.

Martin, Wendy. 1983. *Once Upon a Mine: Story of Pre-Confederation Mines on the Island of Newfoundland.* Montreal: Canadian Institute of Mining and Metallurgy.

McCann, L. D. 1981. The Mercantile-Industrial Transition in the Metals Towns of Pictou County, 1857-1931. *Acadiensis* 10 (2): 29-64.

Morris, I. C. 1899. A Ramble on Bell Island. *Daily News* [St. John's, NL], September 8.

―――. 1906. The Sound of the Steam Whistle Told of New Order of Things. *Daily News* [St. John's, NL], July 14.

Neary, Steve. 1994. *The Enemy on Our Doorstep.* St. John's, NL: Jesperson Press.

Newfoundland and Labrador Statistics Agency. Profiles, Local Area 12: Bell Island. *Newfoundland and Labrador Community Accounts*, 2015. nl.communityaccounts.ca (accessed May 21, 2015).

Newfoundland Directory Company. 1913. *St. John's Newfoundland Directory 1913*. St. John's, NL: Newfoundland Directory Company.

Nova Scotia Steel and Coal Company. 1912. *Scotia: How Canada's Pioneer Steel Corporation Was Evolved From a Country Forge*. Halifax, NS: Imperial Pub. Co.

Queen's University (Queen's University, Institute of Local Government). 1953. *Single-Enterprise Communities in Canada: A Report to Central Mortgage and Housing Corporation*. Ottawa: Central Mortgage and Housing Corporation.

Small House Designs. 1957. Ottawa, ON: Central Mortgage and Housing Corporation.

Submarine Miner. 1954a. C. B. Archibald Posthumous Award. *Submarine Miner* 1(6): 6.

———. 1954b. A. R. Proudfoot Retired after Fifty-one Years Service, 1 (1): 6.

Tye, Diane and Peter Latta. 1989. Symbols of Change: The Legacy of Two Early Twentieth-Century Nova Scotian Builders. *Nova Scotia Historical Review* 9 (2): 18-34.

Weir, Gail. 2006. *The Miners of Wabana*, 2nd ed. St. John's, NL: Breakwater Books.

Lucie K. Morisset and Jessica Mace

Arvida: From Socio-Industrial Utopia to Urban Heritage

The History and Contemporary Challenges of an Identity Project

Arvida was founded in 1925 by the Aluminum Company of America in the Saguenay region of the province of Quebec, downstream from the immense Lac Saint-Jean watershed. Given its remote location, in its early years Arvida was often described as "four hundred and fifty miles north of Boston." As the brand image of the company and pet project of its president, Arthur Vining Davis (who lent it his name), the model city is known as one of the last great industrial utopias of the Western world. As a backdrop to the rich and varied social and industrial framework that Arvida offered its residents, the built landscape of the "aluminum city" testifies well to the considerable attention paid to its design and conservation.

The citizens of Arvida have been campaigning for a number of years for both the protection and development of its architectural and urban heritage, in an effort to fulfill promises of the former company town's visionar-

Fig. 1 – An Arvida street. Photo by Guillaume St-Jean / Canada Research Chair in Urban Heritage.

ies and respond to the still-viable industrial locale. To its dedicated citizens, this has become all the more necessary given that, since 1975, Arvida has twice been amalgamated into new, larger municipalities, thereby surrendering its name and further challenging its identity. The desire of Arvidians of all stripes to preserve their heritage is largely echoed throughout the former city, even more so now that Arvida is a rarity among company towns, in that there is a major renewal of its mother industry, revitalizing the original industrial project of Arvida. Indeed, it is now home to a renewed aluminum smelter equipped with cutting-edge technology and is geared to produce 460,000 metric tonnes of metal. Although there are fewer workers now than in the forty smelting potrooms of the original city—which was built for 35,000 inhabitants and known as home to the world's largest aluminum smelter—Arvida is nonetheless a special case in the larger, post-industrial world where labour, social segregation and a sense of belonging to a community have often become but bitter memories in the wake of factory and mine closures.

In this regard, Arvida is truly an exception. The year 2002, for example, marked the seventy-fifth anniversary of the Syndicat national des employés de l'aluminium d'Arvida (National Union of Aluminum Workers of Arvida), which was accompanied by a large-scale public celebration featuring an outdoor exhibition, titled *Travailleurs de l'aluminium d'Arvida: Un savoir-faire en images* (Arvida's Aluminum Workers: Know-How in Images). Despite some embittered labour disputes in the past, such as strikes in 1941 that led to a royal commission of inquiry,[1] the festivities of 2012 were notable for their jubilant community atmosphere, with citizens lining up to share memories and to write songs in praise of Arvida's industrial history. Another public event is the traditional Arvida Day, which was reinstated three years ago and which has attracted more than 10,000 people. Not only were the citizens of Arvida presented with the Prix Thomas-Baillairgé, a conservation award, by the Ordre des architectes du Québec in 2011, but the municipality also received the National Trust for Canada's Prince of Wales Prize for Municipal Heritage Leadership in 2012. The municipality has initiated an ambitious heritage program, including the classification of 733 private properties as historical monuments in 2009. In 2011, the Arvida Historic District was designated a National Historic Site by the Government of Canada and, since then, the community has intensified its pursuit of designation on the UNESCO World Heritage Site list.

On a similarly global scale, another noteworthy illustration of Arvidian heritage can be found in the context of globalized finance and corporate succession: what began as Alcoa (Aluminum Company of America) in Arvida, then Alcan (Aluminum Company of Canada), was acquired by Rio Tinto, in 2007,[2] and, notably, a redevelopment project of that British-Australian multinational corporation carries the names "Aluminerie Arvida" and "Arvida AP60 Technology Centre." This act of naming was a "direct reference to the history of the complex [...] and to the city of Arvida that emerged in the 1920s, known the world over." Such acts reinforce the corporation's slogan: "L'histoire se poursuit avec vous" (History Continues With You)[3] (Rio Tinto 2011).

Our hypothesis is that the root of this shared and rather paradoxical enthusiasm for heritage (paradoxical since it does not emerge from disaffection, loss or disillusionment) is an identity project that has very quickly turned Arvidian heritage housing into a catalyst for civic pride and sense of ownership. Over the course of a century, Arvida, conceived as a company town, has come to transmit a legacy for which its public officials are now the guardians, acting on behalf of all Arvidians. To better grasp the nuances of this phenomenon, this chapter reflects upon the ways in which this calculated company town gradually ingrained itself as the self-conscious social project of its residents. This examination will be carried out using a historical-interpretative perspective and urban-history methodology. Then, in suggesting that urban heritage in the 21st century may represent a transposition of the socio-industrial utopia of bygone centuries, this chapter explores the contemporary challenges of heritage-making. It also explores "heritage interest" in Arvida—born long before the phrase was ever coined—as well as the ways it has extended from the past into the present, and might extend into the future. Through all of this, this chapter seeks to initiate a discussion of the political, cultural, social, imaginative and material issues involved in preserving the landscape of a company town by evaluating modern methods of heritage-making—from legislative frameworks to mechanisms of physical development—using the special case of Arvida, and what the former model city has become over time. From a perspective of public research, we hope to suggest potentially interesting pathways

toward the heritage re-evaluation of other company towns. It is hoped
that these alternate pathways will be followed in the context of collaborative knowledge construction, in which civic cooperation and
leadership replace the all-encompassing power of national institutions
and become a spearhead for heritage, thereby ensuring its collective
recognition and transmission.

A Heritage Project, An Identity Project

As a model city designed for 35,000 inhabitants, and as a "factory
town,"[4] Arvida represents an unparalleled synthesis of different types
of urbanist research of company towns. Its charming, spacious and
original workers' houses, wide and shady avenues, modern architectural features and infrastructure, including the "first aluminum
bridge in the universe," have been lavishly praised in dozens of scientific articles as well as in geography and urban-planning textbooks
in North America and Europe. We have already examined Arvida in
various publications, for instance, and have notably published one of
its most symbolic images, its urban plan, of a rare graphic and conceptual sophistication, in chromolithography in order to showcase its
magnificence. Typically, company towns from the 19th and the first

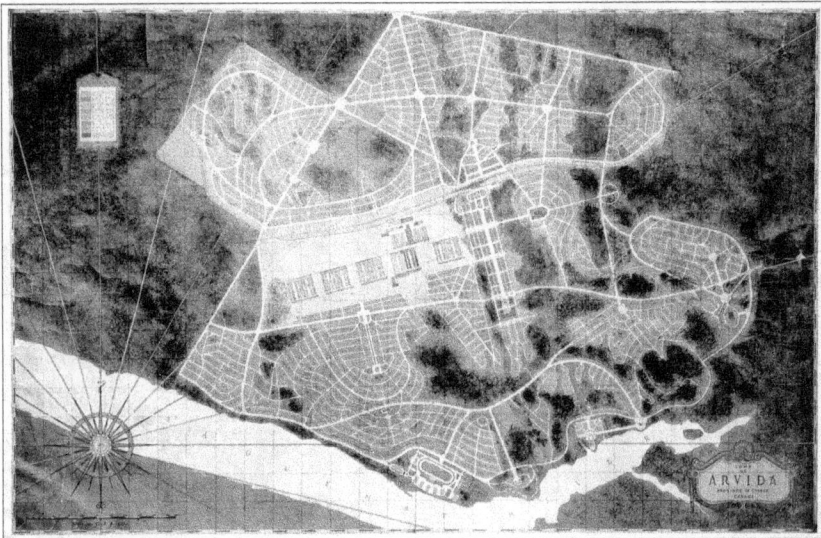

*Fig. 2 – Arvida city plan, Hjalmar Ejnar Skougor and Harry Beardslee
Brainerd, 1926. City of Saguenay.*

half of the 20th century held clear divisions in terms of both class and race, and between bosses' and workers' homes. Examples include the segregation of white neighbourhoods and "coloured" towns in the American South, or in Canada between western European skilled workers and both French Canadian and eastern European workmen. By contrast, Arvida stands out once again, boasting residents from more than thirty ethnic backgrounds and accommodating all workers, regardless of their social status, in single-family dwellings designed for eventual purchase by the workers themselves.

Initially proposed by Davis, then designed by dozens of engineers and architects,[5] Arvida began to make its mark as an identity project. Having become the world's number one aluminum producer during the Second World War, the city—which by 1944 boasted 921 war gardens, also known as victory gardens, created through a citizens' committee initiative—subsequently celebrated its 25th anniversary in 1950 as if it were its 400th. Complete with an anthem and a coat of arms, and imbued with authentic citizen pride, the so-called porcelain city (as jealous neighbours sometimes called it) thus was conceived as an urban utopia down to every last detail. Though it was inextricably tied

Fig. 3 – Arvida's neighbour, the pulp and paper town of Kénogami, is characterized by a clear division between the workmen district and the district reserved for employees, superintendents, engineers and other managers, the quartier des Anglais, or English district, as it is referred to in the French-Canadian context, an area out of bounds for workers. Here we see a section of the English district. Private collection.

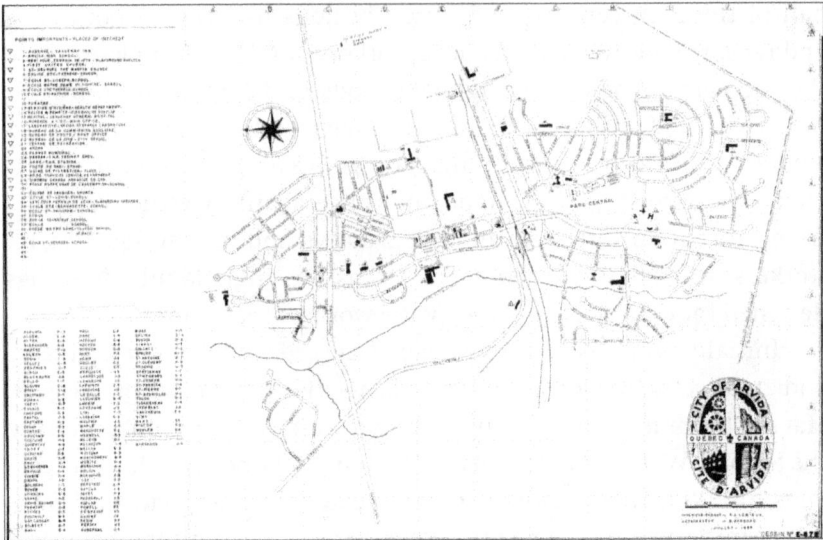

Fig. 4 – Outline of a tourist map for Arvida, circa 1950. The document is stamped with the city's first coat of arms, depicting the industrial era (machine mechanisms), a dam crossed by flowing waters, houses near the plant, and a worker piling up aluminum ingots. City of Saguenay.

to its great industrial potential, the resource town was determined not only to showcase its industrial output but also to express its historical roots and civic pride. This would, in part, be achieved through the built landscape, which was invested with local peculiarities and was remarkable for its exceptional architecture. Indeed, the avant-garde buildings and carefully constructed aesthetic would serve to invent and represent the identity of the aluminum city as both Canadian and modern.

In order to address Arvida's current heritage-making as a manifestation of the genetic makeup of the model city, however, it is first necessary to explore the makings of the original planning process that defined the parameters of the citizenry's involvement in matters of heritage. We propose that the model city was originally invested with what the art historian Aloïs Riegl described as "commemorative value" or "intentional rememoration value."[6] This type of value "claims immortality, in the eternal present. The natural degradation opposed to the realization of this claim [is] therefore ardently combated and unceasingly held in check" (Riegl 2003 [1903]: 89). Among other values, such as age or historic value,[7] this commemorative value that

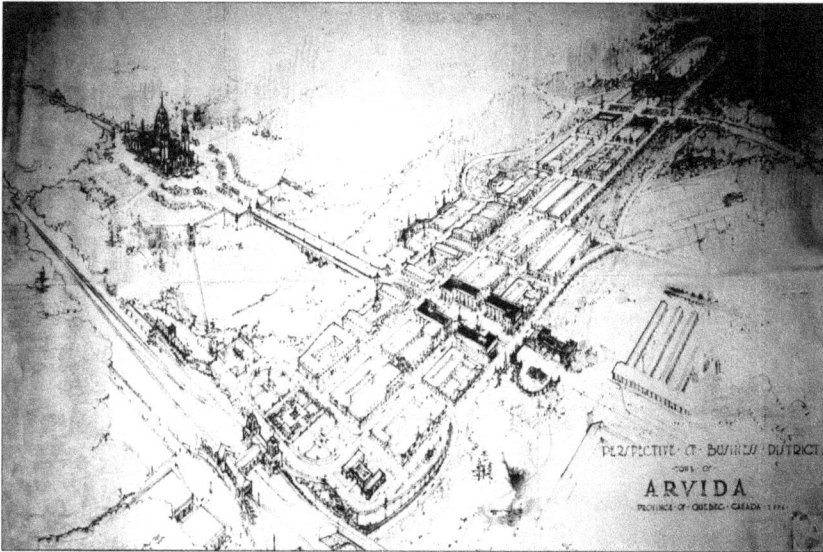

Fig. 5 – Arvida Business Centre, Harry Beardslee Brainerd, architect, 1926. Rio Tinto (Saguenay).

can be attributed to the creation of Arvida "does not appreciate past time in and for itself." Beyond this, it does not "tend ... to designate and showcase it for us as if it belonged to the present," but rather "is intended, as soon as the monument is erected, to ensure that it will never belong to the past but will remain anchored in the minds of future generations" (Riegl 2003: 89). Writing around the same time as Arvida was founded, Riegl was describing a new societal phenomenon, the "modern cult of monuments" (*der moderne Denkmalkultus*), which is known today as heritage. This definition, then, can be of use here because, other than simply directing our present consideration of heritage toward past circumstances, it also allows us to address the issue of Arvida's heritage-making over time within two time frames and systems,[8] namely, commemorative intent and the cult of age, which can be seen to have grown upon its intentionality. In fact, these two heritage desires seem inextricably bound.

If the aspiration to create a social utopia still guided a few industrial magnates at the time, in Arvida it took shape largely through the combination of the material nature of the city and local social participation in heritage-making. From the outset, these were linked together in the model city with the figure of a *moderne Denkmalkultus*.

This assertion may seem surprising, particularly given that the history of company towns is generally composed of paternalistic bosses and clearly stratified social classes, but it must be remembered that Arvida emerged late on the scene. Indeed, it appeared at a time when access to housing, as offered by a company town, increasingly stemmed from public action. In fact, it was in Arvida's housing that the commemorative intention of Alcoa—including Davis and the various other players who presided over Arvida's creation—was manifested most clearly, or at any rate it is what distinguished this intention from that of classic socio-industrial utopias. Indeed, this is what would produce a model city intended to allow individuals to thrive, with an original nucleus of some 270 houses, built in 135 days, that would expand over the course of 25 years so that by 1950 there would be some 2,000 homes, based on more than 100 different models.

Of course, Arvida also stood out for the impressive media frenzy surrounding it and for the distinct impression held by all of its stakeholders, chroniclers and builders that history was in the making. This is also reflected in the financial and construction strategies that turned a monopolistic aluminum company into a reputable and enviable city builder, though these factors will not be discussed further here. The

Fig. 6 – This post card, published in about 1950, conveys the Arvidian identity project. With an old Arvida street, photographed by Studio Lalime, as a background, the card reads "Arvida, Quebec. Population 12,000. The majority of houses rent for $20 to $30 a month. Increasing numbers are owned by aluminum workers." Private collection.

real distinction of Arvida lies in a concept formulated incrementally by Davis and his acolytes at the beginning of the 1920s, that of a "desirable place to live." Although the city's relative isolation and its underlying utopian vision may explain the ambitious plan, it should be noted that the intention was never to create a working-class satellite village or a garden suburb, but, instead, to create an all-encompassing city, complete with a business centre and renowned institutions. The concept of a "desirable place to live," however, went well beyond the mere diversification of assets that led various resource-based companies to build more beautiful or welcoming cities. So, contrary to the vast majority of company towns the world over, Arvida's homes were, in effect, meant to be purchased by workers and, more often than not, to be inhabited by the same families for generations, much like in the remote company towns of Sweden and Norway. Here we touch upon the original legal definition of heritage: property owned by ancestors that is then passed on to descendants. This notion can be found in the commemorative intention of Alcoa. In Arvida, then, we find a special context of "double heritage," which has blended this commemorative intention, visible in various forms throughout the city, with the civic pride of its residents and exhibited in each and every dwelling.

Giving Substance to Civic Pride

Designing this housing, therefore, meant making it recognizable as such for its eventual owners. In other words, it was necessary to ensure that it corresponded to the cultural aesthetic and lifestyle of the workers, and to translate the individuality of family life into architectural terms so that residents would embrace it as their own. Since the First World War, this consideration led to the choice of a single-family dwelling—namely the cottage—as the embodiment of domesticity.[9] This precedent was first set in a few American working-class housing developments where property was sold, then in the first speculative developments of the 1920s (cf. Loeb 2001). But whereas most of these new developments and company towns featured three to four (and generally fewer than ten) models for houses, Arvida displayed an exceptional architectural variety, thereby reinforcing the notion of the individualization of the home. In order to construct the first neighbourhood of the model city, the company draftsmen designed thirty-nine model houses, many of which were mirror-image adaptations, or "left hand" and "right hand" versions. Of these, all but four were built. Aside from a four-family flat, a four-family row house and two duplexes, the entire original housing complex was made up of cottages. The contemporary state of the only four-family flat built—the least well preserved of Arvida's buildings—moreover testifies to the wise selection of a freehold tenure, single-family dwelling for the majority of housing in the city. The abundance of such cottages, then, calls for both architectural and legal research.

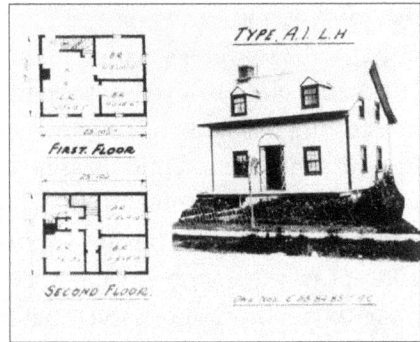

Fig. 7 – Illustration of an Arvida house in the company's Townsite Houses catalogue: this neo-Quebec model is among those that adopted a typical French-Canadian architectural image and dwelling space. Rio Tinto (Saguenay).

In sharp contrast to the image of a brand-new city, this sort of architectural diversity—offering a kind of North American counterpart to Tomás Bat'a's early-20th-century Zlín, in today's Czech Republic—also contributed to the city's sense of historicity from the outset, making it as picturesque as any other town site built gradually and over time. From 1927, Arvida's street names likewise served to confirm this manufactured sense of history: Deville, Hall[10] and other inventors of the aluminum industry rubbed shoulders with Davis and Mellon (bankers and financial partners at Alcoa), along with La Salle, Marquette, Cabot and Cartier, among the names of other North American explorers and pioneers. Local players who were instrumental to Arvida's creation would soon join their ranks. Along this road to identity Arvida also went one step further by giving a distinct and meaningful character to each of its homes. For instance, Harold Wake, the engineer in charge of Arvida's construction in 1926, proclaimed that "One hundred [of the first 270 houses built] are typical Quebec houses with the flared eaves and with one large room across one half of the house serving as a living room, dining room and kitchen" (Wake 1926: 462).

All of this indicates that Alcoa was rather sensitive to the spirit of the place. This is reinforced in that they had taken local considerations into account in their projects elsewhere; for instance, Alcoa hired the planner Morris Knowles to create housing adapted to the tropical conditions in Mackenzie, British Guiana. Although the highly influential Raymond Unwin[11] was at the time promoting the English Gothic or English Domestic Revival as a means of achieving harmonious design while avoiding the monotony of regularity (Unwin 1909: 367-68), the invention of neo-vernacular architecture (known as regionalist in certain contexts) remained embryonic (Morisset 1995, 1996; Loyer and Toulier 2001). Indeed, outside of world fairs and universal exhibitions, it was confined to the work of only a handful of architects. While variations on the theme of American colonial architecture proliferated, the small New Mexican houses of Bertram Goodhue or Irving Gill in southwestern United States remained the exception to the rule. As Margaret Crawford has pointed out, the American cottage, reinvented by Grosvenor Atterbury in the model community of Indian Hill, Massachusetts, instead became the instrument of an architectural nationalism, one aimed at immigrants in particular. Before the First World War, the planner John Nolen, struck by the cultural diversity of the workers in Kistler, Pennsylvania, declared that: "The population being so largely foreign in its make-up, there is a distinct necessity for a lead to be given in the direction of Americanism" (Nolen 1927). As the American cottage gained popularity internationally, so too did the innumerable examples of the English Domestic Revival, which serve as a reminder of the immense fortune of the Garden City model and of Unwin's rather overused proposals.

The invention of Quebecois-style houses by Arvida's American planners is thus rather astonishing. Indeed, in 1927, the Canadian planner Alexander Walker pointed out that:

> In a company town, remaining as it does in one common ownership, there is an unsurpassed opportunity to achieve a wonderful community feeling among its inhabitants by the simple process of carrying out a uniformity of treatment in the many elements of the town's structure. (Walker 1927)

The neo-vernacular aesthetic of Arvida's housing is all the more surprising given that it is linked to both private inhabited space (illustrated by the traditional French-Canadian family room) and to international architectural achievements. In some cases, the architecture was influenced by the American cottage, characteristic of a number of industrial housing complexes of the era, and in other cases by the cottages of Norwegian hydroelectric and metallurgic company towns, as if the entire initiative at Arvida involved the creation of a "northern" style in direct contrast to the tropical bungalows common to American resource towns (Morisset 2013). Of course, Alcoa representatives did indeed diligently visit Norway, as reported by the company's vice president, Edwin Fickes, an engineer, who described having been to the towns of Rjukan, Tyssedal and Høyanger (Fickes 1938). The Danish-born engineer Hjalmar E. Skougor (one of the two principal designers of Arvida) was no doubt familiar with this type of piecemeal identity. A short time earlier he wrote of his work for the Mexican town of Nueva Rosita: "In deciding upon the building material for the town site the natural development of building operations in this territory for the past fifty years was strictly adhered to" (Skougor 1921: 985).

The conditions of the invention of the Arvidian neo-vernacular, however, highlight the purpose of the exercise and reveal, in the more general context of the domestic architecture of international company towns, the identity project of Arvida's builders and the intended destiny of each home to foster a sense of civic pride. In fact, it was on site and not in the company's American workshops that all of the plans were designed, while the original American blueprints "were all discarded and ... the new designs were much more acceptable" (Wake 1926: 462). The experience of chief engineer Wake probably also affected the design of Arvida's houses. Wake came to Arvida from Badin, North Carolina, where Alcoa distinguished itself by its respectful attitude toward its African American workers.

Even though the hydraulic and geological potential of the Saguenay region allowed the aluminum company to develop the world's largest electrolysis plants in tandem with the most powerful hydroelectric stations,[12] one crucial resource seemed much more difficult to acquire than all the rest: the workforce. As opposed to older forms of industry, aluminum production necessitated sophisticated handling and required specialized workers who would be willing to accept difficult and uncomfortable working conditions, particularly in the potrooms. In short, this is what caused Alcoa leaders—with Davis foremost among them—to pay careful attention to the living conditions of workers, and to their local customs, in order to maintain a skilled and stable workforce.

In 1926, the population of Arvida was described as comprising hundreds of Poles, Swedes, Norwegians, Finns, Czechoslovaks and Italians, but few French Canadians were inclined to settle there with their families. Originally, Alcoa had counted on easily attracting the local French Canadian population, but they soon discovered that French Canadians were much more reticent than expected when it came to settling in the industrial town. The engineer Thomas L. Brock recalled that "It took a number of years to coax them off the farms in any large number to work indoors, particularly in the pot-rooms or carbon plant" (Brock 1971). During the first fifteen years of the town's existence, historians have pinpointed a "founding nucleus," composed of a little more than 50 per cent French Canadians, a third of whom came from the immediate vicinity of Arvida (curiously equivalent to the percentage of Quebec-type houses). Otherwise, the founding nucleus consisted of eighteen different nationalities (Igartua 1996: 73-74).

Although the unfavourable economic situation at the end of the 1920s likely drew workers to Arvida from industrial facilities that were closing throughout the region, a key factor was clearly engineer Wake's architectural about-face, which was intended to enhance the model city's drawing power by affirming its French Canadian character. Indeed, it should be noted that a few years earlier, the architect Perry MacNeille asserted that:

Fig. 8 – Like hundreds of other photographs and promotional documents produced by the company to showcase Arvida, this winter view, staged in 1927 on one of the city's first streets, testifies to the company's commemorative intention. Alcoa Papers, Library and Archives Division, Heinz History Center (Pittsburgh).

Rest for the mind and soul, not just for the body should become the principal aim in designing workingmen's houses.... An artistic house in a picturesque village makes a pleasanter home to return to, is more restful, more inspiring and increases the family's pride. (MacNeille 1917: 72)

While it may seem difficult to distinguish labour-retention factors from various other demographic characteristics, what is important above all is that the housing analysis—combined with the fact that a quarter of the "founding nucleus" was assigned to aluminum production—seems to indicate a metamorphosis from a socio-industrial utopia to an "aluminum society" project. This project includes a mosaic of various cultures assembled, like Arvida's homes, in a unique landscape and a shared egalitarian living space, characterized by both diversity and a sense of rootedness. The proliferation of nationalities, as described in the company's employment records, and that the heads from Alcoa were themselves foreign to the Canadian landscape, no doubt served to erase typical social and racial segregation. In fact, these were abolished from the moment the city project was announced: "The City," reveals Arvida's charter, "shall comprise but one Ward."[13]

The identity project espoused by Alcoa thus took shape through a certain type of naturalization, but territorial mediation was not solely restricted to architectural aesthetics in the creation of civic pride.

Heritage-building

Whereas the neo-vernacular structures in Arvida may have led to an immediate desire for ownership, civic pride and loyalty were forged over time. The creation of desirable housing was not enough to induce everyone to readily identify with "their" home, and certainly not enough for the worker—whether Polish, Norwegian or Canadian, Catholic, Protestant or Orthodox—to assume the role of active heritage guardian. Above and beyond aesthetics, these dimensions of Arvida's identity project were attained by way of law. This was achieved through a system of access (leasing, financing, etc.) to the original property and by subjecting properties to the conservation requirements registered in the acts of ownership in the form of constraints, or servitudes, of a rather unconventional nature. The project thus involved creating both a desire and the resources for heritage.

The complexity of undertaking a cadastral survey (of the extent, value and ownership of land) for Arvida's first neighbourhoods (which took four years to complete) attests to the rarity of such an operation. Two successive cadastral maps were created, including one of a clearly interim nature, since it subdivided dozens of parcels of land into hundreds of lots crisscrossing the territory. These also illustrate the obvious eagerness to sell the properties, which led Wake to declare (1929) that, in spite of the regrettable economic slowdown, "We have 88 properties under sales contract at the present time and have collected $68,607.02."[14] Even though the possibility of purchasing a home may encourage a region's residents to settle in a company town, it is nonetheless rather unusual for companies to sell the houses they built for their workers. As late as 1927, for instance, discussions around the creation of Mariemont, Ohio—where "The individual ownership of homes is contemplated; the workers will be given favorable terms for purchase" (Nolen 1927: 125)—testify to the exceptional character of these ideas. Presented as a work of philanthropy by its creator, John Nolen, the aforementioned contemplation nevertheless seems to contradict how the project was outlined four years earlier, that is, as "a community in which working men and men with small incomes will be provided with homes, either by rental or purchase, at a cost that will be properly proportionate to their wages or salaries" (Nolen 1923: 4).

In Arvida, aside from twenty or so lots that were kept in the company's hands (no doubt for use by some of the more itinerant company executives) the entire building project was subdivided into roughly equal lots to be sold. The near abandonment of the only two housing models more-or-less designed for rental purposes—the four-family flat and the row house[15]—illustrates the clear choice in favour of single-family dwellings toward

Fig. 9 – View of the Moritz ice rink, one of many facilities built by the company in Arvida; the alignment of the houses around it also illustrates the prevalent architectural variety, including on this street, the closest one to the plant. Private collection.

131

worker ownership. This tendency was indeed confirmed during the first year of the town's construction. Thus, when Wake reported that "in April 1929 we started to sell property in Arvida," he wrote that "our houses are built on lots 50 ft. x 100 ft. [15 x 30 m] with common driveways between every two houses and without alleys at the rear" (Wake 1929). Yet, three alleys remain from the original town plan, in which a certain number of lots were narrower, speaking to the on-site evolution of Alcoa's priorities. It does not seem far-fetched that Arvida as planned—as opposed to Arvida as eventually claimed (via municipal amalgamation)—was originally to include a small sector of densely packed rental housing, located close to the aluminum plant itself.

In any case, this was not the parent company's first foray into real-estate sales. In its company town of Alcoa, Tennessee, the project to sell houses at cost to both African American and Caucasian workers was held up as an unprecedented egalitarian accomplishment. But that operation's relative lack of success, in spite of payment terms of up to ten years, served as a reminder of what the press deemed "America's next problem: the housing of the unskilled wage earner" (Wood 1919). Here we see the source of this distinctly Arvidian trait, related both to the Mariemont ideal and to the product of a cross between company intentions and local usage. This was lease financing extended according to the worker's capacity to pay. Wake praised the formula as follows:

> A form of lease with promise of sale which was drawn by Messrs Prud'homme and Bell and Notary Lacroix. None of our employees has sufficient capital to make an outright purchase or pay more than a nominal amount on the purchase of property. Therefore we had to adopt a policy of selling on a monthly payment basis. We find out the maximum monthly payment which the purchaser indicates he is able to pay and if that shows a reasonable margin over the rent charged we make the contract. (Wake 1929)

The local newspaper, *The Arvidian–The Saguenay Valley Democrat* (itself a company product), added its own observations to the mix:

> Company employees have shown a great deal of interest in taking advantage of the company's offer to sell their homes to them. Up

until now approximately 81 people have purchased their house in Arvida, and J.-M. Lacroix, the public notary, has worked day and night for the last three weeks drafting the contracts of sale.... In a famous speech in Oyster Bay, N.Y., the late president Theodore Roosevelt stated that when they own their own homes the citizens of a country are entirely trustworthy. Under the circumstances, Arvida promises to have a good many solid citizens for, up until now, approximately a third of them have taken possession of their own homes, which is a sign of great things to come for the town moving forward. (*The Arvidian* 1927)

The land ownership archives, however, contain few traces of the acquisition of houses as a result of this financing formula.[16] A few titles to property evoke lease financing, stipulating, as in one title deed of 1931, that:

The buyer must pay and is moreover committed to paying all the taxes ... that are or will be levied for the said property from the date of the lease and a promise of sale granted in favour of the buyer through the seller before J. Miville Lacroix on November 24, 1927. (Land Register of Quebec, number 56640: July 4, 1931)

In most cases, it is the rental contract that references the leasing agreement, if indirectly, to which later official documents of sale rarely refer. So, the lease for a model C3 house, granted in 1927, is tied to a 204-month rental period in the monthly amount of $47.20:

The tenant may at any time pay the entire remaining sum.... To this remaining sum will be added interest at the rate of 5% per year from the date of payment, until 1944, and the total will be deducted from the unpaid balance of $9,628.80 at that time, but the payment of this sum will not free the tenant from the obligation to make the successive monthly payments required to pay the remainder of the $9,628.... Any tenant who fulfills all the conditions may complete the purchase for $1. The price mentioned in this act of sale will be $5,300. (Rio Tinto (Saguenay), rental lease, lot 42-b-78)

The relatively high cost of purchase—in this case about $10 above the monthly cost of rental to cover interest charges—must not obscure the true intentions of the company. Indeed, Alcoa clearly intended to establish a population of owners with strong ties to their property, but they needed to do so without frightening investors. To further foster these ties, a number of incentives to encourage pride in ownership were put into place in Arvida, such as competitions for the most beautiful gardens. These incentives attest to the same commemorative and heritage intention that linked the entire town and each property that gradually became a part of it. "Starting in 1928," pointed out Wake, "we offered prizes for the prettiest yards, both front and back, and considerable enthusiasm has been generated which has resulted in improving the appearance of the town" (Wake 1929: 2).

Although the economic slowdown at the end of the 1920s deprived Arvida's new proprietors of the wages that would have enabled them to agree to a contract of sale (as well as of boarders, who could have helped them cover the additional monthly fees associated with lease financing), various discrepancies in the archives point to informal agreements favourable to the worker-buyer. In the case of the C3 house mentioned above, for instance, the documents that refer to a cancellation of the sales contract in 1932 also announce the foreclosure of the property by the company, which nevertheless offers to reimburse the difference between the amount paid under lease financing and what would have been paid in rent. Yet, a few years later, the same worker is recorded as still living in the same place, apparently without any new monthly payments. In any event, as early as 1929, Wake was pleased that "quite a number of our people have been paying for a sufficient length of time that they now have real interest in the property" (ibid.).

Even so, this building of a heritage that belonged to both a private estate (under the aegis of Alcoa) and to private individuals (subdivided among a large number of owners) needed to avoid one of the most common pitfalls of ownership in a company town. As a number of people have noted, the sale of dwellings in such towns has generally resulted in various alterations that, in the end, have left the town or village unrecognizable. Indeed, in the vast majority of celebrated industrial complexes, preservation is limited to tiny portions of neighbourhoods that were generally reserved for company managers and executives. Such preserved historic properties have typically only recently been sold to private citizens—for instance, in the city of Bourlamaque, in Quebec, which is one of the most striking examples in this regard. In Arvida, however, the lease-financing formula contained ideas similar to contemporary notions of heritage: although each worker could construct his or her own heritage, each house was also understood as a kind of public property, in that it was subject to the exercise of power, not (yet) by any government authority, but by the company. At the end of the 1930s, this division of property became more formal as the company abandoned the somewhat informal lease-financing model in favour of mortgage loans.[17]

It is interesting to note that the second of Arvida's two main planners, the architect Harry Beardslee Brainerd (who was responsible for the plans for the town's business centre), stood out in his professional circle for his position in favour of architectural regulation. "Architectural Control," he wrote, "is a public welfare measure intended to enhance the amenities of life in the field of physical, economic, and social planning.... [I]t may be understood to mean regulation of buildings and structures at all stages" (Brainerd 1938). A number of his contemporaries objected to this idea, arguing (in a tone reminiscent of the anti-heritage discourse of today) that regulation systematized a reproduction of the past (Ackerman and Weinberg 1938). In any case, Brainerd's argument concerning "tax revenue" and the "stability of property value" (Brainerd 1938) was clearly reflected in the aims—if not always commemorative, then, at the very least, economic—of the capitalists of Alcoa. In Arvida, even before the creation of the town, they had specifications added to Quebec's *Cities and Towns Act* that would grant the municipal council the following powers:

> To regulate the place where traffic facilities, businesses, industries and buildings for specific uses are to be located within the city limits, as well as the use of real estate within these limits; to divide the city into districts or zones whose name, shape, and area will appear most appropriate for purposes of this regulation, and as regards these districts or zones to regulate and prescribe the architecture, dimensions and symmetry of the buildings constructed therein, the area of lots that these buildings may occupy, the space to be left between buildings, at what distance from the building line of the road the buildings must be constructed; and regulate the type of commerce, business and industry, as well as the uses ascribed for buildings and real estate in these districts. (16 George V, chap. 78, section 48)[18]

Even though, as chief engineer Wake lamented, "it [took] constant supervision and endless patience to get the buildings constructed according to the plans [in the downtown area]," the notary Miville Lacroix's expertise in matters of civil law[19] successfully tailored Alcoa's commemorative intention to the territory, applying it to each house sold. In fact, well before public action in the field of heritage was inscribed in the handbook of town planning, each of Arvida's deeds of ownership included specific conservation provisions in the form of servitudes (restrictive covenants). In civil law, these are defined as perpetuating the "use intended by the father of the family." In terms of inheritance, when the head of a family transfers part of his land to one of his children, the property is to be in some way preserved as long as the father's land remains unchanged.[20] These constraints subject the ownership of the Arvidian home, designated as "servient estates," to include another form of ownership, called "the dominant estate," which in Arvida is the factory complex of the industrial city (lot 8050 in the example below). In other words, the future of each Arvidian home was determined by the model city's maintenance of its industrial function, itself guaranteed by the property titles of the homes. Relatedly, the appearance of each home was, in turn, guaranteed by that of neighbouring houses. For instance, in 1931, when the company sold a 50 ft. by 100 ft. (15 x 30 m) lot to Petter Hjertholm (lot 3993),[21] a contractor of Norwegian origin who would build one of the very first and very rare "private" homes in Arvida, the title deed (similar to all the others, including for the previously mentioned C3 house) provided the following specifications:

> Said lot shall not be used for any other purpose than that of private residence and no structures other than one (1) dwelling house of not more than two full stories in height with the privilege of an attic or mansard [roof] in addition costing at least six thousand dollars ($6,000.00) for material and construction, with roof having a fire-proof covering of metal, slate, asbestos shingles, tiles ... and built for and adapted to the use of not more than one family shall be erected or maintained upon said lot except that a garage of not exceeding two car capacity.... Any such dwelling house shall face Taschereau Road, shall be located that no part thereof is nearer than thirty (30) feet to the front line of said lot or eight (8) feet to the side line of said lot.... No garage ... shall be erected or maintained upon said lot within seventy-five (75) feet from the street.... 2- No structure or sign of any kind,

except the small ornamental structures above mentioned, shall be erected or maintained upon said lot or be materially altered unless the same shall be erected and the alterations, be made in the location, position, manner, and of the design and material approved in advance in writing by the owner of said lot number eight thousand and fifty (8050) ... nor shall any structure erected or sign displayed on said lot be painted at any time without such approval.... (Land Register of Quebec, number 56185, April 7, 1931)

In each conveyance, servitudes of the same nature assigned the company the role of public authority with respect to the development of urban infrastructures.[22] For instance, the ownership of animals other than those of a domestic variety was prohibited, and, perhaps more directly related to Arvida's social project, the sale or transportation of any "habit forming drug, distilled or rectified spirits, wine, fermented or malt liquor" was forbidden. It should be noted that these strict regulations were very unusual, and forced each homeowner to take on the role of guardian of his or her own property, which was to be kept in the state that it was received. These were repeated from one deed to the next, and acquired some slight differences during the 1940s, possibly because the first contracts of sale subject to lease financing had come to term, leading to a multiplication of formal sales. At this time, the City of Arvida adopted its first planning regulations, which in the company's title deeds would take the form of certain regulatory specifications, as reflected in this typical conveyance of a J3 house:

The present sale is made subject to the following servitudes, namely:

The right to maintain and operate the works as now constructed and operated by the vendor, its subsidiary and affiliated companies in the City of Arvida, for industrial purposes and to maintain and operate the same as enlarged, altered or replaced from time to time without any liability to the owners and/or occupants of the property hereby sold, for any injury, damage or inconvenience to them or to the said property or any part thereof or anything thereon by reason of the emission or production of odour, dust, smoke, gas, vapour, fumes, vibration, explosion or noise in connection with the maintenance and/or operation of said work ... the above-described property hereby sold shall be used in accordance with the dispositions of the land-use and building by-law n° 125 of the city of Arvida, adopted 22 May 1950. It is expressly understood and agreed that no fence shall be erected anywhere on the front portion of said property within the set-back distance specified in said by-law. It is further agreed that no construction, changes, additions, modifications or rebuilding shall be carried out on said property before plans and specifications for same have been submitted to and approved in writing by the vendor. (Land Register of Quebec, number 123156, December 1, 1954)

In short, by setting up a residential-housing development and property sales for houses or lots (very rarely, given the lack of lease-financing support), the company established and perpetuated the industrial city, the planned city and its society. For the industrial city, this was achieved by the creation of the dominant estate and the preservation of the plant's function; for the planned city, by a demarcation of strictly residential neighbourhoods and aesthetic control; and a society was established by fostering a willing population to inhabit and sustain it. Above all, the Arvidian homeowner became a heritage transmitter, spurred on by architectural and legal conditions, in keeping with Alcoa's commemorative intention and its integration with the Quebecois economic and cultural landscape. At the same time, the built landscape took shape as a common good, protected by the upkeep of the industrial property, the management of a public authority, the owner's own desire and the watchful eye of thirty or so of his neighbours.

A Public Good Administered by Public Authorities

Before the expiry date set by the company of January 1, 1960, as noted in Petter Hjertholm's title deed, Alcan (as the company was registered in Canada in the 1940s) made sure to systematize the building restrictions of its servitudes through public action. The impressive thirty-five-page Arvida land-use and building bylaw confirmed in detail the provisions outlined in the city charter and stated that title deeds for houses would henceforth refer to the bylaw. Instigated by Arvida's town manager, the regulations drew on those of Sillery, Quebec, and controlled the city's functional zoning, the height and size of buildings, building density, yard size, billboard advertising and aerial structures, and the administration of building permits. It also reiterated restrictions imposed in title deeds concerning the functional, architectural and landscape characteristics of dwellings. Conveyances for houses continued to be subject to other servitudes that were likewise intended for heritage conservation, and were applied to each specific house as well as to the city as a whole ("no fences ... no construction, changes, additions, modifications or rebuilding").

With the increase in the number of property owners, and consequently in taxpayers and voters, the municipal government gradually emancipated itself from the company, at least in appearance. In 1949, for instance, an Alcan engineer said that "We ran the town openly at first. Now we do so from behind the scenes" (qtd. in Cronin 1949: 5). Nevertheless, though the company succeeded, in 1926, in replicating the model of governance at Arvida that it had previously implemented in the city of Alcoa, Tennessee (consisting of a municipal council made up three elected officials, who selected a mayor from their own ranks), the minutes do not reveal any particular harmony between the municipal administration and the company (aside, of course, from the official use of English,[23] which was no doubt the legacy of the three Alcoa engineers who happened to form the first council). The municipality's prerogatives, however, seemed to become distinctly clearer with the growth of the city, which had reached more than 10,000 inhabitants by the beginning of the 1940s and boasted the most powerful aluminum plant in the world. By this time, the official exchanges between the company and the municipality were, on the whole, characterized by a relative separation of these two "public" bodies in the model city. This is illustrated, for instance, by Alcan's proposal to the city council to build new houses:

> Mr. G. W. LaMountain, Superintendant of Properties, Aluminum Company of Canada, Limited, Arvida, dated 18th of September, 1942, stating that the Aluminum Company of Canada, Limited is building to the West of Davis Street a certain number of houses and requesting the City to build concrete sidewalk in front of those houses. The letter states also that as the City has no appropriation in its current budget to cover the cost of this

work that a special assessment covering the cost of said work will be accepted and paid by the company. After consideration, on motion of Alderman D. P. Ross seconded by Alderman J. E. Bouchard, the abovementioned request was approved and the City Manager was instructed to carry out the said work.[24]

Of course, the company, which was pursuing both its housing program and its history-making project—as attested by a series of commissioned photographs of the plants and workers by the British photographer Ronny Jaques during the tumultuous war years—had no intention of leaving to chance or to outside players the commemorative intention that motivated the creation of Arvida. This is why, in 1943, the company created a town-planning commission with the municipality, to which it assigned, among others, Harold Lea Fetherstonhaugh, the well-known architect with whom it did business during that time, and the highly celebrated landscape architect Frederick Gage Todd, known as a student of Frederick Law Olmsted and as the father of landscape architecture in Canada.

It was this planning commission that drew up the zoning and construction regulations that were initially outlined in 1945 and adopted in 1950, in order to accompany "the company's policy ... to encourage private property and small industry" (Commission 1964). Incidentally, as of 1938 the company officially mandated one of its employees "to lease [the company's property] with or without promise of sale and/or to sell" (Land Register of Quebec, number 64274, May 27, 1938).[25] In a context of increasing power with respect to state institutions in public space, the company seemed to want to legitimate its town-planning leanings. In fact, this is how the Arvida Planning Committee and the town's legal adviser explained the decision to opt in favour of the zoning and construction regulation model provided by Sillery rather than that of the company town of Baie-Comeau, Quebec, which was deemed inadmissible by the provincial government. During a discussion concerning the municipal powers of intervention, the legal adviser and the committee did not hesitate to mention the

necessary amendment to the *Cities and Towns Act* ... the law should be amended ... the idea [should be submitted] to the City Managers Association or other influential groups at their respective conventions so that sufficient pressure could be brought to bear on the ministers concerned.

On a broader scale, the Arvida Planning Committee took on the task of "studying the development of Arvida for the well-being and benefit of all citizens, of Alcan and of any other owner," to the extent that the town manager was officially appointed one of its five members "in order to create a certain interest among citizens and to obtain the consent of the town council."[26] The *Le Lingot* newspaper (which succeeded *The Arvidian-The Saguenay Valley Democrat*) confirmed this focus on the architectural and town-planning regulation that was intended to generate the "eternal present" (borrowing again from Riegl's definition of commemorative value) of Arvida:

> The role of the Planning Committee will also be to prevent the town of Arvida from building houses that disfigure a city.... Arvida's citizens, and especially the town's future home own-ers, may count on the Planning Committee, which is made up of highly experienced technicians able to develop the very best town-planning principles. (*Le Lingot* 1944)

In concert with municipal initiatives, public power exercised by the model city's mother company was thus maintained, along with the notion of the common good that justified it. This power was main-tained in both the socio-industrial utopia as continually envisioned and in the bustling aluminum city as lived. The company was respon-sible for perpetuating the original idea of the city and its impacts on the Arvidian landscape, housing and living environment, ensuring that Arvida would be preserved as a whole and that its worker-owners,

Fig. 10 – Work of the architects Fetherstonhaugh and Durnford, the Saguenay Inn, built in 1939 as a company hotel. Photo by Guillaume St-Jean / Canada Research Chair in Urban Heritage.

with their crucial role in the heritage project, would continue to feel a powerful sense of civic pride.

The indigenization that was initiated by the reformulation of the cityscape and of the housing of the 1920s was also continued throughout the 1940s and 1950s by the perpetuation of a type of architecture that came to be increasingly characteristic of Arvida and its region. This also produced some original neo-vernacular masterpieces. Léonce Desgagné and Ernest Isbell Barott, for instance, would adopt the local preferences for their work in Arvida, even though their original proposals were of a distinctly modernist bent. The designs of new house models likewise confirmed this aesthetic of belonging, for instance, in the work of the architects Henry Ross Wiggs and Alexander Tilloch Galt Durnford, who were well known for their vernacular sensibility. With the generous financial support of the company, the commemorative intention—and the feeling of identity it engendered—was also translated into religious, commercial, school and industrial buildings, and even to road infrastructure.

In the sphere of property and of the home, Alcan also maintained its somewhat informal ownership-incentive policy. Even with the extremely rapid acceleration of sales between 1954 and 1960, the company was still as attentive as ever to the model city. When certain houses were threatened by the city's densification, for instance, Alcan moved some in order to preserve them. This was also the case during the extension of a downtown street in 1960.[27] The sale of a greater number of houses also did not prevent the continuation of former practices, whether it was the registration of so-called heritage servitudes (using contemporary language),[28] the spreading out of payments over a maximum term of seventeen years (204 monthly payments) or financial support provided by the company. Alcan continued to oversee the collection of monthly payments in their entirety, although they

Fig. 11 – The Saint-Jacques church, built in 1949 based on plans by the architects Desgagné and Boileau. Photo by Marianne Charland / Canada Research Chair in Urban Heritage.

made a financial agreement with Canada Life, to which the company increasingly transferred balances of sales and mortgage loans. This was the case, for instance, in the 1955 sale by the federal crown corporation Wartime Housing Ltd. of one of the 561 homes built in Arvida, which Alcan subsequently acquired and set up as a business:

> Alcan hereby sells and transfers to Canada Life, present and accepting, for the prices and consideration of $3,600 payable in the manner that the parties have moreover agreed upon, a portion of the sales price owed to Alcan, by the purchaser in accordance with the previous provisions of this act, equaling $3,600 including interest on the said portion of the sales price as of the present date and all the appurtenances guaranteeing payment of the said portion of the balance of the sales price....

> Each monthly payment of $38.40 payable in accordance with the title price will be divided proportionately between Canada Life and Alcan such that Canada Life will be entitled to receive $27.11 and Alcan, $11.29....

> Canada Life hereby establishes Alcan as its agent to collect all sums owed by the purchaser in accordance with the present agreement and authorizes Alcan to discharge the purchaser of all sums paid. The address of Alcan as an agent will be the office of its property department in Arvida.[29] (Rio Tinto [Saguenay], AS1081)

In public and institutional space, Arvida's schools stood out among all of Canada's educational institutions for their innovation and accessibility, and were also established and funded by Alcan. In such places, the Arvida anthem, written for the 25th anniversary of the model city, resonated as a reminder of its utopic origins and deeply rooted Arvidian identity:

> Receive our songs and praise / You, our brilliant city / Our vocal phalanxes sing your praises / Prosperous City of Arvida.

> With pride, you dispense to us / Your rich gifts and blue waves / You pour them out in abundance / Oh majestic Saguenay! / Bathed in your limpid waves / Gathered on your enchanting shores / Grow splendid towns and cities / Centres for peace and hard work.

Noble and prosperous garden city / You have known the devotion / Of proud-spirited, virile men / Smitten by a provident love / Your founders made you beautiful / At once peaceful and full of good cheer / No matter what their name / With us, they're right at home.

Let's especially praise the diligence / Of our ever-so-devoted pastors / And let's also praise the vigilance / Of the leaders of our city.[30]

In 1975, however, Arvida's social project was hit by a major setback. A territorial-organization reform orchestrated by the provincial government was imposed on the model aluminum city, and it was forced to amalgamate with its neighbours, the pulp and paper town of Kénogami and the older settler town of Jonquière. It must also be kept in mind that in 1970 Arvida had already absorbed the neighbouring village of Saint-Jean-Eudes,[31] which had been populated over the years by "para-Arvidians" who were either unable or unwilling to live in the porcelain city. And so, in the midst of the resulting social chaos and despite thundering protests on the part of its residents, Arvida took on the name of Jonquière and disappeared as a municipality.

Rupture and Resiliency: From Identity Project to Civic Determination

The impact of the amalgamation upon the porcelain city affected far more than the name of the place. Arvidians were disheartened, having fiercely resisted the municipal reorganization and the erasure of a name and an identity that they knew was internationally renowned. Further adding to the disappointment was the complete termination of fifty years of "Arvidianity" (which many still remember vividly)[32] that resulted from the dissolution of Arvida's integral space in the wake of this political restructuring of territory. Nearly forty years later, it is possible to confirm that Arvida was the target of a deliberate identity-erasing campaign. This is attested to by the financial success of the municipal reorganization, which obtained the impressive Arvidian tax base, and also, if only a little, by a certain envy built up over the years in Arvida's neighbours. Indeed, the amalgamation left scars on the heritage tissue of Arvida's togetherness and built environment. That the reorganization took place shortly after the tragic 1971 catastrophe at Saint-Jean-Vianney—a landslide on the opposite shore of the Saguenay River swept away some forty homes, with hundreds of survivors relocated to Arvida—certainly did not help to alleviate social dislocation, or the effects of provincial legislation. That very same year, 1971, the province of Quebec exempted Alcan from paying municipal property taxes on its dams, thus draining Arvida's coffers of half of the municipal assessment value in one measure.[33]

The years following the amalgamation were coloured by antagonism, revenge, rationalization and adjustment, all of which affected the redistribution of facilities, infrastructures and investments. Arguably, Arvida lost out in the arrangement, becoming the poor relation in the amalgamation. At first, however, the terms of the municipal reorganization seemed to favour the former model city: the transfer of civil servants and permanent employees entrusted the City of Jonquière with Arvida's court clerk, treasurer, police chief and fire chief, while only the manager and director of public works came from the former Town of Jonquière. But this bureaucratic representation had a symbolic counterpoint: the first session of the new municipal council was slated for the town hall of the former municipality of Kénogami.

The municipal reorganization also triggered a reorganization of the Arvidian landscape, its political space and the democratic representation of its citizens. Although they generally respected the logic of the previous territorial divisions (especially parishes) of Arvida's two "rivals," Jonquière and Kénogami, the electoral subdivisions of the new City of Jonquière seemed to divide the population of Arvida without any regard for historical territory and housing plans. After provincial legislation stipulated that a municipality the size of Jonquière should have a minimum of twelve and a maximum of sixteen electoral districts, the seven electoral districts dividing the area, represented by two councillors each, were re-divided in 1979. At this time, fourteen districts were formed, represented by a single councillor each (Ville de Jonquière, bylaw number 349, July 30, 1979), including five on

Fig. 12 – Chez nous c'est chez nous *(our home's our home): another view by Marc Ellefsen during the anti-municipal-reorganization campaign in Arvida.* Library and Archives Canada.

Arvidian soil. Then, barely six years later, two subsequent reconfigu-rations of these five districts (Ville de Jonquière, bylaw number 391, May 25, 1982; regulation number 576, May 26, 1986) produced a result revealing of the upheavals of the political space in question: in 1986, the Arvidian parishes of Saint-Jacques and Saint-Mathias were com-bined and renamed as "Vaudreuil," and the space known to Arvidians as the "Vaudreuil neighbourhood" was swallowed up by the "district of Saint-Philippe." Similarly, the "district of Sainte-Thérèse" sliced the territory of this parish in two and, most strikingly, excluded the church bearing the name of its patron saint. In short, none of Arvida's new districts ended up corresponding to the historical geography of the former city. In 1994 and 1998, during a new subdivision of the city into ten districts,[34] Arvida saw its number of districts reduced to three, and confirmed the now longstanding trend of nonsensical boundary changes (Ville de Jonquière, bylaw number 1005, May 9, 1994; regulation number 1245, April 27, 1998).

As such, the municipal reorganization sparked a dynamic of historical discontinuity that was contrary to the inherent historicity of the commemorative intention of the Arvidian project, which was still vigorously embraced by municipal actors in the early 1970s. The company maintained relative control over Arvida's housing stock by continuing to explicitly subject all property that it sold to the perpetual servitudes that were by now characteristic of buildings sold as servi-ent estates (e.g., Land Register of Quebec, number 124311, February 9, 1955; number 21952, November 7, 1968). Resale by individuals, however, was often limited by "an industrial servitude to the effect that Alcan is not responsible for the emissions of its Arvida plant" and the "use of the building as a private residence" (Land Register of Quebec, number 60311, July 17, 2002). Furthermore, faced with a certain degree of confusion that had slowly crept into acts of owner-ship with regard to servitudes of industrial operation and of public utility (Land Register of Quebec, number 219956, 1968), notaries would soon restrict reminders of servitudes as "subject to rights as-signed in accordance with registered titles" (Land Register of Quebec, number 343471, April 4, 1979), or simply "to all servitudes, active or passive, apparent or hidden, that may affect it" (Land Register of Quebec, number 368350, November 19, 1980; number 112925, 1953). No additional detail was provided in such cases, and others neglected to mention servitudes at all, likely the result of notaries from outside the region who were no doubt unfamiliar with the process (Land Register of Quebec, number 225565, August 7, 1969). And so heritage knowledge dissipated, little by little. What remained was confined to the imagination and practices of a diminishing number of first-generation owners in a context that was unsympathetic to their civic pride.

More generally, public action in the Arvidian community (formerly exercised by the company and gradually delegated to the municipality) was discarded and subject to a municipal governance that was marked by rivalry. Above all, it was replaced with a cultural and town-planning logic foreign to the community and to the heritage mediation and conservation mechanisms that had prevailed there. With the new municipality's professed goals of equity and uniformity, rather than of difference and singularity, the denial of Arvida's existence, and influence on the international stage, would continue well after the erasure of its name. Indeed, the fruit of the commemorative intention that gave life to the city all but vanished in the refusal to give the former city any sort of priority with regard to the development and management of its built landscape. Pride and memory gradually bled out of the Arvida "sector," which now included Saint-Jean-Eudes, lacking distinction or difference. Less than twenty years after the amalgamation, all that remained of the heritage project was a rumour that the Arvida area appeared as an "A" shape when seen from the air. This translation of the idea of a planned city into the public imagination, however, carried forward the notion of identity and contained the seed of an already nascent Arvidian resurrection.

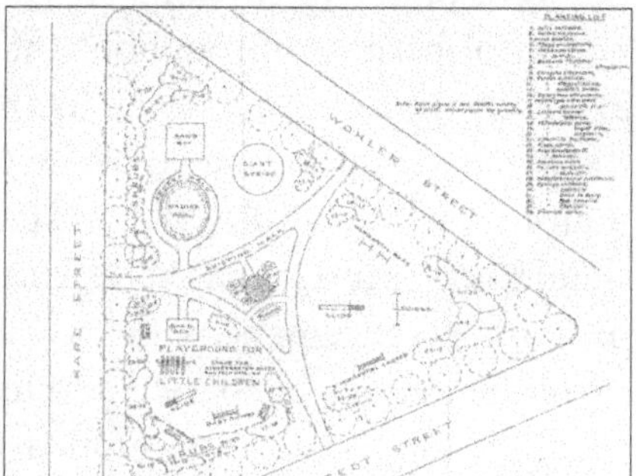

But the phoenix must nevertheless die before being reborn from its ashes. As early as the 1970s, the rupture of the heritage project was confirmed by the unceremonious storage of the former model city's original plans in a quickly forgotten base-

Fig. 13 – Frederick Todd's design, when he served as chair of the Arvida Planning Committee, for one of the numerous parks in Arvida. The park was restored in 2014 according to his original plans. City of Saguenay.

ment. These plans numbered in the thousands and had guided the meticulous construction of Arvida down to the smallest architectural and urban detail. At this point, territorial development had diverged significantly from these comprehensive plans of 1926,[35] and if the new visions for the municipality had carried on unimpeded, they probably would have threatened the 1,400 or so hectares that were already built up, as well as the 1,000-hectare greenbelt. But, at the heart of the city, the aluminum plant—still renowned as the largest in the world at the beginning of the 1970s, with an annual production of 432,000 tons and 5,000 employees—was experiencing difficulties as it was slowly being superceded by new technologies. Although the company would open two new plants in neighbouring towns, production in Arvida plummeted, reaching only 266,000 tons in 1990, with nearly 2,000 fewer employees (Lapointe 1992). In the socio-political context of the 1980 provincial referendum on Quebec sovereignty,[36] rumours of a plant closure were enough to incite a mass exodus of aluminum company workers, notably to Kingston, Ontario, where Alcan announced (1972) that it would build a new 80-hectare industrial complex.[37] Torn apart by quarrels regarding equity within the confines of Jonquière, and now anonymous, silenced and discredited, Arvida lost a good many of the Arvidians who had remained its only guardians. Indeed, from 1971 to 1982, the population of the historical territory dropped by 30 per cent.

Collective Knowledge to be Reiterated

Thus put to the test, the heritage project that gave life to Arvida and its residents had to face the challenge of modernity. Although it carried the seeds of the identity and social participation that would shape the notion of heritage throughout the 20th century, the company town evidently remained anchored in an older political space, animated by the company's governance of the territory and its resources more so than by the free will of the Arvidians themselves. In this respect, it should not be surprising to learn that, in 1948, when the town planning and management of the city increasingly became the responsibility of the municipal council and less of Alcan, an innovative housing program for Arvida was nipped in the bud.[38] The loan regulation that was to permit the municipality to acquire land and to finance construction was put to a referendum and was defeated by a margin of 106 to 57 by voter-owners.³⁹ Though egalitarian in its aspirations, the identity project was thus hijacked by a select few. Perhaps, in the end, the municipal reorganization by the province forced a reorganization, a reawakening, of Arvida's citizenship.

In the first decades of the 20th century, commemoration dominated heritage practice, as Aloïs Riegl testified. Situated in an eternal present, or in a linear, continual historicity, it was nevertheless akin to a new idea that wished to place the historical components of heritage in a relatively distant past. Throughout the Western world (and probably in an even larger portion of the planet), the Second World War clearly propelled this second set of values—related to the more distant past—ahead of the first. In Arvida, it was the 1975 amalgamation that produced this kind of temporal rupture and that toppled the heritage system. Henceforth, the once self-sufficient identity project, which had previously relied on the congruence of territorial governance and on the relative permanence of Arvidian society, would measure itself against the guidelines of modern notions of heritage.

In opposition to the commemorative intention that prompted Arvida's creation, modern notions that situate heritage squarely in the past took hold in Quebec in 1972 with the adoption of the *Loi sur les biens culturels* (*Cultural Property Act*). This both established the role of the state in public initiatives concerning heritage and confirmed the French-style classification system; that is, the designation of a legal status that subjects property to government supervision, as a measure to protect, for example, assets, monuments and historic districts. But while in certain regions of the world first-wave deindustrialization sparked a growing interest in architecture and industrial or proto-industrial complexes, in Quebec the situation was rather different. A context of French Canadian empowerment had been gaining steam since the Quiet Revolution, and public authorities increasingly came to value the heritage of "New France," which had been supposedly lost to "les Anglais" so many centuries ago. In Saguenay, the 1984 classification of the Pulperie de Chicoutimi—an industrial pulp and paper complex that, beginning in 1930, was progressively decommissioned—was a notable exception in this regard, revealing both the exceptional imprint of industrialization on territorial development in the region and, consequently, a certain predisposition for this type of heritage. But neither this regional peculiarity nor the delegation of certain powers to the municipalities in the 1985 *Cultural Property Act* was enough to attract the attention of the City of Jonquière or the provincial authorities to Arvida. Lacking in defunct industrial buildings, the model city had nothing in common with the historic districts of the province, of Old Quebec City or of Old Montreal, but the denial of Arvida and its seemingly ordinary appearance also, no doubt, led to the belief that interesting heritage necessarily had to be found elsewhere. So a search was initiated in an attempt to find anything in Jonquière that might be similar to the venerable built landscapes of Quebec City or Montreal. It was not until the turn of the millennium that the municipality officially recognized a building in Arvida in accordance with the "citation" power it held under the law—the Église Sainte-Thérèse-de-l'Enfant-Jésus, the first church built in the aluminum city. Although it was certainly not the most representative building of Arvida's storied past, the gesture by Jonquière was significant.

In a process similar to the management exercised by Arvida in the past, Quebecers began to equip themselves with new heritage development and conservation tools that privileged local authorities. Meanwhile, the political project that presided over the 1975 municipal reorganization gradually waned. Soon, being "from Arvida" (a claim that residents never relinquished) took on a whole new meaning: the built landscape could act as a framework for a better community. This is most likely how the city of Arthur Vining Davis took on the shape of an imaginary "A"—it began to be viewed from above, as it were, and from elsewhere, just as it had when its industrial and

Fig. 14 – In front of a J3 house designed by architect Alexander Tilloch Galt Durnford and registered in 1944 in the Inventaire des œuvres d'art de la province de Québec *(Quebec Works of Art Inventory), the municipal councillor Carl Dufour poses with an Arvida family for the front page of the brand-new* Arvidien.

town-planning feats attracted the attention of the world.

In 1995, an exhibition of planned industrial towns was organized by the Canadian Centre for Architecture in which Arvida was showcased alongside just two other company towns. This no doubt served as a catalyst for public action by making use of documents that local actors had until then considered trivial; Arvida was suddenly back in the spotlight.[40] Indeed, at the end of the 1990s, Arvida's town planning and heritage gradually emerged from the shadows—for instance, in two studies commissioned by the province of Quebec, an overarching *Report on the Conservation of Built Heritage of Jonquière* of 1994 that was superseded by a much more specific *Plan for the Conservation and Development of Urban and Architectural Heritage of Arvida*

Fig. 15 – View of the outdoor exhibit Travailleurs de l'aluminium d'Arvida (Arvida aluminum workers), organized in 2012 in honour of the 75th anniversary of the National Aluminum Worker's Union of Arvida; the photographs of workers taken by the artist Ronny Jaques provide a step-by-step rediscovery of the city's downtown area, while a QR code for each panel directs the visitor to a second exhibit, a virtual one this time. Photo by Marie-Blanche Fourcade / Canada Research Chair in Urban Heritage.

in 1999 (Noppen and Morisset 1994; Ville de Jonquière 1999).

Thus it was that Arvida would be approached as a singular object, both from town-planning and heritage perspectives, although this required getting to know the object better. While regulatory measures such as the Plans d'implantation et d'intégration architecturale (Site Planning and Architectural Implementation Program), under the *Loi sur le patrimoine culturel*,[41] promptly ensured the immediate protection of sectors threatened by renovation gentrification or increased population density, a local series of inventories established specific provisions for classifying the built landscape of Arvida. Interestingly, these were not just based on external criteria, but also took into account the community's distinctive features, and notably those of the overall housing

plan. A first-stage analysis of the built landscape and of historic documents, therefore, helped establish descriptive categories that in turn
helped in measuring the state of the built environment as well as of
housing needs in the heritage sector. By comparing the existing housing in relation to their models, the exercise was intended to evaluate
which transformations would be desirable, acceptable or prohibited,
keeping in mind that one of the special qualities of the site of Arvida
was in its sixty or so original housing models. The intervention
resulted in a restoration guidebook that reiterated the premise that
heritage was a project and, in this case, a lived project. By targeting
the built landscape as it was designed and constructed over a period of
about fifty years of the 20th century, the objective was both to remain
close to the original and to seek tolerable mitigation measures that
took into account the needs of modern Arvidians.

Since then, three central ideas have served to structure Arvida's
heritage history, based on an increasingly explicit strategy: conservation, citizen participation and the development of knowledge and
know-how. As was the case with the launching of the inventory of
buildings, public action proceeded hand-in-hand with a renewal
of knowledge and practices, and was now backed by educational
institutions from the perspective of innovation, development and
harmonization with the historical era. Indeed, the town-planning
adventure of the industrial city had already merited a dissertation and
two monographs during the 1990s.[42] By the end of the first decade of
the 21st century, this approach had reached new heights, spawning,
for example, ten or so studies, the adoption of a half-dozen architectural and integration plans and support for Arvida's property owners,
with thanks to a consulting service dedicated to renovation based on
knowledge compiled from the inventories. But first, Arvida would
have to go through yet another amalgamation.

In 2001, a decree of the government of Quebec ordered the
merging of Jonquière with the cities and towns of Chicoutimi, La
Baie and Laterrière, and with the municipalities of Lac-Kénogami
and Shipshaw (Decree number 841-2001, June 27, 2001). The resulting city, named Saguenay, contains approximately 150,000 residents
and covers an area the size of the island of Montreal,[43] making it
the seventh-largest city in the province. Saguenay includes nineteen

districts, which range from 1,512 to slightly more than 8,000 electors, and the former city of Arvida is home to 10 per cent of this entire population. Arvida, including Saint-Mathias and Saint-Jean-Eudes, is divided into two districts of 7,497 and 7,466 electors, respectively, with a standard deviation of 4.6 per cent of eligible voters, compared with the other subdivisions. And so, having gradually rediscovered its identity as the effects of the 1975 municipal reorganization dissipated, it seems that Arvida was not lost after all, even if its political representation obeys territorial logic that remains incomprehensible from a historical and a heritage perspective. Indeed, it seems that the effects of globalization—which elsewhere has erased national borders to the benefit, in some cases, of planetary metropolises, rediscovered lands and local particularities—have also had an impact on the microcosm of Saguenay.

Freed from the distrust of the 1970s, and no doubt simmering since the company distanced itself from the town, the voices of Arvidians have reclaimed public space. In 2008, the periodical *The Arvidian–The Saguenay Valley Democrat* was reborn as *L'Arvidien–le journal des gens d'Arvida* (The Arvidian–Newspaper of the People of Arvida) and Arvida would soon be the subject of three publications in three consecutive years, published by born-and-bred Arvidians (Hartwick 2007; Michaud 2009; Archibald 2010). Then, in November of 2009, a municipal councillor with a promise to protect heritage was elected. Six months later—in accordance with the powers conferred upon it by the *Cultural Property Act*—the municipality designated an area comprising more than 700 private houses as a heritage site; this included the oldest part of the model city and about one-third of all of the homes of the Arvidian territory. This became, then, the most important heritage site of its kind in the province. Imposing a significant degree of architectural and landscape control, this sort of measure requires public consultation and, importantly, the consent of an enthusiastic population.

Arvida's heritage conservation and development initiatives have intensified ever since, around the three central ideas of conservation, citizen participation and the development of knowledge and know-how. These are supported by a parallel proliferation of preservation distinctions and official recognitions, as attested by, among others, several inscriptions put forward by the municipality to the Canadian Register of Historic Places and the designation of Arvida as a National Historic Site of Canada, another initiative taken by the municipality.

Based on the principle of the co-construction of knowledge put forward since the turn of the millennium, municipal officials have continued to establish heritage inventories and collaborative preservation measures.

During the re-evaluation of Arvida's downtown, and with Arvida's increasing attention in academic studies, museums and industry, the municipality, in partnership with the Quebec Ministry of Culture and Communications, sealed its commitment by investing in the restoration of Arvida's residential housing stock. Some $260,000 per year has been paid out since 2011, which is more than half of the provincial funding allocated to heritage in the entire Saguenay region. In order to inscribe such actions within a sustainable political framework, the City of Saguenay created the Comité pour la reconnaissance patrimoniale d'Arvida (CORPA) (Arvida Heritage-Recognition Committee) in the summer of 2009. CORPA is a multi-party roundtable that brings together a cross-section of community actors, ranging from representatives of Rio Tinto to private citizens and local merchants, along with participants from the cultural and town-planning sectors of the municipality and the provincial government. Having been limited, for a time, to timid quotations in a few brochures, public action concerning heritage in Arvida has finally recovered the all-encompassing dimension that characterized the commemorative intention of the founding private company. Grounded by Arvidian involvement and with the help of innovation and locally developed resources, the commemorative intention touches on culture and planning, as well as on the economy and society, and brings together specialists, researchers and contributors from such fields as heritage, tourism, ethnology, real estate, museology and urban development. Far from being conceived of as a last hope or as a perishable memory, this heritage is not received or managed as a preserved artifact, but instead as a living environment and a vision of the world, as befits the socio-industrial utopia that produced it. From this point of view, the heritage recognitions that have grown recently have transmitted a sense of belonging and pride to Arvidians that was never completely extinguished. Just as the

1995 exhibition at the Canadian Centre for Architecture reopened Arvidians' frame of reference beyond the borders of Jonquière, the present deeply rooted drive of residents and their representatives to obtain UNESCO recognition is in line with the heritage desire that has peppered Arvida's genesis and growth.

Certainly, the re-conquest of the Arvidian heritage project is not without challenges. The venture touches upon the principles of conservation (e.g., how to ensure the conservation of two semi-detached houses in relation to one another) and is unfolding in an ever-changing social and political context. As such, while the new *Loi sur le patrimoine culturel* (*Cultural Heritage Act*) adopted by the National Assembly of Quebec in 2011 recognizes citizen participation as the main catalyst of heritage, the management framework that the *Act* promotes has yet to be appropriated and translated into a means to be implemented by the municipality. In this respect, although the new category of *paysages culturels patrimoniaux* (designated cultural landscapes) seems like a straightforward way to recognize the inter-relationship between Arvida and the surrounding area, beyond municipal boundaries, the changes resulting from heritage governance are accompanied by notable technical and political challenges. The longstanding partnership between the city and the academic community, through its ongoing research, is a major advantage when it comes to providing solutions for heritage problems that may arise. But the participation of Arvidians—the cornerstone of this heritage—has yet to be better incorporated into mechanisms of protection and sustainability, so that citizens are not just the recipients of activities and services, but active legatees of Arvida's heritage as well. In concert with competitions and various events designed to encourage civic expression, the recent expansion of local heritage considerations into the realm of intangible heritage produced by the Arvidian utopia is among the means being implemented to foster heritage participation and transmission.

In fact, neo-Arvidians, no matter how enthusiastic they may be, have not had access to the knowledge held by Arvida's first property owners, nor do they remember the heraldic celebrations, coats of arms and anthems. The company's commemorative intention has not fully reached them. From this point of view, Rio Tinto's initiative and its program under the theme of "history continues with you" is to be applauded. But it remains that the ranks of the memory bearers are thinning and the reconstruction of the heritage project will require the participation of individuals with identities as multifaceted as (if very different from) those who lived in the American, Nordic or Quebec-style cottages of Arvida's first district. Moreover, considerations such as those that led to the foundation of CORPA will, from time to time, have to confront a resurgence of the levelling reflex that emerged during the first amalgamation, and that spread throughout public space and to the municipal administration. Indeed, there are still those (even if their numbers are dwindling) from Chicoutimi or Kénogami who believe that everything that is beautiful is to be found elsewhere and that everything of heritage value has already been recognized.

But Arvidians know better.

Notes

A great many organizations, entities and people have been indispensable to the research work carried out concerning Arvida over the past twenty or so years. From the Ville de Saguenay, Rio Tinto Alcan, the Canadian Centre for Architecture, UQAM or the John Heinz History Center, these persons have particularly helped in the preparation of this article: Nathaniel Bolduc, David Carrier, Paul Chénier, Julia Dawson, Carl Dufour, Chantale Francoeur, Marie-Blanche Fourcade, Nicol Guay, Normande Lapointe, Roger Lavoie and Art Louderback. This note represents a small token of our gratitude.

1. "The Royal Commission to Inquire into the Events which Occurred at Arvida, Quebec, in July 1941" was struck upon the recommendation of the prime minister of Canada to examine the circumstances surrounding a work stoppage at the plants of the Aluminum Company of Canada, including, in the context of negotiations concerning working conditions, rumours of sabotage that led to a significant halt in the production of this war industry.

2. Alcan, with strong ownership ties to Alcoa prior to 1950, was purchased by Rio Tinto in 2007, as noted, and reincorporated as Rio Tinto Alcan.

3. Translator's note: This and all other quotations in the chapter and notes are translations from the original French, except those from original English sources.

4. It was called a "ville-usine" by the French historian of architecture, Pierre Lavedan.

5. Interestingly, Davis originally wanted to build an observation tower in the city.

6. Based on two German-French translations, by Jacques Boulet of Aloïs Riegl (2003 [1903]) and, prior to that, by Daniel Wieczorek (1984). The original German refers to "Der gewollte Erinnerungswert."

7. Respectively, "der Alterswert" and "der historische Wert" in the original.

8. Concerning the conceptual framework underlying this choice of vocabulary, please refer to Lucie K. Morisset (2009, 2010).

9. Concerning this subject, please refer to the experience of Grovesnor Atterbury and of the Norton Company in Indian Hill, in Margaret Crawford (1995, 101s).

10. Henri Sainte-Claire Deville is known to have invented a process to extract alumina from bauxite, first step into the aluminum production. Charles Martin Hall is known, in America, to have developed the electrolysis process on which part of the aluminum production is based.

11. For instance, Lawrence Veiller (1926) advocates a return to traditional types and local traditions, referring to the case of Bournville, model city of the Cadbury chocolate factory.

12. Not to mention both the underlying commemorative intention and an influx of the best engineers that Alcoa had to offer.

13. *An Act to Incorporate the City of Arvida*, 16 George V, chap. 78, March 24, 1926, section 5.

14. Or $884,592 in 2013 dollars. Bank of Canada calculations based on the Statistics Canada price index. Statistics Canada.

15. Only one of each was built.

16. Few sales were completed, likely due to the unprecedented nature of the purchasing method in which the title property was transferred only when paid in its entirety. As such, only a few garages were registered as fully purchased in the 1927 assessment roll. Ville de Saguenay, Service du Greffe, assessment roll, 1927.

17. As stipulated in the transfer deeds uncovered for this period, for example, concerning a lot on Rue Davy in 1939 and a B1 house at 909 Rue Moissan in 1941. Later deeds registered in the 1950s, for example, also mention prior collection of this equivalent of 15 percent of the sales price (Land Register of Quebec, number 66407, November 3, 1939, and number 68524, March 26, 1941).

18. This insert replaces the following passage from the *Cities and Towns Act* (chap. 102, section 426): "to regulate the architecture, dimensions and symmetry of buildings in certain streets."

19. Civil law, the legal system in force in Quebec, was foreign to the Americans.

20. Code civil du Québec, Sections 692, 693 and 694.

21. When Hjertholm bought the Arvida building, he was already living in Montreal, perhaps a sign that this was a one-time act of real-estate speculation. He would return to Arvida on a few occasions, especially in the service of the architect Ernest Isabel Barott during the building of the Sainte-Thérèse school, in 1937. From correspondence kept in the Barott fund, at the Canadian Centre for Architecture, we have learned that Hjertholm left to settle in Oslo in 1938. The land register tells us that he sold his Arvida property at that time.

22. As such, it reserves

> The right to construct, maintain, use, repair and replace beneath the surface of the ground across the entire width of said lot within three feet of the rear line thereof, gas, water, sewer ... and/or beneath the surface of the ground within the said three foot strip wired, cables, conduits, poles ... necessary or convenient for the transmission of electric current or impulses, for the furnishing of light, heat, power, telegraph, telephone, fire alarm and police alarm. (Land Register of Quebec, number 56185, April 7, 1931)

23. Until the end of the 1940s.

24. City of Arvida, Minutes of the two-hundred and forty-second (regular) meeting held at the City Office, Wednesday, October 14, 1942. Ville de Saguenay, Service du Greffe.

25. The listing is registered in the chain of title of each residential property held by the company in Arvida. It will subsequently be repeated or registered at a later date in the title of certain properties. For example, see Land Register of Quebec, number 24 038, December 17 (1949).

26. Commission d'urbanisme d'Arvida, 1964 (January). Ville de Saguenay, Service du Greffe.

27. According to the city's permit file and the Land Register of Quebec, this referred to a F7-type home built in 1940 to the west of the downtown area of the day, and moved between July 18 and August 20, 1960, to a street that would only be parcelled out and registered on the assessment roll two years later. Alcan would sell the house in 1964.

28. In the Francophone world, at any rate, where it refers both to the legal concept of "heritage" and the transmission of the servitude. See, for example, Leniaud (2001: 113). In Canada, the Heritage Canada Foundation designates under this rubric (especially in Ontario, under "heritage easement"), an obligation to conserve that subjects owners to "accepted national standards" as regards work carried out on their property.

29. This refers to a W model house located on Rue Labrecque (RTA [Saguenay], AS1081).

30. Lyrics by Lionel Girard and music by Daniel Rioux. Original in French:

Reçois nos chants et nos louanges / O toi, cité remplie d'éclat / Nos voix t'acclament en phalanges / Prospère Ville d'Arvida.

Avec orgueil, tu nous dispenses / Tes riches dons et tes flots bleus / Tu les déverses en abondance / O Saguenay majestueux ! / Baignées par tes ondes limpides / Groupées sur tes bords enchanteurs / Grandissent des villes splendides / Foyer de paix et de labeurs.

Noble cité jardin prospère / Tu as connu le dévouement / D'hommes virils à l'âme fière / Épris d'un amour prévoyant / Tes fondateurs te firent belle, / Paisible et gaie tout à la fois. / De quelque nom qu'on s'appelle / Chez nous, ils ont place de choix.

Louons surtout la diligence / De nos pasteurs si dévoués. / Louons aussi la vigilance / Des dirigeants de la cité.

31. The resulting entity adopted the official name in French "Ville d'Arvida"; the designation "City of Arvida" remained unchanged in English given that the former name of the municipal entity in French was "cité." Department of Municipal Affairs, Letters Patent, Quebec Official Gazette, 102, 33, 1970 (15 August): 4639. In 1962, Arvida had also annexed the village of Saint-Mathias, in the southwest, with an inventory of some fifty buildings. This would become the so-called Dubose district.

32. During interviews with old-stock Arvidians (as opposed to natives of other localities) between 2010 and 2012 as part of the "Arvida Memories" project, the question "Do you remember the amalgamation?" elicited spontaneous responses pertaining to the municipal reorganization of 1975, not the more recent reorganization of 2002.

33. National Assembly, Official report of debates of the Commission de l'aménagement and des équipements (Land-Use Planning and Facilities Committee), 34th legislature, 1st session, December 13, 1989.

34. As a result of the province's *Act* respecting elections and referendums in municipalities (RSQ, cE-3.3).

35. The folio of a plan with revisions, dated 1966, and with others that may have preceded them, contains a sketch of two sectors, including the Deschênes plateau, whose urban contours are the polar opposite of Arvida's, especially as regards its dead-end streets and lots divided with little consideration for topography, independent of the contour plan in force to that time.

36. Some works have clearly documented the emigration out of Quebec that took place in this context, especially involving Anglophones and qualified workers, and even more so with regard to middle-income population

groups, a certain percentage of professionals, people owning homes with a certain property value, those with links to the financial sector, and communities with a higher-than-provincial-average segment of residents having at least a college diploma—a population mix typified by Arvida. See, especially, Pettinicchio (2012).

37. It was to be built next to a factory built during the Second World War (Grenville et al. 2011).

38. At the beginning of 1948, Roland A. Lemieux, the municipal manager, informed council that he had managed to amend the Charter of Arvida such that council would henceforth have the power to authorize house construction. At that point he envisaged the building of 50 or so homes and proposed that about 60 lots spread across the city be purchased from Alcan (Ville de Saguenay, Service du Greffe).

39. City of Arvida, motions number 1577-79.

40. All the more so since the exhibition was subsequently presented in the region, at an exhibition centre located in the former city of Jonquière.

41. Provided for since 1989 under the *Loi sur l'aménagement et l'urbanisme* (*Land-Use Planning and Development Act*).

42. Excluded here are the equally numerous scientific studies and the various research reports that have proliferated since the 1950s. See Igartua (1996) and Morisset (1996: 406; 1998: 272).

43. A little over 100,000 hectares, or 1,136 km^2.

References

Ackerman, Frederick L. and Robert C. Weinberg. 1938. A Brief for Architectural Control: Discussion. *The Planners' Journal* 4 (4): 94-98.

The Arvidien. 1927. "Grand nombre de ventes de propriétés à Arvida." December 19.

Archibald, Samuel. 2010. *Arvida*. Montreal: Le Quartanier.

Brainerd, Harry Beardslee. 1938. A Brief for Architectural Control. *The Planners' Journal* 4 (2): 41-42.

Brock, Thomas L. 1971. *Alcan in the Saguenay: The Formative Years*. Montreal: Aluminium Company of Canada.

Crawford, Margaret. 1995. *Building the Workingman's Paradise: The Design of American Company Towns*. London and New York: Verso.

Cronin, Fergus. 1949. Arvida: Ace Company Town. *Saturday Night*, December 13.

Fickes, Edwin S. 1938. History of the Growth and Developments of the Aluminum Company of America. Unpublished manuscript. Library and Archives Division, Heinz History Center, MSS 282, 50:3.

Grenville, John H., David C. Kasserra, Jennifer McKendry, William J. Patterson and Edward H. Storey. 2011. *Chronology of the History of Kingston*. Kingston: Kingston Historical Society.

Hartwick, John M. 2007. *Out of Arvida*. Kingston: Citoxique Press.

Igartua, José. 1996. *Arvida au Saguenay: Naissance d'une ville industrielle*. Montreal: McGill-Queen's University Press.

Lapointe, Paul-André. 1992. Modèles de travail and démocratisation. Le cas des usines de l'Alcan au Saguenay, 1970-1992. *Cahiers de recherche sociologique* 18-19:155-83.

Leniaud, Jean-Michel. 2001. Politique du patrimoine en France : pour une redéfinition du rôle de l'État. *Chroniques patrimoniales*. Paris: Norma.

Le Lingot. 1944. "Commission d'Urbanisme." January 29.

Loeb, Carolyn S. 2001. *Entrepreneurial Vernacular: Developers' Subdivisions in the 1920s*. Baltimore: John Hopkins University Press.

Loyer, François and Bernard Toulier, eds. 2001. *Le régionalisme, architecture and identité*. Paris: Monum.

MacNeille, Perry. 1917. *What Types of Houses to Build*. Washington, DC: National Housing Association.

Michaud, Gilles L. 2009. *Club Saguenay Arvida. Quatre-vingts ans d'histoire*. Gilles L. Michaud.

Morisset, L. K. 1995. À la recherche d'identités: usages et fonctions du passé dans l'architecture au Quebec. In *Architecture, forme urbaine and identité collective*, ed. Luc Noppen, 103-33. Sainte-Foy/Sillery, QC: Éditions du Septentrion.

———. 1996. "Arvida, cité modèle, ville moderne, ville de l'aluminium. Histoire de la forme urbaine et de l'architecture, 1925-1950." Thesis, Université de Bretagne occidentale.

———. 1998. *Arvida, cité industrielle : une épopée urbaine en Amérique*. Quebec City: Septentrion.

———. 2009. *Des régimes d'authenticité. Essai sur la mémoire patrimoniale*. Rennes: Presses universitaires de Rennes.

———. 2010. Patrimony, the Concept, the Object, the Memory and the Palimpsest. A View from the History of Architecture. *Architecture Canada* 35 (2): 53-62.

————. 2015. Le "métal magique" porteur d'utopie. La genèse aluminière d'un idéal urbain. In *Aluminium. Du métal de luxe au métal de masse*, ed. Dominique Barjot. Paris: Presses Universitaires de Paris-Sorbonne.

Nolen, John (reputed author). 1923. A Demonstration Town for Ohio. *The Journal of the Town Planning Institute of Canada*, 2 (3): 4.

————. 1927. *New Towns for Old*. Boston: Marshall Jones Company.

Noppen, Luc and L. K. Morisset. 1996. À la recherche d'une architecture pour la nation canadienne-française : entre le paysage and la patrie. De la Crise à la Seconde Guerre mondiale. *Cahiers d'histoire du Québec au XXᵉ siècle* 5 (spring): 19-36.

Pettinicchio, David. 2012. "Migration and ethnic nationalism: Anglophone exit and the 'decolonisation' of Quebec." *Nations and Nationalism* 18 (4): 719-43.

Riegl, Aloïs. 2003. *Le culte moderne des monuments : sa nature, son origine.* Trans. Jacques Boulet. Paris: L'Harmattan. (Original work: Aloïs Riegl. 1903. *Der moderne Denkmalkultus. Sein Wesen und seine Entstehung*. Vienna: W. Braumüller).

Rio Tinto. 2011. Aluminerie Arvida. Centre technologique AP60, note de service, August 23.

Skougor, Hjalmar E. 1921. Rosita, Mexico, a Carefully Planned City; Pleasing, Comfortable and Hygienic. *Coal Age* (June 2): 985.

Statistics Canada. N.d. Consumer Prices Indices for Canada, Monthly, 1914-2006, V41690973 series.

Unwin, Raymond. 1909. *Town Planning in Practice: An Introduction to the Art of Designing Cities and Suburbs*. London: T. Fischer.

Veiller, Lawrence. 1926. *Cottages: Their Planning, Design, and Materials.* London: Country Life.

Ville de Jonquière. 1999. *Plan de conservation and de mise en valeur du patrimoine urbain and architectural d'Arvida*, Ville de Jonquière and Ministère de la Culture and des Communications.

Wake, Harold. 1926. "Building the City of Arvida." *The Engineering Journal* (November): 462.

———— (reputed author). 1929. Analysis of Procedure at Arvida in Connection with City Development. Unpublished manuscript, October 1. Ville de Saguenay, Service du Greffe.

Walker, Alexander W. 1927. Company Towns. *The Journal of the Town Planning Institute of Canada* (June): 97-101.

Wood, Edith Elmer. 1919. *The Housing of the Unskilled Wage Earner: America's Next Problem*. New York: MacMillan Company.

Chapter Five

Tom Urbaniak

The Intentional Cultural Settlement as a Company Town: The Contested Heritage of Kaszuby, Ontario

This chapter examines a particular kind of company town—what we now would call an "intentional community": a place with high social cohesion, organized not around a heavy industry but planned around common lifestyle, cultural or linguistic characteristics. Although the retention or reclaiming of heritage is a specific goal, even a founding goal, of such a community, questions of identity, cultural loss and conservation may be perceived by residents as even more delicate, and even more controversial, than the problem of finding new uses for old buildings.

This is the story of Kaszuby, Ontario. It is the story of a founder with a vision. It is the story of the rise of a self-contained town in the 1950s, with its own name, socioeconomic vocation, post office and public services. Kaszuby was built using many of the same legal instruments and infrastructure-development patterns as an industrial company town. But its mission was not industrial. It was cultural.

This settlement was not built around a factory. Many of the residents were seasonal. The "boss" was a priest. And the town was a kind of heritage project in its own right. Catering to newcomers to Canada of Polish descent, it claimed the name, the folk culture and the symbols of the area's rural residents, descended from settlers who came almost a century earlier, many of them from the Kashubian region of Poland, a country under occupation during the 19th century by Prussia (Germany), Russia and Austria (Austria-Hungary).

Kaszuby is not at risk of being abandoned. For many Canadians of Polish descent, it is a kind of spiritual home. But for the rural descendants of the original Polish Kashub settlers, many of whom were living on marginal farmsteads and losing their young people to larger cities, was it a welcome cultural infusion? Was it cultural appropriation? When we speak of heritage conservation in Kaszuby, whose heritage is being conserved?

Competing visions and narratives threaten to erase some of the rich and complex layers of heritage of this part of Renfrew County, in southeastern Ontario. Here, heritage is not just the built heritage, it is also the intangible heritage. It is not just memory, but how one chooses to define an ethnic identity. And yet, place always matters: heritage cannot easily be put into silos. It is about buildings and landscapes, but also languages and dialects. It's about the names of places and of people. It's about the labels for holidays and about the ways in which residents (however one defines *residents*) choose to present themselves to the world. Sometimes, all of these things are intertwined.

Since childhood, I have been a frequent visitor to Kaszuby and the surrounding area. I have witnessed changes, including recent changes, to how many local residents view their cultural identity and define their sense of place. I began looking more deeply into this "glocalization" (local identities being rediscovered or redefined due to the ease of global contacts)—after returning to visit the region in 2008, following a nine-year hiatus. Personal observation and communication, subsequent visits, linked with documentary research of local histories, local reporting and studies of the Kashubian region of Poland, have helped me to try to better understand these changes. As this book was in its late stages of editing, and with this chapter drafted, Joshua C. Blank's new book, published in May 2016, came to my attention: *Creating Kashubia: History, Memory, and Identity in Canada's First Polish Community* (McGill-Queen's University Press). It is a more extensive academic study, covering similar themes, which I highly recommend.

The Road to Kaszuby

If you travel along the 19th-century colonization road into the interior of eastern Ontario known as the Opeongo Line, or along the paved, less jagged Highway 60, which runs mostly in parallel, you will come upon small, scattered villages, abandoned logging camps, small and seldom prosperous farms, decaying or gentrified log cabins and an increasing number of craft businesses,

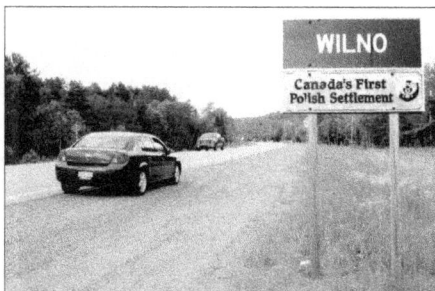

Fig. 1 – Wilno – Canada's First Polish Settlement sign. Photo by Emily Urbaniak.

hobby farms, art studios and bed-and-breakfasts. Along the numerous small clear lakes, summer cottagers and seasonal residents occupy little portions of what they consider a piece of Canadian paradise. It is reminiscent of some of the rugged landscapes painted by the Group of Seven artists.

About 200 km from Parliament Hill, Ottawa, at the boundary of the townships of Madawaska Valley and Killaloe-Hagarty-Richards, you will encounter the village of Wilno. It bills itself as Canada's first Polish settlement, ca. 1858. The railway station has been gone almost forty years, but the former Exchange Hotel, once serving the railway passengers, remains. It is now the Wilno Tavern, continuing a hundred-year tradition of serving hearty old-country meals and functioning as a social meeting place for locals who gather to play cards or music (cf. Bartul 1997).

To this day, the names of the side roads and on the rural mailboxes are Slavic names that were given anglicized orthography by 19th-century immigration registrars: Yantha, Peplinskie, Smeglinski, Lepinski, Stoppa, Shulist and Divazie, among others. It is impossible to miss the twin steeples on "Shrine Hill"—those of Our Lady of Czestochowa, Queen of Poland Roman Catholic Church—built in 1936 in the Polish Cathedral style, replacing the burned St. Stanislaus Kostka Church (ca. 1875), named after Poland's main patron saint (Visutskie 2005). In nearby Barry's Bay, St. Hedwig's Church bears original stained-glass windows depicting the failed 1863 January Uprising against Russian rule in Poland.

When the first settlers arrived in this part of Ontario, they did not come from Poland as such. Poland had been carved up among its three powerful neighbours, Russia, Prussia and Austria. Those arriving were from the Prussian-held area, but they were adamant that they were not Prussians. Some of the Canadian immigration officials took to calling them the "Polish Prussians." By most accounts, they were content to be known just as Polish and to make the most of the inhospitable soil and topography, a far cry from what they had been promised to lure them to homesteading in Canada.

They formed distinctive village communities. They preserved their language and a popular form of piety. They shared and adapted legends and artistic traditions from the homeland.

In 1950, Fr. Rafal Grzondziel visited the region. A veteran of the Second World War—including the legendary battle of Monte Cassino, Italy, where Poles distinguished themselves as part of the Allied forces—he spent some time in the United Kingdom and the United States. Ordained a Franciscan priest, he had already sketched out a vision for a "new town," a retreat and formation area for displaced Polish youth. A veteran of the Polish scouting movement, he saw that very movement, with its multi-faceted commitment to education, faith, culture, survival and good living, as an ideal partner for such an enterprise.

Fig. 2 – Grzondziel's headquarters. Photo by Alison Etter.

For a time this remained only a dream. Grzondziel was searching for a place. Hearing that some former senior scouts, who had been part of the anti-Nazi Polish underground but who were now living in Toronto and Montreal, were camping near Wilno on the farm of the descendant of one of the original settlers from the Kashub region, he soon paid a visit himself. Grzondziel, who was not a Kashub, befriended Monsignor Piotr Biernacki, long-time pastor of St. Hedwig's in Barry's Bay, and a descendant of early Kashub settlers. Biernacki, himself a former scout, was intrigued by Grzondziel's vision, and before long the Franciscan Order and Grzondziel were buying and receiving from the Crown large tracts of wilderness along the Old Barry's Bay Road, mid-way between Barry's Bay and Combermere.

Grzondziel's "youth centre" was in the form of a rustic log chapel with meeting rooms "in the pines" (*pod sosnami*) on Wadsworth Lake. An outdoor altar and seating followed, then designated picnic areas and beaches. Then came lease agreements with the growing number of scouting groups—Karpaty, Giewont and a host of others named after well-known locales and regions in Poland. They took over pieces of lakefront, back country and sometimes even the abandoned barns of early settlers, but all in the same cluster midway between Barry's Bay and Combermere. More barracks and cottages would be built over the years.

To many Polish immigrants and refugees fleeing the post-war communist regime, and to Polish displaced persons who had found a home in Canada, this place was a little piece of Poland. The scenery was actually reminiscent of parts of the countryside in Polish Kashubia (*Kaszuby*), complete with the rural residents descended from the origi-nal Kashubs, who had preserved what seemed to the newcomers to be a quaint and particular way of speaking. Their homes exhibited the crafts and art forms reminiscent of the old country. Colourful Kashub motifs, for example, adorned many of the barns. And so "Kaszuby" was born. That label was attached to the several hundred acres around Wadsworth Lake and Kaminiskeg Lake that were set aside to be a kind of little Poland.

Grzondziel successfully petitioned to have the name Kaszuby officially assigned to his settlement around Wadsworth Lake. A post office was established. The first postmaster was the energetic priest himself.

In 1955, a building committee was set up in Toronto to raise funds and acquire surrounding Kaszuby properties. It was under the auspices of Zwiazek Harcerstwa Polskiego (Association of Polish Scouting). The vision remained of a "scrap of Canadian ground that resembles Poland." With the camps, the cottages and the new perma-nent residences, the region's visual identity soon changed.

Grzondziel and Biernacki had envisioned a "Polish, Catholic place for scouts" and immigrants (Blank, Lorbetskie and Prince 2014). The church and the scouting association operating in Kaszuby had quite literally become a company—providing the plans, the tone, the rules and the local economic engine. They had done so with reference to the region's Polish/Kashub cultural heritage. But, alas, the rapport between newcomers and old-timers was limited. At any time, hundreds of campers would join hundreds, and then thousands, of cottagers and retirees, clustering around this settlement. When Biernacki died, the *Eganville Leader*, a Renfrew County newsweekly, printed a tribute from a parishioner who recalled the monsignor's involvement with the scouting movement *before* the expatriates developed the colony. "After taking our pledges we sat down to a supper that looked more like a banquet than the rustic type of fare that we as scouts expected" (F. J. Ritza, 1959, in Connolly, n.d.: 20). But the rustic was now becoming permanent. And the pre-Grzondziel scouts were not the nucleus of the new settlement.

This area became famous among Canadians of Polish descent, a place where they could be immersed in their culture. Major scouting jamborees were organized, including an international one in 1976. To this day, barracks are bustling, and there are cottages and permanent homes around them. Kaszuby carries on Grzondziel's vision of an intentional community, a Polish town, with culture as its raison d'être.

But some descendants of the original settlers feel detached from, perhaps even somewhat displaced by, this settlement, which uses their names and their people as a backdrop for an enduring heritage project that has helped to transmit the Polish language and culture to a younger, urban generation.

In the past twenty years, some of the Kashub descendants, whose identity and folk culture became the inspiration for this intentional community and many of its symbols, have come to insist—stridently, sometimes—that they are not of Polish descent at all, that "Polonization" is a potential threat to their way of life, and that their Kashubian heritage should be recognized as a separate and distinct ethnic category. In Wilno, 12 km from

Fig. 3 – Grzondziel Memorial. Photo by Alison Etter.

Fig. 4 – Grzondziel's Polish chapel in the pines. Photo by Emily Urbaniak.

Grzondziel's settlement, "Polish Day" (May 3, which is celebrated in Poland as Constitution Day and the Feast of Mary, Queen of Poland) became "Kashubian Day."

Visitors from Kashubia, cut off for so long from the diaspora communities by occupation and communism, began to appear for lectures and workshops about the cultural identity and language of the Kashubian people. On February 14, 2001, the local newspaper, *Barry's Bay This Week*, ran an advertisement of the Wilno Heritage Society for a lecture by Wojciech Etmanski, "Kashubian Historian-Poland." The advertisement bore the Polish and Canadian flags and explained that Etmanski spoke "Polish, Kashub (low Polish), and English." A blurb at the bottom of the advertisement read, "Wojciech is asking Canadian Kashubs, What is low Polish? And Canadians are asking Wojciech, What is Kashub?"

That advertisement was the last reference of the Wilno Heritage Society to "low Polish." Etmanski's visit included not just a defence of the language but a strong case for regional autonomy and an explicit differentiation of the ethnic identities of the descendants of the early settlers and the post–Second World War members of the intentional community. It struck a chord.

The case of Kaszuby, Ontario, puts into sharp relief some much larger phenomena: the threat to local cultures posed by modern media and global consumption, but, on the other hand, the opportunity offered by contemporary means of communication to connect with distant relations and faraway cultural activists; the impact that seemingly unrelated internal political decisions in one country can have on local politics in another, such as Poland's adoption of the European Charter on Regional or Minority Languages; the continuing cultural and spiritual meaning attached to place, and the political consequences of that; and how terminology (such as cultural labels), symbols (such as flags and icons) and particularly assertive figures can serve to reshape debates and catalyze a new understanding of identity.

From Kashubia to Canada

The Kashubians are a Slavic people who established themselves in what is now northwestern Poland and northeastern Germany between 600 CE and 900 CE. The relationship with the Poles was always close, and there was never a Kashubian nation state. In the 10th century, a Kashubian prince married the daughter of Polish King Bolesław Chrobry (Bolesław I the Brave), and Kashubian nobles were incorporated into the Polish nobility. There was significant intermingling and intermarriage.

During the Protestant Reformation in 16th-century Europe, the Poles largely remained Catholic, and most of the Kashubs with them, but a portion of Kashubia became Protestant. And it is on the Protestant side that we see the first sacred texts in the Kashubian language, including vernacular translations of a Lutheran prayer book and Martin Luther's ninety-five theses. Most students of the Kashub people, however, have observed a very high level of assimilation of the German/Prussian Kashubs with Germans.

On the Catholic side, a Kashub literary awakening was pre-empted by the Prussian takeover of the Polish Kashubian lands in 1772, followed by the complete disappearance of the Polish state in 1795, partitioned among the Prussians, Russians and Austrians. There was a brief period in the 1840s where a policy of Germanization was relaxed, leading to the prominence of works by some Kashubian nationalists, most notable among them being Florian Ceynowa. But this period was short-lived, and was not to be revisited until the two decades between the world wars, when Poland was again independent.

During the Nazi occupation of Poland, the German authorities tried to encourage an anti-Polish form of Kashubian nationalism, but this was largely resisted by the Kashubs, who remained faithful to the idea of a free Polish state. The post-war communist authorities in Poland discouraged Kashubian cultural expression, especially if it had even slight political overtones. Alas, a free Polish state would have to wait until 1989.

After 1989, the post-communist period saw a wide range of new contacts between the Polish Kashubs and their Canadian cousins. There were frequent visits back and forth (visa requirements were eased in 2002). The leaders of cultural organizations were attentive to developments in each other's jurisdictions.

In 1972, Jan Perkowski completed a controversial study on Canada's first Polish settlement in this corner of Ontario. *Vampires, Dwarves, and Witches Among the Ontario Kashubs* is noteworthy not so much for recounting local lore on ghosts and hauntings, but for its observations of tight-knit communities that had maintained distinctive ways of life. The onslaught of mass media and modern technology, not to mention seasonal residents, was being felt in Kaszuby in the 1960s, but still Perkowski estimated that only 3 per cent of marriages were mixed ethnically. Most of the descendants of the first homesteaders a century earlier still spoke their mother tongue, and about 20 per cent had difficulty with English. "There are even several fourth generation monolingual Kashubian speakers," Perkowski noted (1972: 13, 20).

These observations were similar to those of William Makowski in his *History and Integration of Poles in Canada*. Writing in 1967, he found in the region many continuing traditions. People would assemble for wakes at the death beds of loved ones. Weddings could last many days. There were about 2,500 Kashub descendants in the area.

Today, there are no monolingual Kashubian speakers in Renfrew County, and the language is in danger of disappearing in the region. The parish halls are quieter than they were, and the area's permanent population is not growing. But the local assertion of Kashubian identity, as distinct from the Polish, is stronger than ever. Indeed, it could even be said that many residents have redefined their ethnic identity in recent years. What factors have contributed to this phenomenon?

From 1892 to 1896, about two hundred and fifty Polish families from Galicia arrived, but, as Anna Zurakowska notes, this cohort was largely "absorbed and assimilated by the existing community. They even learned to use the Kaszubian dialect" (Zurakowska 1991: 39). In the late 1890s and early 1900s, more Kashub families arrived, mainly by way of Massachusetts. This whole group considered itself to be ethnic Poles, to the point that specific memories of regional origins seemed to fade.

Fr. Aloysius Rekowski, who would become a keen student of the Kashubian identity, remembered growing up in the 1930s: "We were definitely Polish, of that we were certain, but what kind of Polish and where from Poland, we didn't know" (1997: 3).

In 1938, the aforementioned Msgr. Biernacki of Barry's Bay gave a talk in Montreal on the situation of the "Poles of Ontario." He gave no hint of anything other than a Polish identity. The Poles in Barry's Bay-Wilno numbered about four thousand and had retained their faith, their Polish language and their customs, despite economic adversity, Biernacki asserted (Connolly, n.d.: 7-8).

In 1961, the Village of Barry's Bay adopted its coat of arms. A Polish eagle was prominently featured. Anna Zurakowska observed that "Canadian Kashubs have always stressed their Polish origins. In

Fig. 5 – Kashub barn with folk motifs. Photo by Emily Urbaniak.

later years many of their descendants did not clearly understand the meaning of the term Kaszub" (1991: 91).

In 2008, I visited Kaszuby for the first time in nine years. It was the 150th anniversary of the first Polish settlement. The changes were not hard to discern. The black and yellow Kashubian flag was being displayed prominently, whereas previously it was not seen. The Kashubian griffin seemed now more prominent than the Polish eagle. Books on the Kashubian language and culture were being produced locally. Representatives of the Gdansk-based Kashubian-Pomeranian Association were visiting regularly. A statue of Matka Boska Sianowska, Queen of Kashubia, was unveiled at Our Lady of Czestochowa (St. Mary's) Church in Wilno.

I heard Fr. Ambrose Pick, who is of Kashubian descent, celebrate part of a mass in the Kashubian language. I often heard it remarked by local residents that former priests had told them—and that they had assumed themselves—that the language of their ancestors was a form of "low Polish." Now it was understood as a complex and distinctive language in its own right.

Many of the cultural initiatives were and are being led by the Wilno Heritage Society. It was founded in 1997, and in 2002 it opened the Polish Kashub Heritage Park in Wilno. The society's high-profile president, David Shulist, who became the mayor (2010-2014) of the amalgamated Township of Madawaska Valley—which since 2001 includes Barry's Bay, Wilno and the Grzondziel-founded Kaszuby settlement—made several trips to Poland and has described how he had not been fully aware of his Kashub identity as a child. He noted that because of language he felt a close kinship with his distant cousins in Poland: "If it was not for the Kashubian language, most of us could not speak to each other. We don't understand Polish and they don't understand English, so Kashub was the one that connected us" (*Barry's Bay This Week*, August 16, 2009).

Back in Canada, Shulist is also known as "Johnny Kashub," a local radio personality who hosts a show on Kashub culture. He had previously been a Polish cultural activist, and his father, Martin, had been active in having the Wilno area recognized as "Canada's first Polish settlement" by the government of Ontario, which erected an official plaque to that effect on Shrine Hill. But now Shulist believes that he and his father were in error.

"It is very hard to correct 154 years of history," Shulist said, but he believes he has a responsibility to explain that Kashubs are not Poles. "They are close cousins," without always a happy history together, he noted. He believes that the Polish priests led the local people to believe they were something they were not. He lamented that Polish symbols had become so prolific. Even the name of the church was an imposition. Our Lady of Sionowo (the icon of the Queen of Kashubia) should be the prominent symbol, according to Shulist. On the other hand, the area where the Polish scouting camps are clustered could reasonably be called "Polonia," Shulist said, but it should not be called Kaszuby. It should not appropriate the Kashubian name (personal communication 2011).

What Shulist says he wants most is recognition that the Ontario Kashubs are part of a distinctive people. He is concerned that when people see the work done—in the museum, in preserving cultural traditions, in organizing a multicultural hockey tournament, complete with a "Kashub Griffins" team—they still congratulate him for what he is doing to preserve Polish culture. Essentially, his project is not the same one as Fr. Grzondziel's. The Kaszuby settlement that Grzondziel founded, dedicated to preserving a culture, is seen by some, including Shulist, as appropriating another culture.

Some of the Kashub elders have not yet been persuaded to reconsider their identity, Shulist conceded. And indeed I encountered some of these skeptical residents at the church. They told me that the Polish element is an integral part of their lives, even if they are descended from Kashubs. They grew up with a Polish liturgy and Polish symbols, and their ancestors genuinely felt themselves to be Polish, praying for an independent Poland, where their relatives—persecuted for being Polish—would be free. Shulist's own father, who had been a leader in pushing for the "first Polish settlement" designation, was also skeptical, but Shulist said he finally persuaded him on a trip to Poland that their ethnicity is in fact Kashub.

The cross-national links have become much stronger since Poland emerged from communist isolation in 1989. Two pioneer buildings from Ontario's Kaszuby were donated to businessman Daniel Czapiewski, who has developed a museum in honour of Kashub culture in Szymbark, Poland. But there is more: Some of the most active and outspoken Kashubian leaders have been attracted to this area of

Ontario, where the Kashub language and traditions, although under threat, are still in evidence. They were able to hold up the Ontario Kashubs as an example of cultural perseverance. Likewise, the Ontario Kashubs are hearing from some of their Polish contacts that they are indeed a distinctive ethnic, and not simply regional, group.

The Kashub movement in Poland can point to an endurance of identity despite formidable obstacles. In the estimation of one sociologist, they are today "the most distinctive indigenous linguistic-cultural group in Poland" (Synak 1998: 10).

The main advocacy group, the Kashubian-Pomeranian Association, has not called for separation from Poland. Indeed, there is no *voivodeship*—province—and only a relatively small number of towns where the Kashubs are in the majority. But they have called for forms of self-governance in education, municipal affairs and the like. There are elements within the movement that are considered radical and others moderate. The more strident leaders, including association past president Artur Jablonski, who had established very close contacts with the Ontario communities, sought recognition for the Kashubs in Poland as an "ethnic minority" (Galus 2009). This alarmed the moderates, who were concerned that such recognition might lead to a marginalization of Kashubs from the national life. Although the Kashubs are a tiny minority in Poland, some Kashubs, including former Polish Prime Minister Donald Tusk, who is now the president of the Council of Europe, play a prominent role in public affairs.

These cross-national linkages appear to have been strengthened following Poland's ratification, in 2005, of the European Charter for Regional or Minority Languages. After a debate on language versus dialect, Poland recognized Kashubian as a language, the only officially recognized regional minority language indigenous to Poland. With this came an enhanced program of linguistic education, the option of taking high-school-completion examinations in Kashubian and additional funding for cultural organizations. This has arguably helped to strengthen the links between Kashubs in Poland and with the diaspora communities.

Poland's present geopolitical situation is also conducive to these cross-national links. Through most of the history of the settlement of the Kashubs in Ontario there has not been a viable interlocutor in

Poland. During periods of occupation, the Kashubs were generally eager to identify themselves as Poles. A brief phase of Polish national independence (1918-1939) was followed by Nazi and Soviet invasion and then, after the Second World War, communist rule. There was not much space or freedom for regional and minority identities to assert themselves.

The globalization of commerce and communications means that there is, on one hand, a loosening of national boundaries and national sovereignty and a more homogenous global, consumer culture, notable in the predominance of English and of common brands and certain common tastes. On the other hand, there is also a reclaiming of local and regional identities, and even the development of disparate, sometimes virtual, communities based on those particular identities.

Alas, in the case of Ontario's Kashuby it may be even more complex than that. Differences between native residents and newcomers may be playing a role. Robert Klymasz writes that many of Kaszuby's seasonal residents are urban professionals looking for a retreat reminiscent of "the simple ways of rural folk." The local population was like a backdrop. It offered to "Polish urbanites the continuity, stability, and comfort represented by old country ways" (1993: 160).

But the seasonal residents and the long-time permanent residents do not appear to have a very close relationship. In none of the Township of Madawaska Valley's published economic development literature is there reference to the local Polish identity as a means of investment and business to be further cultivated. Kashubian descendants often insist that they are non-ambivalently Canadian; they are unhyphenated Canadians. The Wilno Heritage Society's logo has the Kashubian griffin holding the Canadian flag. Is there perhaps a subtle message here? A message that the local Kashubian population, maybe in contrast to some of the seasonal residents or more recently installed newcomers, is of this land and is rooted in this Canadian soil.

In 2012, when Prime Minister Tusk visited the region, the cultural differences in the region were readily apparent. The municipality and the Wilno Heritage Society organized a major welcome, ushering Tusk to sites associated with Kashubian settlement. There were no major events at the Grzondziel-founded Kaszuby settlement, but at some of Tusk's stops there were protestors complaining about his policies and even his government's handling of the investigation into the 2010 airplane crash at Smolensk, Russia, that resulted in the death of the Polish president and numerous dignitaries.

In 1997 and 2011, Henryk Bartul produced two documentaries on the history of the region. The first dealt with the original settlers and their descendants, the second with the post-war generation. He tried to tie the two together, but the main common links in the documentaries were that the post-war settlers were intrigued by a region that reminded them of rural Poland as well as the historical research activities of the Polish Heritage Institute Kaszuby. The latter was driven mainly by Anna Zurakowska, a post-war settler based in Barry's Bay in "Kartuzy Lodge," named after the unofficial capital of the Kashubians in Poland. She built it with her husband, the famous Polish Canadian Avro Arrow test pilot Jan Zurakowski.

The Polish narrative of the region became largely one of the wartime and post-war experience of urban professionals. The reassertion of Kashubian regionalism and even nationalism became a kind of reassertion of a community that saw itself as marginalized in this corner of Renfrew County.

Kaszuby has its solitudes, perceived more by the Kashubians than the post–Second World War Polish settlers. The post-war generation sees itself as fully complementing and enriching the Polish character of the region. They do travel the back roads. They do sometimes venture into Our Lady of Czestochowa Church (St. Mary's) and dine at the Wilno Tavern. Some have become active in civic life. But they may not be fully seized of the concerns of the Kashubian descendants. Can both heritage projects co-exist in a more active collaboration?

Both the post-war Poles and the Kashubian descendants have used signature landmark

PRESENTING

WILNO HERITAGE SOCIETY'S
NEWEST BUILDING PROJECT

LATNICA (Lat Neet sa)

An open-sided 16' x 24' multi-use park building - Cedar timber frame design with Kashubian inspired vented capped cedar shake roof
Completion date - Summer (Lato) 2014

The WHS is selling each of the twelve building support posts @ $300 apiece to interested heritage families. When the building is completed each purchased post will be marked with a permanent plaque bearing the surname of the sponsoring family. If you and your family would like to purchase a "Latnica" post please talk to a Wilno Heritage Society executive member.
Thank You. Bóg Zapłać.

POST SOLD

Fig. 6 – A recent addition to the Polish Kashub Heritage Park in Wilno. Photo by Alison Etter.

projects to promote an authoritative history of this place. Grzondziel called his settlement Kaszuby and built sites to endure. His successors built a series of monuments, such as the memorial to the 1944 Warsaw uprising and to scouts who fell during war. The Kashubian descendants built the explicitly Kashubian heritage park by collecting and interpreting various rustic farm buildings in a well-designed prominent cluster across from the Wilno Tavern on Highway 60. The society even dismantled an original farm building and shipped it to a similar Kashub heritage park in Poland, with great fanfare.

But what if these efforts tried to branch into telling a more organic history rather than an authoritative one? The *Ontario Heritage Act* allows municipalities to maintain a heritage inventory of properties for planning purposes. These properties are not designated for mandatory preservation, but they get flagged when demolition or development permits are requested, allowing the municipal heritage committee to examine other options with the owners.

The main point of this inventory would be to tell a multi-layered story of the places, buildings and landscapes. All communities could make inputs, and the short descriptive texts could be in Polish, Kashubian and English. This could help to foster an awareness of places and personalities that is more than superficial or folkloric.

A lesson here is the importance of accepting ambiguity in heritage. Shulist is involved with a website (www.kashub.com) in which there are some stark pronouncements: "The most dominant culture that influenced the Kashubian culture was by the Polish people, who immigrated to the area after the Second World War," the website says. "We started to become Polonized." The notion of Poland as occupier and assimilator in fact appears to be the minority view among members of the Kashubian community in Poland, who largely embrace a dual ethno-linguistic identity (Galus 2009) and acknowledge close inter-mingling over centuries, forged through a common pride in Polish national identity and through long-common struggles against occupying powers.

Shulist was defeated in the 2014 Madawaska Valley municipal election. He had been previously elected on the strength of his profile as past president of the Wilno Heritage Society, and as someone who was trustworthy and helpful in addressing constituent concerns. His defeat was not sparked directly by questions over Kashubian nationalism, except that his contacts with international dignitaries were seen in some quarters as a distraction. He arguably did not fully succeed in making a direct connection between culture and economic development in a rural region.

For the post-Second World War generation, Kaszuby, Ontario, served as an "intentional community" where the Polish language could be nurtured, along with a new generation, schooled by elders, who would keep the flame of freedom burning during the communist era in Poland. The narrative that was transmitted was a heroic one in which the Polish nation was unified and courageous. Regional differences were quaint vestiges. Seldom did these youth visit local Kashub homes to learn local skills and internalize the local memories.

Canadian Polish organizations have tended to represent the newcomer group and not so much third- and fourth-generation Polish Canadians. Their mandates have been more concerned with immigrant settlement than showing solidarity with endangered communities of Polish extraction on Canadian soil. This contrasts somewhat with Polish organizations in the United States. The current president of the Canadian Polish Congress, Teresa Berezowski, has recognized this dichotomy and has articulated the need for a more pan-Canadian, place-based approach. This would see the congress working more in tandem with organizations like the Wilno Heritage Society and bringing the support of the Canadian Polish community to bear in profiling and reinforcing Kashubian identity and language.

Kaszuby offers some valuable lessons as an intentional community. It had a clear cultural thread and sense of purpose. It was chosen with reference to its history and surroundings. It was planned, but it was flexible, allowing for part-time stays and permanent residencies. It had leaders and champions, but a kind of federated structure in that each of the scouting organizations and voluntary groups elected their own leaders. It was effectively promoted through word of mouth, and managed to link youth with elders.

But it had limited engagement with the original local population. And so this settlement's cultural project, designed with reference to the existing local population, came to be questioned by members of that very population. That may be a healthy process—so long as it remains a process. Sometimes, heritage and place are not meant to be finally and authoritatively defined, but continually redefined, questioned and explored.

References

Barry's Bay This Week. 1997-2014. Back issues at Barry's Bay Public Library.

Bartul, Henryk, dir. 1997 *Kaszuby Canada – Part One: The Story of Canada's First Polish Settlers* (DVD).

———. 2011. *Kanadyjskie Kaszuby/Canadian Kaszuby*, Part II (DVD)

Blank, Joshua C., Angela Lorbetskie and Theresa Prince. 2014. *Sto Lat: One Hundred Years of Faith at St. Hedwig's Parish*. Barry's Bay, ON: St. Hedwig's Parish.

Connolly, Shirley Mask. [n.d.] *A Giant Among Us: Msgr. Piotr Biernacki.*

Galus, Henryk. 2009. *Spolecznosc Kaszubska: Odrebnosc i Przynaleznosc.* http://henryk.galus.vot.pl/hgalus/tom.09.htm (accessed on December 27, 2014).

Klymasz, R. B. 1993. Review of *The Proud Inheritance: Ontario's Kaszuby*, ed. Anna Zurakowska. *Canadian Ethnic Studies* 25 (2): 159-61.

Makowski, William. 1967. *History and Integration of Poles in Canada*. Toronto: Canadian Polish Congress.

Obracht-Prondzynski, Cezary. 2007. *The Kashubs Today: Culture, Language, Identity*. Gdansk: Instytut Kaszubski w Gdansku.

Perkowski, Jan L. 1972. *Vampires, Dwarves and Witches Among Ontario's Kashubs*. Ottawa: National Museum of Man.

Rekowski, Aloysius. 1997. *The Saga of the Kashub People in Poland, Canada, U.S.A.* Privately published.

Synak, Bruno. 1998. *Kaszubska tozsamosc: Ciaglosc i Zmiana*. Gdansk: Wydawnictwo Uniwersytetu Gdanskiego.

Visutskie, Lynn. 2005. *Wilno – First Polish Parish in Canada*. Wilno Heritage Society.

Wilno Heritage Society newsletters. 2005-2014.

Zurakowska, Anna, ed. 1991. *The Proud Inheritance: Ontario's Kaszuby*. Ottawa: Polish Heritage Institute.

Chapter Six

Barbara Hogan, Lyn Bleiler, Anne Leckie,
Rob McIntyre and Marc Johnston

Elsa and the Mines of Keno Hill

Six hours north of Whitehorse, drivers heading to Elsa, Yukon, turn off a "chip-sealed" highway onto a rutted gravel road, drive another hour, and may notice a fork in the road. A sign there warns: "Do Not Enter." Large convex mirrors and a faded sign saying "All Visitors Must Check in At Office" are the first hint of what was once a thriving, dynamic mining camp. Elsa evolved from a rough log cabin at a hand-worked mine to become the site of one of the largest mines in Yukon, and Canada's second-largest silver producer.

Today, the town site is gone and the residences are dismantled, leaving only the mining-camp buildings and infrastructure. Narrow gravel roads wind along the hillside of Galena Hill, terraced with tailings held back with log cribbing. Pan-Abode buildings, two-storey frame structures and a 20-metre (65-ft.) high water reservoir are the most apparent connections to what once was. Deemed a contaminated site, the most imposing and significant building, the mill, must come down. Bunkhouses have been demolished, making room for the construction waste of the mill itself.

The core of the United Keno Hill Mines Ltd. (UKHM) operations is evident: the administration building, the assay office, the engineering office, the store, the fire hall, the power house, the boiler house and the snack bar. The vernacular architecture is typical of buildings constructed in the late 1940s and 1950s: simple, unadorned, functional. The modest assemblage reflects a time and place of the past. Thirty years later, food specials for a long-past week remain advertised at the store; bulletin boards still offer directions, contacts and notes. But the ink is faded and a blanket of dust has settled, enveloping all that remains inside.

The view is spectacular, looking down over the valley, with white-topped mountains not far away. The wind rustles through leaves, the lots now overgrown, changing the site to a greener, softer place. Some of the buildings in the mining camp are used by the company that purchased the mine and is overseeing the demolition of the mill and other contaminated buildings. Their offices can be found in the old recreation centre; drill reports and assay records are stored in the engineering offices and in the market, and trucks roll in and out of the remaining garages.

Conversations continue among local residents of nearby Keno City, the UKHM claims-owner and the Canadian and Yukon governments about maintaining an effective balance of remediating environmental threats and saving the vestiges of Yukon's last company town, an industrial giant of the past.

This chapter provides a glimpse of the mining company and the people that developed this remote mountainous site, an important part of Yukon's history.

Introduction

The discovery of gold in the Klondike in the 1890s put the Yukon Territory firmly on the North American map. Thousands of people headed over the Chilkoot Trail, between Alaska and British Columbia, built their boats at Bennett Lake and struck out for Dawson City to seek their fame and fortune. Robert Service's poem "The Spell of the Yukon" echoes in the heads of generations of Canadian schoolchildren:

The land, have you seen it?
It is the cussedest land that I know,
From the big dizzy mountains that screen it,
To the deep deathlike valleys below.

To this day, "the Yukon" evokes a sense of adventure and calls to the imagination in all of us. While it was the gold that brought the stampeders, it was that other precious metal, silver, that built the Yukon economy and fed, housed and clothed generations of Yukoners. It was the silver ore that came out of the Keno mining district and the associated mining camps that was the catalyst for the territory to build the roads, prolong the steamboat traffic and for the company to build a new town, complete with a school and a general store. Between 1913 and 1989, a number of camp communities arose and were abandoned, each one having a lifetime associated with the quality and quantity of the silver ore being taken out of the ground.

The earliest camp was at the top of Keno Hill, followed by Wernecke, Elsa and Calumet, with operations later centralized in the Elsa camp. The Elsa camp evolved to become a hamlet in 1985, until the mine closed in 1989, and with it the company town.[1] There are still vestiges of occupancy at most of the camps. However, the mill, administration and operations-related buildings—the heart of the company—are in Elsa. Although this chapter concentrates on Elsa, it is impossible to tell the story of the rise of the camp without telling of the associated rise and fall of the others. Silver production from the

Fig. 1 – Map of the Keno area adapted from United Keno Hill Mines annual report, 1986, by E. L. Bleiler.

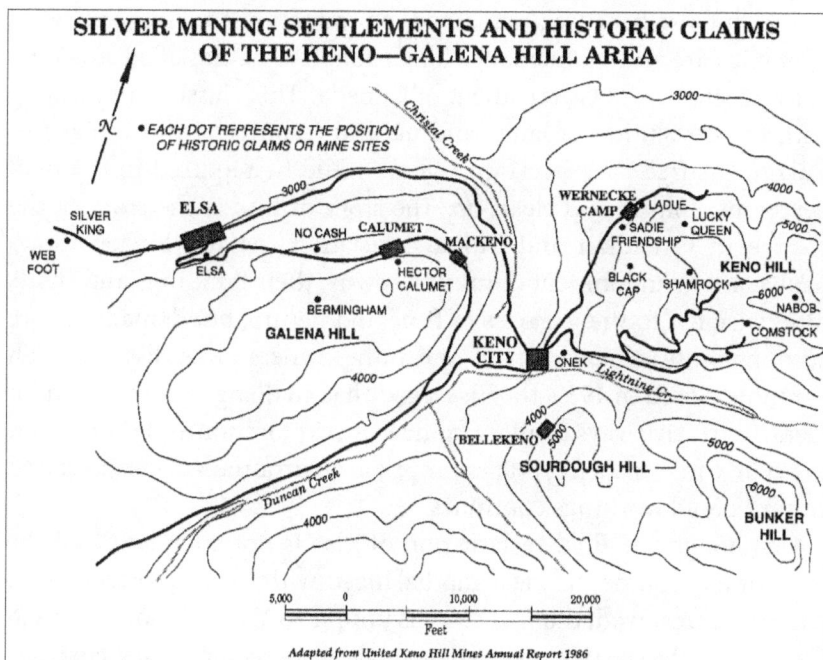

SILVER MINING SETTLEMENTS AND HISTORIC CLAIMS
OF THE KENO—GALENA HILL AREA

Adapted from United Keno Hill Mines Annual Report 1986

Keno mining district generated more wealth in the Yukon than the Klondike, which was one of the richest placer-gold-mine districts in the world (Cathro 2006). Between 1920 and 1975 (except during the Second World War), silver production from this area provided much of the economic base for the entire Yukon.

From 1914 to 1989, a total 217 million ounces (6.1 million kg) of silver, 710 million pounds (322 million kg) of lead, and 437 million pounds (198 million kg) of zinc were mined from the Keno mining district (Copland 2006). Following a small amount of hand mining between 1913 and 1917, larger-scale production was almost continuous from 1919 to 1989. Well into the 1950s, Keno mining district companies provided a huge amount of permanent employment for Yukoners. All told, it was two companies that produced most of the ore, Treadwell Yukon Corp. Ltd., from 1925 to 1941, and UKHM, between 1947 and 1989 (Cathro 2006: 1). In fact, the story continues, with renewed exploration and extraction starting up in 2006.

While other mining camps came and went in the Yukon, most other camps were abandoned and dismantled prior to any regulatory requirement for clean-up or historic preservation. The privately owned company town Elsa is unique in Yukon, not only because it produced longer than most other mines and was granted hamlet status later in its life, but also because it remained in production and in the purview of public care and maintenance long enough to be classified as a Type II Mine site by the Government of Canada. This classification, along with the devolution of lands and natural resources from Canada to Yukon, ensured that a certain rigour would be required in the final decommissioning and clean-up. The story of Elsa is the story of the change in Canadian and Yukon legislation that no longer allows haphazard abandonment of mining towns, their buildings and shafts otherwise left to the vagaries of time and nature, but demands more accountability of government and mine owners alike. Even though the mine closed in 1989, the Elsa legacy has challenged government to identify creative ways to allow for new ore exploration and production to occur while ensuring that appropriate environmental clean-up and control of old workings continues.

Although the final reclamation of Elsa is not complete, and the issue of environmental clean-up balanced with historic preservation remains unresolved, the Elsa story is unique to Yukon, and perhaps to Canada, as the parties involved struggle to implement new environmental and heritage regulations to resolve the impact of a hundred years of silver mining in the district in a way that is mutually beneficial.

The First Silver Strikes

The first silver strike in the Keno mining district was in 1903. The claim was called "Hell's Gate," and the man to discover the silver-lead ore in Yukon was Jake Davidson. He gave his samples to a fellow prospector, Harry McWhorter, and asked him to have them assayed. Then, Davidson, ever the prospector, let the claims lapse and headed off to Cobalt, Ontario, in search of a rich silver deposit he had heard about there. McWhorter held true to his promise to have the results assayed, but never answered Davidson's queries regarding the property, because while the assay results were an astounding 300 ounces per ton of silver the focus of the mining in the area still revolved around gold and there was, as yet, little interest in silver (Bleiler, Burn and O'Donoghue 2006: 111). McWhorter didn't return until 1913, when, based on the assay of the 1903 samples, he re-staked Hell's Gate as the "Silver King" claim on February 23.

In the meantime, the enterprising Gene Binet had moved from Dawson City in 1903, surveyed and built a town, which he named Mayo after Alfred H. Mayo, one of the early traders in the area and a riverboat captain. The town sat at the confluence of the Mayo and Stewart Rivers, close to the head of navigable waters, and in an area of quiet water where steamboats could dock. Mayo was ready for the steamboats to come, and come they did, bringing goods and supplies to prospectors searching for the silver ore. In June 1914, the steamer *Vidette* left the dock carrying the first shipment of fifty-nine tons of ore. The net smelter returns on the shipment came back that September at $269 per ton, and the silver stampede was on. In short order, more than ninety-five claims were staked and prospecting had begun in earnest (Aho 2006: 66-70).

McWhorter mined the Silver King for several years, until Thomas Aitken, one of his partners, exercised his option to purchase the claim; it was optioned several more times in the coming years to other partners. Five more lode claims were staked in the surrounding area in 1916 and 1917, but no ore was located. It was prospector Louis Bouvette who found a silver-rich galena float[2] on Sheep Mountain (later named

Keno Hill) in 1918. He traced the float up the hill and staked the "Roulette" claim. Bouvette knew he had something bigger than he was able to develop alone so he sent his samples to Dawson City with the hope of interesting Fred Bradley, president of the Alaska Juneau Gold Mining Company. Bradley had just left Dawson, so Bouvette's findings were taken to the Guggenheim's Yukon Gold Company (YGC) in Dawson City, where the assay was completed by Alfred Schellinger and indicated 200-300 ounces (5.6-8.5 kg) of silver per ton. Schellinger immediately

Fig. 2 – Silver King Mine. Yukon Archives, E. Forrest fonds 80/60 #5432.

sent people to stake the surrounding ground and went to Mayo to create an agreement with Bouvette (Bleiler et al. 2006: 112).

The Corporate Players of the 1920s and Keno City

Now there were big players in the arena and a rush ensued. As prospectors flocked to the Keno Hill area, the YGC bought their claims and conducted prospecting activities of their own. In the winter of 1919-1920 more than 500 claims were staked, including claims that would later yield some of the highest-grade silver in the world. In 1920, a subsidiary to YGC, Keno Hill Ltd., was formed to direct the parent company's operations in the Keno Hill district. The barren, windswept top of Keno Hill became a very busy place as shafts were blasted down into the earth to reach the rich veins of ore. Living conditions were difficult; wood for heat and mine timbers had to be hauled up the hill. Water was scarce, as it was frozen for much of the year. The tent camp located near the main shaft of the "Top of the Hill" mine housed company workers in abysmal conditions, the lead/silica dust contaminating their food, clothing and bedding.

Fig. 3 – Workers at mining camp. Courtesy Yukon Archives, Schellinger fonds 82/30 #5829.

Finally, in 1921, a two-week labour strike led to improved conditions, shorter workdays and construction of a framed wooden bunkhouse (Bleiler et al. 2006: 113). During the same year, a $13,000 warehouse was built in Mayo, and 325 feet (99 m) of waterfront along the Stewart River was leased for stockpiling ore. It was intended that steamboats would take the ore downriver to link with a rail line for points south.

A power plant was built on Duncan Creek near the junction with Lightning Creek, to supply the mine with electrical power. The first plant opened in December 1920, and after its wood-fired boiler exploded a second boiler was brought in from nearby Highet Creek. By 1922, the first five-ton Holt gasoline-powered Caterpillar tractor was brought to the district by Keno Hill Ltd. to haul wood for the power house boiler.

High-grade ore was hand-sorted and hauled down the hill to a collection of buildings at the bottom, now called Keno City. Greenfield and Pickering, freighting contractors, devised a method of transport called "rawhiding." When snow was deep during the winter, a dozen heavy sacks of ore would be tied up in a cowhide, hair side out. A horse would drag a few of these at a time down the mountainside to the road. Then two sets of four-horse teams took wagonloads in four stages to Mayo, where the ore was stacked on the riverbank to await the steamboats that would arrive in the spring, when the ice went out. There were four relays on the forty-mile (64 km) trip from

Keno City to Mayo, each outfit made ten miles (16 km) a day and then returned. The winter freight rate to Mayo was $50 per ton, and from there to the smelter in San Francisco the cost was another $22 per ton. The ore had to be very rich to recover the costs of mining and freight. Cordwood and mine timbers were carried on the back-haul from Mayo as wood had become scarce around Keno given all the building, heating, shoring up of underground mines and burning of fires to thaw the permafrost (Bleiler et al. 2006).

Fred Bradley, president of the Treadwell Corporation in San Francisco, had been following the developments in the Keno silver district since Bouvette's discovery, and in 1921 sent his mining engineer, Livingston Wernecke, to investigate the silver prospects. Wernecke liked what he saw; the company invested almost $500,000 in properties and soon had fifty to sixty miners tunnelling into both ends of the "Sadie-Ladue" vein on Keno Hill. This vein was 130 yards (118 m) long and averaged 20 inches (50 cm) wide, assaying 295 ounces of silver per ton (more than 10,000 grams/tonne).

By the early 1920s, Keno City had grocery, ladies apparel and novelty shops, a post office and several hotels. People could play tennis, pool, baseball, or watch silent movies or dance. The Jackhammer Band drummed out music for Saturday-night dances at Jackson Hall, which included a spacious dance floor upstairs, over the bar, and which featured a stylish English prospector who gave ballroom-dancing lessons. Keno City also became home to bars, gambling halls and houses of ill repute. Several of Yukon's famous madams, including Dawson City's Bombay Peggy and Ruby Scott, had houses in Keno City in the 1920 and 1930s (Gaffin 1982: 41). While Wernecke disapproved of the raucous activities in Keno City, he realized the need for his men to "let off steam" and engaged with such business owners in Keno City to ensure the safety of his men. His personal doctor routinely examined the women who catered to the workers, and the women ensured the men were sober and back to camp in time for shifts. As the town became the centre for recreational activities, the increased traffic up and down Keno Hill led to brawls between miners. To reduce this friction, the camps coordinated their operations and gave their workers alternate days off.

Wernecke realized that greater efficiency was needed to ensure the success of the mines. He brought in two ten-ton Holt tractors in the fall of 1923 to reduce the cost of hauling the ore to Mayo. The tracked vehicles ended the Greenfield and Pickering horse-and-wagon contracts and were said to have replaced ninety-six horses. The Holts halved the freight cost of $50 per ton and then subsequently shaved costs to $8.50 per ton (Yukon Development Corporation 2004: 18).

Wernecke Camp

Keno City's population declined as the tractors replaced the stables, horses and drivers. Roadhouses closed as there was no need to stop along the route. Wernecke established a one-hundred-ton-per-day milling and concentrating plant in January 1925 on the northwest flank of Keno Hill, where the Sadie-Ladue and "Friendship" claims contained a substantial reserve of low-grade ore. The mining camp located there came to bear his name.

Wernecke and his wife lived in the manager's house with their two children. He encouraged movies, dances and any form of recreation at Wernecke Camp, other than the drinking, gambling or prostitution that took place in Keno City. His camp had bunkhouses, an excellent cookhouse for the single men, a machine shop, framing shed, mill buildings, residences, a recreation hall with a pool room, bowling alley, indoor tennis and badminton courts, a library, a soda fountain, laundry facilities, radio sets, and outdoor skating and curling rinks.

It was a family community, and wives and children were welcomed. It was, in short, much different than the community of tents and bunkhouses that had grown up at Keno City.

Fig. 4 – Wernecke camp. Yukon Archives, Cooper-Carr Collection 99/48 #31.

The prosperity at the silver camps resulted in a building boom in nearby Mayo. The village quickly established itself as the main transfer point for the silver-ore shipments. Eventually it was a terminus for the first telephone between Mayo and Keno City. The first radio-telegraph system in the Yukon was installed in 1923 between Mayo and Dawson, and after the radio station opened in Edmonton, in 1924, the radio-telegraph quickly replaced the Yukon Telegraph System land line between Dawson and the outside world (Bleiler et al. 2006: 15).

Between 1921 and 1923, stern-wheel steamboats hauled 12,000 tons of sacked high-grade ore from the YGC and the Treadwell Yukon Corp. The ore was transported on the Stewart and Yukon Rivers to Whitehorse. The White Pass and Yukon Route Railway carried the ore from Whitehorse southward, across the U.S.-Canada border over the mountains to the port at Skagway, Alaska. The ore was then loaded onto ocean-going ships that transported it down the west coast to smelters in California (Bleiler et al. 2006).

Keno Hill Ltd. ceased production in 1923 when its senior mining engineer, Fred Hellman, concluded that the quality of the ore was degrading at the No. 9 and the No. 3 workings at the Top of the Hill mine. The company shut down operations on May 31, 1924. This left Treadwell Yukon as the only corporation on the hill. However, the Keno Hill area remained alive with activity, and the local Yukon infrastructure continued to grow to meet the needs of transporting the ore and bringing in supplies. Deals were struck with government to build roads and other necessary infrastructure (Aho 2006: 66-70).

Elsa's Beginnings and the Treadwell Yukon Years

The development that ultimately created the success story of the Keno mining district and led to the creation of the company town at Elsa, rather than isolated camps, was the discovery of silver. In 1924, Charlie Brefalt staked the "Elsa" silver claim on Galena Hill. He might have named it after his sister in Sweden, but others recalled that a girlfriend in Keno City was also named Elsa, who, perhaps on the strength of Brefalt's sudden fortune, agreed to marry him. We do know that when the first boat left Mayo after the ice went out in 1925, both his erstwhile wife and his winter earnings were on board while he remained behind.

Later that year, while grouse hunting, Brefalt, now known as the "lucky Swede," stumbled on his "Lucky Strike "claim that adjoined the Elsa claim. The ore assayed at 3,000 ounces (85 kg) of silver per ton (Cathro 2006). It was indeed a lucky strike, and mining in the region was guaranteed to continue with the discovery of this high-grade strike.

Brefalt sought $250,000 for the Elsa claim, but Wernecke had just committed Treadwell Yukon to heavy development on the Sadie-Ladue veins and could not afford the asking price. However, recognizing the potential of the Elsa claim, he did influence the Yukon government to build a winter road and a bridge over Galena Creek so Brefalt could haul ore to Mayo. By October 1925, Brefalt had fifty tons of high-grade ore sacked and shipped to Mayo.

By 1928 it appeared that they had mined out all the high-grade ore and Treadwell Yukon optioned the property for $150,000. In that same year, Treadwell Yukon expanded the operations at Elsa from Brefalt's log cabin and barn to include a messhouse, a bunkhouse for thirty men, a change house, a blacksmith shop and a compressor on the steep slopes of Galena Hill. A road was built over the Williams

Fig. 5 – Approximately 12,000 tons of bagged silver lead ore near the water-front in Mayo, ready to be shipped. Yukon Archives, Gordon McIntyre fonds, 82/441.

Creek summit, connecting the Elsa camp to the existing road system (Bleiler et al. 2006: 114).

In 1929, living in Elsa was noisy and rough, with few amenities. Single men lived in nearby bunkhouses and were able to walk to work, to the mess hall and to the clubhouse. A couple of staff houses were constructed, likely for foremen and managers. Life was simple and the company provided the necessities. However, the stock-market crash of the same year caused silver prices to plummet from $0.65 per ounce (28 g) in 1925 to $0.25 per ounce in 1931. Wernecke worked hard to keep people employed through the Depression. Nevertheless, by 1932 he had to shut down the Wernecke camp and mill. Only independent prospectors, mostly grubstaked by Wernecke, continued to explore the area.

In 1935, silver prices rose to $0.70 per ounce and Treadwell Yukon restarted operations under Wernecke's management. The ground was mined out at the Sadie-Ladue claims near the Wernecke camp, but the area around Elsa looked promising. There was a steady vein at Calumet, the known rich ore at Elsa, and new workings at Silver King. The decision was made to move the mill from the Wernecke camp to the Elsa camp. Yukoner John Scott, a newly graduated mining engineer, used his mining engineer's handbook and a U.S. Bureau of Mines bulletin on tramlines as guides as he designed and supervised the construction of an aerial tramline connecting the Calumet mine with the Elsa mill (Aho 2006: 203-204).

The tramline had 14,200 feet (4,328 m) of line strung down slopes as steep as fifteen degrees on forty-two towers. A third of the way down, buckets loaded ore from the "No Cash" mine before clanking into Elsa. At the Elsa mill, ore was processed from the reopened Silver King and Elsa veins, and later from the Hector and Calumet veins, all on Galena Hill. A new road was constructed between Mayo and Elsa. It was now faster and cheaper to move more ore down the hill to the mill and transport the ore concentrate to Mayo for points south.

The mill was a gravity mill and the incline of the land assisted in the movement of ore through the mill machinery. Tailings—mining residue—were used to terrace the hillside, allowing the construction of support buildings close to the mill. The power plant, assay office, cookhouse, bunkhouses, warehouses and roads were built along the contours of the land, while the ore was moved straight down the hill,

Fig. 6 – Elsa ca. 1935. Yukon Archives, Geological Survey of Canada Collection #150.

with the tailings dumped below. The mill was central to Elsa in the early days.

Not only were the operations buildings nearby, so were the bunkhouses, staff houses, clubhouse and mess hall (Aho 2006: 204). These buildings were constructed quickly or moved in from the Wernecke camp, seventeen miles (27 km) away.

In 1935, working in the mill paid $5 a day, plus room and board, which was considered good money at the time. Labourers worked eight hours a day, seven days a week. Single men lived in the company bunkhouse, which consisted of one large room upstairs and one large room downstairs, with about forty men on each floor. There was no indoor plumbing: the men washed in one common washroom and pulled water from five-gallon (19-litre) drums. There was an outhouse, a 6-8 holer, near the bunkhouse, as well as others strategically located in different areas of the camp. The sole source of fuel for cooking and heating was wood (Hicks [n.d.]: 30).

By 1936, the camp boasted a machine shop and compressor house, a framing shed, bunkhouses, staff housing, first-aid facilities, a clubhouse and a mess hall. The majority of buildings were light-frame construction with medium-sloped gable roofs that were of simple design, functional and economical to build. Except for the mill, most buildings were oriented east/west along the road and were finished with corrugated sheet metal or were painted. The gabled roofs and the bright white trim around windows and doors made them distinctive from the green slopes of Galena Hill. As the camp matured, small single-storey residences appeared on the outskirts of the operations centre. These homes were built in an informal manner, scattered along the muddy trail that connected the Elsa mine to the Calumet mine, or across the hillside above the mill.

Conditions remained challenging. There was no clean water supply for the camp. The mill used water generated from the mine, and water was hauled for the bunkhouses, residences and mess hall until the creeks froze. In winter, forty-five-gallon (170-litre) gas drums were placed behind the wood stoves and filled up with snow—along with sticks, leaves and whatever else happened to be in the snow. Hot water was recycled, first used for baths, then for washing clothes and finally for washing floors (Hicks [n.d.]: 35-37).

The Elsa camp ran on a month-by-month basis as silver prices continued to fluctuate. Nobody was ever sure if they were staying, so families didn't tend to accumulate furnishings. Even with these uncertain circumstances, the married men were allowed to build their own shacks on company claims, and did so after work with the help of their friends.

Livingston Wernecke, the company superintendent, was developing other properties in the United States and consequently was spending less and less time in the Yukon. The company had never invested heavily in the exploration and development of new ore bodies, and was now beginning to suffer. The efficiency of the mill and company mines was decreasing and Treadwell Yukon needed to find more financing to continue their Yukon operations.

In April of 1939, an economic recession started in the western United States and that country cut back silver purchases to a month-by-month basis. The Elsa mine continued to produce some of the richest ore in Canada, with the Hector and Calumet mines steady producers; the Silver King was now mined out. Treadwell Yukon's management in Juneau, Alaska, decided to close the operations in the Mayo district. Silver was at $0.35 per ounce and the outbreak of the Second World War was followed by the U.S. government's announcement that it would no longer buy foreign silver. Word was sent to Mayo, and Wernecke began selling all company assets (Aho 2006: 213). The staff was focused on shutdown procedures and compiling inventories when Wernecke and his pilot, Charles Gropstis, were tragically killed in a plane crash on their last flight out of Mayo, en route to San Francisco, in late 1941 (214).

The company dissolved the following year, ending Treadwell Yukon's twenty years of silver production in central Yukon, and Elsa was left with the mill, the power plant and the aerial tramway for future restart.

The War Years and the 1950s

When war with Japan broke out in 1941, the United States began construction of an all-weather gravel highway through the Yukon, connecting the lower forty-eight states with Fairbanks, Alaska, where the Americans were building a $10-million air base. The U.S. Public Roads Administration, stationed in Whitehorse, purchased some diesel engines from the defunct Treadwell Yukon mines for use in the construction of the Alaska Highway. They also bought the complete machine shop with all its supplies, tools and equipment.

After the war, the previous Treadwell Yukon shareholders joined other mining companies to form Keno Hill Mining Company Ltd. This company had eighty-seven claims, including Elsa, Calumet and Hector, and the remaining buildings, shops, machinery, mill and tramlines. However, many of the workings had caved in or were iced in, the Elsa mill was in poor shape and the Calumet tramline was inoperable.

The summer of 1946 was a period of high activity for Elsa. Eighty men were working, thawing mine shafts, conducting repairs to the mill, shops and tramline and securing staff housing. The winter of 1946-1947 was the coldest in recorded history, with temperatures reaching -82 Fahrenheit (-63 C). These were hard times in the Keno mining district. The cold cracked down and the camp was blanketed in deep snow, shrouded in ice fog and hoarfrost with only five hours of daylight on winter days. Hungry wolves were sneaking into camp and killing dogs.

Work progressed, although it was difficult as local labour was scarce and not many outside miners wanted to work this far north. The men hired were often inexperienced and required much more supervision than the independent prospectors and locals who had worked in the pre–Second World War era (Hicks [n.d.]: 41).

With the arrival of spring, production at the mill started up, the tramline was repaired and silver prices had risen. Operations continued even though the company again experienced financial difficulties. Corporate reorganization and refinancing carried on; the sale of the property was finalized, with the Elsa mine included in the assets assumed by UKHM in 1948. Development and expansion continued and profits climbed. The Hector-Calumet No. 1 mine, uphill from the Elsa mine, was projected to be the largest mine in the company with the strongest showing of millable ore. The Calumet camp was expanded with Pan-Abode and frame buildings built to house the engineering, geological and mining staff, plus the underground workers for that mine. Both Elsa and Calumet had churches, curling rinks and recreation halls.

Buildings shifted continuously due to thawing permafrost and it was not until the late 1940s that construction methods were refined to minimize the effects of building on permafrost. New buildings were built above ground with post-and-beam foundations. Gravel or fill was laid down on top of the moss that provided an insulating layer over the permafrost. Posts were dug in below the frost line so they would freeze in place, supporting beams were placed between the floor joists and posts, and well-insulated floors stopped the heat loss, thereby maintaining frozen ground under the buildings. This technique proved effective and lessened the shifting the buildings would have otherwise experienced. The footings for the larger machinery were excavated several feet below the frost line, filled with concrete and reinforced with steel bars (Skuce 2011: 6-7).

Restarting the mine to have concentrates ready for the 1947 production season was quite a formidable undertaking as the mine buildings had been earlier stripped of any saleable items, including the sheet-iron roofing. However, new sources of ore and outstanding technical staff quickly made a success of the enterprise and assured a profitable operation.

In 1948, a coal mine 155 miles (250 km) south, near the village of Carmacks, was reopened to supply UKHM with fuel for heating. The company generated all of the power for their mines with a new 500 horsepower electrical plant installed at Elsa, and the machine shop there was expanded in 1949. The federal government allocated funds for an all-weather road from Minto to Mayo in 1948, thus eliminating the steamboats that previously hauled the ore south via the Stewart and Yukon Rivers.

The UKHM transportation division was created with a fleet of truck-and-trailer units. Groups of eighteen flatdeck trucks accompanied by a tow truck made the run from Elsa to Whitehorse in nine to twelve hours, instead of the five to six days by sternwheeler. Each truck carried eight tons of concentrates, which were then hauled by train over the White Pass and Yukon Route Railway to the port in Skagway, Alaska. The world's first container ship, the S.S. *Clifford J. Rogers*, also owned by the White Pass and Yukon Route, then took the cargo to Vancouver. From there it went on to smelters at Trail, British Columbia, or to East Helena, Montana. Ferries operated at the three river crossings on the road to Whitehorse during summer and ice bridges were used in winter, with pauses in traffic every year during freeze-up and breakup. Eventually, bridges over the Pelly, Stewart and Yukon Rivers were built by the government over a period of four to six years, further reducing delays and costs. The completed highway connecting Whitehorse to Mayo was officially opened on October 9, 1960 (Bleiler et al. 2006: 116).

Disaster struck on June 11, 1949, when the mill caught on fire and burned to the ground. Insurance covered the loss. Using local labour, UKHM management drew up construction plans and a new concentrator mill was up and running by October 24, before the final architectural plans were completed. Later, the same team enlarged the mill to 450 tons per day and designed and built the cyanide plant (Aho 2006: 234).

The People

UKHM recruited men, and much later women, from Toronto and Vancouver, often from immigrant communities. Federal policy stipulated that groups of post-war immigrants in Canada could not work in a city until they had worked for two years in a remote community. This was a strategy popular with UKHM, which hired and sent immigrant labour up to Calumet or Elsa with one-way tickets. The company would pay their way and then deduct the cost of their incoming fares from their first few paycheques. As an incentive for them to stay, the company would return the fares if they were on the job for three months. However, their outgoing fares would not be paid until they had worked a full year. Once the workers arrived at the camp they were given a slip to take to the warehouse or the company store for rubber boots, clothing and whatever else they needed for work. This too would be deducted from their paycheques (personal communication with Horst Moritz, October 2012).

The miners and labourers who came to Elsa after the war were mainly single men from Europe, primarily from Germany, Austria, Poland and Czechoslovakia. Many were officially classified as displaced persons, and they assumed an important role in the economic boom of the post-war years throughout Canada. The role they played in Elsa was no different. Many had significant trauma associated with the war, and most viewed their departure from Europe as the beginning of a new life. Language barriers, separation from family and assignment to labourer jobs on the Canadian frontier made for difficult transitions. There was also a tendency for many English-speaking Canadians to underestimate the abilities of immigrants, and resentment was often apparent when the newcomers sought to move into jobs more in keeping with their ability and training. Many of these immigrants stayed in the Yukon long after the mines closed. They started businesses and became stalwarts of Yukon society.

The Elsa camp of the post-war years became a melting pot of Europeans and was known as "Little Europe" in the 1950s. There were men from both sides of the European theatre of war in Elsa, and many a tense moment in the bunkhouses and mess halls was reported in personal stories from miners of the 1950s. There were former Walfen-SS soldiers whose tattooed forearms told a different story from their tattooed co-workers who had been prisoners in German concentration camps; there were former members of the Hitler Youth who found their way to Elsa via stays in South America; and there were people from Eastern Europe who had walked to freedom through Mediterranean and Atlantic ports. The mostly male, single immigrants worked hard for many years so that they could return to their home country to bring back a bride to Canada.

Sometimes, they married women of the First Nation of Nacho Nyäk Dun, in whose traditional territory UKHM operated. The resulting ethnic mix had a significant impact on the development of cross-cultural families in central Yukon, and this led to its own set of prejudices. First Nation women who married into the immigrant population were sometimes shunned by their own families, and their children were labelled by others as "half breeds." The children tell stories of dad making borscht on the weekends and mom serving up moose meat and bannock. They also remember not being accepted by either parent's culture and their young women being used as "entertainment" in the bunkhouses. Despite these trying years, and perhaps because of a better understanding of prejudices, a number of these children have gone on to become government leaders in the First Nation of Nacho Nyäk Dun, now a self-governing First Nation under Yukon land-claims agreements that are protected by the Constitution of Canada.

Elsa, the Family Town

With an increase in population, and workers being encouraged to bring their families to town, UKHM faced the difficult task of housing and feeding everyone. By 1950, the population numbered more than 500 people (327 of whom were on the payroll). The mill town was remote and isolated; there was a dearth of almost all services and it was hard to not only get a workforce into the area, but to keep that workforce fed, housed and clothed. Management made some extraordinary decisions to ensure that the town and its people survived. UKHM concluded that the best way to recruit and retain good workmen in such a remote part of the Yukon was to provide lots of good food.

In the early years, before road transport was established in 1948, this was not easy, particularly with respect to fresh meat and vegetables. The twice-weekly plane into Mayo was of limited capacity and often grounded by bad weather. There were no roads from Whitehorse to Mayo and no refrigerated transport. Sternwheel steamboats were used to transport groceries and materials during the summer. Self-sufficiency was the name of the game when operating a mine in this isolated region. The company grew crops of potatoes, carrots, cabbages and greens in their own market garden in Mayo. Efforts to provide fresh meat included the employment of a full-time moose hunter (legal at that time). Moose steaks and roasts were augmented by a steady supply of trout from nearby Mayo Lake. These local offerings were not popular with the miners who expected beef and pork, with salt cod on Fridays. The miners accused the company of trying to save money when, in fact, the fresh food cost the company three times more than the $2.50 per day charged to the miners. After the highway was built and a food supply was available from further afield, the company was able to reduce, but never entirely eliminate, the complaints.

Along with grievances about the food, there were, of course, constant criticisms of the cooking. The head cook was a permanent target of abuse, and in order to vary the cuisine the company rotated kitchen staff between the various camps. The cooks themselves were an endless source of trouble, being by tradition temperamental and frequently alcoholic. This problem was solved in part by engaging the services of a Chinese-food catering firm (Hicks [n.d.]: 29-33).

Life could be monotonous for the single miners and other workmen living two-to-a-room in bunkhouses, with little to occupy their leisure hours. Television was unknown and even radio reception was uncertain, with the strongest signal usually coming from Russia. With the camp perched on the side of a hill, the underlying permafrost made it difficult to gouge out an area for a baseball diamond or a skating rink, though these were eventually built. Few if any of the crew took advantage of these facilities, however, preferring to play poker in the common room at the end of each bunkhouse.

Alcohol consumption was also a problem and it seemed that the lonely life in the bunkhouses made it inevitable. With the proximity of the liquor store in Mayo, UKHM found it impossible to monitor the flow of spirits, and from time to time a bootlegged carload of whisky led to rather serious problems. To get around this, one of the early mine managers persuaded the Yukon territorial government to allow the company to operate bars at the main camps, Elsa and Hector. The readily available alcohol, in pleasant surroundings, significantly reduced the problems, and the profits were devoted to improvements in the recreational facilities (Hicks [n.d.]: 33-35).

In a very cold climate and, indeed, in a very hot climate, there is no better place to work than an underground mine. The temperature varies little with the seasons and it is a relief to enter the subterranean ambience as an escape from either extreme. In general, the company suspended as much outdoor work as possible during the winter months. The miners were exposed to the elements for only a few minutes each day as they moved from bunkhouse to cookhouse or to the mine change house. Much the same applied to the workers in the shops, the mill and the office.

There were a few people who were unavoidably exposed to the worst of the temperatures. UKHM cut timber for mine props and operated its own sawmill, producing lumber for all sorts of construction in the camps and underground. During the record cold spell in 1947, a gang of Scandinavian woodcutters, who were perhaps accustomed to working in the cold, were chopping trees for badly needed mine props. They worked through the day and on returning to camp in the evening sometimes found the coal oil in their lamps frozen.

Families enjoyed a more normal life than the single men, but they also had their problems, not the least of which was keeping the pantry filled. When available, the housewives purchased their fresh meat and vegetables from the camp cook. For staples, the women would get together to put in their orders for a six-month supply of groceries from Woodward's or W. H. Malkin in Vancouver. This would be delivered by steamer to Mayo and trucked to Elsa in the spring and fall (Hicks [n.d.]: 34).

The Pan-Abode houses had a small room built on the back for groceries. The company would give employees an advance for food and deduct an amount each month from their pay until the account was settled. In 1959, the company opened a store in Elsa, in the converted No. 2 warehouse. Starting in the 1960s, a truck would come in once a week with fresh produce and other supplies (personal communication with Robert E. "Dutch" Van Tassell, September 2012).

There was also a curling rink in Elsa, with two sheets of ice, built by the residents. Curling is a very democratic game and it was not unusual to find a senior staff member wielding a broom under the shouted orders of a mine labourer who seemed to thoroughly enjoy the switch in roles. A couple of times each winter the company would host a bonspiel with rinks coming from Whitehorse, Dawson and even Fairbanks, Alaska.

In 1953, log Pan-Abode buildings were brought into Elsa initially for staff bunkhouses; however, within a few years, several more were constructed for family residences. Shipped in from British Columbia, these cedar buildings were easy to move and could be assembled by unskilled labour. Since heating was supplied by the company, families stayed warm even at -50 Fahrenheit (-45 C).

The company carried on a steady program of house building, but the board of directors insisted on a very basic design with no luxuries. The houses were either Pan-Abodes or frame constructions.

Fig. 7 – Calumet ca. 1960. George Hunter photo. Mayo Historical Society UKHM Collection.

The Pan-Abodes were one-storey log homes with a simple medium-pitch gabled roof. They had a concrete foundation and usually had a basement. Building packages were shipped in with everything, right down to the fasteners, from the Pan-Abode Company in Vancouver. Windows, doors, roofing material, logs, framing material and flooring were all part of the package.

At Calumet, the Pan-Abode homes were occupied by the geologists and staff, while the miners built their own simple frame homes on concrete foundations laid out by the company.

The residential area of Elsa was developed west of the mill and was laid out with streets constructed across the slope of Galena Hill. Single-storey Pan-Abode dwellings and frame houses were oriented along streets providing residences with million-dollar views overlooking the McQuesten River valley. Street names such as Bellekeno Lane, Conwest Lane, Comstock Lane, Galkeno Drive and Shamrock Street were derived from the working mines of UKHM.

In 1947, the mine manager's first home in Elsa consisted of a single L-shaped room, the largest portion of which was devoted to living and sleeping space, with the kitchen jutting off at one end. Wood-burning stoves supplied heat for warmth and cooking. There was no running water but a forty-five-gallon (170-litre) oil drum sat beside the kitchen range, which was topped up once a week from a tanker truck, itself filled from a nearby creek. Toilet facilities consisted of a "one-holer" outhouse reached through the kitchen. This had solid walls up to a height of five feet or so for privacy, and above was enclosed by fly screening, leaving it rather open to the elements otherwise.

Over time, living conditions improved for the mine manager: he and his family moved into a renovated four-room house with a flush toilet, even though the house did not have running water. The single water drum in the kitchen was replaced by three in the basement, which were filled twice a week. There was also a cistern in the attic that was filled from the basement by means of a wigwag pump. This type of living was not much different than in the nearby town of Mayo (Hicks [n.d.]: 36-37).

Disposal of wastewater would normally have been by underground septic tanks. Because of the permafrost it was not only difficult to dig these, but, when installed, they simply froze and failed to work. The "septic tanks" were therefore located in the basement of the houses and consisted of three or four gas drums connected together. These worked well and digested their contents in the same way as a more conventional system would have done. When full, a valve was opened and the clear effluent was discharged through a pipe down the hill to a point well below the houses (Hicks [n.d.]: 36-37).

A source of vexation for the tenants was their coal-burning basement furnaces. The company purchased coal from the mine at Tantalus Butte, near Carmacks, to provide fuel for the camps, but it had been hoped that a commercial market would also develop. Despite their best efforts, this didn't happen because the coal was poor quality. It was friable, and by the time it reached the camp after two or three handlings it was about 50 per cent dust. The company could burn it in their main heating plants through the use of sophisticated firing equipment, but as a domestic fuel it was unsatisfactory.

Families at Calumet and Elsa had what some remembered as a pleasant social life with the ladies visiting back and forth during the day, and in the evening couples might get together for a game of bridge. There was a daycare for the children and functions for the children at Easter and Christmas (personal communication with Al Archer, October, 2012).

During the postwar period, warehouses were built, a framing mill, garages, a machine shop, lumber storage, carpentry shop and a fire hall were all new additions to Elsa. The early 1950s were a time of optimism and expansion.

Construction was started on the Mayo hydro dam with an agreement from UKHM to buy power. The mill capacity was enlarged to 450 tons per day and a cyanide circuit was installed to treat tailings from the flotation circuit. Two new two-storey bunkhouses were constructed in Elsa. Camp spirit was excellent. Housing was spacious, comfortable, modern and cheap. Employees were paid $30 per month and were covered for light, heat and telephone. Groceries were ordered in bulk, and families traded dry goods such as spices, oatmeal and tea. Fresh produce and meat were purchased from the company cookhouse twice a week. Elsa had two churches, a school, recreation hall, movies, concerts and dancing groups. In addition to the curling rink, there was a ski hill and tow, and playing fields for summer sports (personal communication with August Pociwauschek, October, 2012).

The 1950s was a time when Yukon's entire infrastructure grew, road systems were improved and expanded, the sternwheeler era ended, and the newly constructed hydro dam near Mayo powered the town, Elsa and the UKHM mine sites. The labour force was relatively stable and the core staff of European immigrants, highly skilled in other trades, quickly adapted and excelled in the silver-mining business. These men brought in their wives and families and some became middle-management mine staff or started their own businesses (personal communication with Al Archer, October 2012). UKHM now held more than 600 claims.

In 1952, mineral production for the area topped $11 million, with silver, lead and zinc providing most of the returns. Once considered worthless, zinc and cadmium cruised into credit brackets. Keno Hill exploded into a havoc of staking posts, prospectors, promoters, opportunists, syndicates and junior companies.

In 1959, a new administration building was constructed in Elsa, west of the original office; its location just uphill from the power plant made it a focal point for the area as it overlooked the operations of the power plant and mill. Elsa remained central to the company operations with the mill, machine shops and transportation division servicing the outlying camps. The next year a new cafeteria-style mess hall was built along with a new assay office. A fire broke out and a

Fig. 8 – Elsa ca. 1960. George Hunter photo. Mayo Historical Society UKHM Collection.

bunkhouse next to the mill burned. This incident convinced the company to install water tanks and buildings in Elsa for fire protection. Sprinkler systems were installed in all the buildings.

The UKHM mines were now heralded as North America's richest and most modern silver-mining operation. They employed not only miners, truckers, mechanics and partsmen, but they now also required accountants, secretaries and other office workers (personal communication with Robert E. "Dutch" Van Tassell, September, 2012).

The 1960s

The ore reserves began to decline in the late 1950s. In the early 1960s, Falconbridge Nickel Mines, which had assumed control of UKHM, launched a rejuvenated exploration program under Robert E. "Dutch" Van Tassell. The program paid off when a new vein system, known as the Husky mine, was found by methodical overburden drilling near the Elsa mine. It was located under 35 feet (10 m) or more of overburden. The Husky was the first major vein discovery in the district in over twenty years, and in its twenty-five-year life produced almost 17.9 million ounces (500,000 kg) of silver, the third-largest producer in the area, behind the Hector-Calumet No. 1 at 96.2 million ounces (2.7 million kg) and Elsa No. 2 at 30.2 million ounces (850,000 kg). Even with this rejuvenation it was apparent that the Keno mining district was diminishing. The first signs of decline appeared in the early 1960s, when it became apparent that the ore reserves were not being replaced quickly enough to sustain the milling rate. From 1960 to 1963, the exploration department expanded and new geologists were hired to identify future mine prospects. Meanwhile, management decided not to budget for housing repairs or maintenance, resulting in poor employee morale. Staff and miners began to leave. In 1963, Alex MacDonald, the UKHM manager, approved home repairs and modernized the camp, but when he left in 1965 problems recurred, causing a major exodus of senior and intermediate staff (Aho 2006: 287).

In an effort to cut costs, UKHM management decided to further centralize operations and selected Elsa as the best option. This was likely due to the investment the company had in Elsa, with the mill, garages, machine shops, administration building and housing. Buildings were recycled, a warehouse was turned into a store and post office, the carpentry shop converted to a fire hall, and the women's staff house was converted to apartments for married quarters. New construction also occurred: a new framing mill was built in 1965, a new water pump house and water tank, a new carpentry shop and a new boiler plant. The boilers were switched from local coal to diesel and electrically operated. The boiler plant provided compressed air for underground tools and other buildings in Elsa, filtered drinking water and provided heat for all of the buildings in Elsa and nearby mines.

In 1966, an 18,000-foot (5.5 km) water line was installed across the McQuesten Valley, providing domestic water for staff housing, fire protection and mining operations. Utilidors, insulated pipe boxes, were constructed to carry the pipes that provided heat and water to each building in Elsa. By the next year, only Calumet and Elsa were still operating; all other UKHM mining camps had shut down. Silver production had dropped in 1966 and again in 1968. Exploration and development were curtailed and all operations were consolidated and moved to Elsa.

In 1971, twenty-one buildings were moved into Elsa from Calumet. Throughout the 1970s, Elsa continued to evolve: a men's staff house was converted into a co-ed residence; a Pan-Abode bunkhouse was converted into the geology/engineering offices; welding shops, the mine dry and the Calumet ore dump were dismantled to make room for the new thaw shed; and a three-storey bunkhouse was built. Meanwhile, silver jumped in price and held steady until the mid-1980s (Skuce 2011: 5).

Fig. 9 – Moving a Pan-Abode house, 1970. Horst Moritz photo. Mayo Historical Society.

In total, from 1946 to 1988, about 5.08 billion grams of silver were produced from the Hector-Calumet, Galkeno, Bellekeno, Elsa, Keno (No. 3 and No. 9), Lucky Queen, Silver King, Sadie-Ladue and Husky mines. Up to the late 1970s, all the underground mines operated by UKHM were tracked mines using small electric locomotives and heavy ore cars. In 1977, open-pit mining was introduced, using bulldozers, backhoes and rock trucks to remove the ore.

The outside world again encroached on the isolated town of Elsa, as it had in the war years and in the 1950s. In the late 1970s, Mary Scholz, a resident, was moved by the plight of Vietnamese people fleeing their homeland and she resolved to do something to help. Her first stop was the mine manager's office, where she asked if he would employ Vietnamese boat people if she signed on as their sponsor. He agreed to give jobs to five men, providing they could understand English and could read safety signs. Next, she went to the Canadian government and was told she needed a committee of five people to sponsor five single men. Mary Scholz and Alla Roberti were the life force of the resulting committee. Together they brought in five single Vietnamese men in the winter of 1979-1980. The Department of Immigration required the committee to put up $100 per month for a year for each man's expenses. The committee paid for the men's warm clothes, boots and safety equipment. Four of the men stayed for the year and one went to Saskatchewan. One of them was a trained machinist and became very successful working in Elsa. He married his Vietnamese girlfriend and subsequently brought her to Canada. After the mine closed, he moved to Whitehorse and purchased a car-parts business, later purchasing a Chrysler dealership there and another on Vancouver Island (personal communication with Mary Scholz, September, 2012).

The Decline of the 1980s

Despite the downturn in the fortunes of the Keno Hill mining district during the 1980s, the area continued to thrive on a social level.

The turnover was very high among unmarried workers, less so with the married. The social divides split along the type of job: union or salaried. There was limited housing, so that was another divide: families or single. The hierarchy within management followed the supervisory chain. The union hierarchy for underground workers was based on the bonus system; the miners who made the most footage were the top of the heap and support positions to the miners were secondary. Claire Briand-Festel, who was the hamlet recreation director from the late 1970s until the close of the mine in 1989, noted that Elsa was a great place to raise a young family. The recreation hall was very close to the family housing, and parents volunteered there at after-school, evening and weekend activities.

The bonds between the women were very strong; they relied on each other so much that their relationships were more like those of an extended family. Briand-Festel also noted that the remoteness, along with the raw, competitive frontier atmosphere, took its toll on some women: some kept to the "company side" of town, only going out to social events accompanied by their husbands; some husbands became overly possessive. It was not unusual for women to have nervous breakdowns. For some, men and women alike, the northern mining-town life was just too tough.

The role of women changed over time. The company hired women in the store, the main office (administrative), and later started hiring women in the assay office and flotation

Fig. 10 – Elsa community event, 1980s. Courtesy of M. Mancini, G.D. Sutter collection 3609-6-2.

mill. These were usually married women. In later years, in the early to mid-1980s, there were enough single women on the payroll that the company had a women's bunkhouse, a six-room trailer. By then, a few single women had started working underground as well. The old-timers resented them, said they were unlucky, but the company needed workers, so the practice continued.

Housing was always an issue in Elsa. Some workers waited years for company housing so that they could live with their families; it was harder for union workers to get housing, so some rented or bought cabins in Keno City.

The single life in Elsa was bunkhouse living, mess-hall eating revolving around shift work. Entertainment was gambling at the coffee shop or signing up for sports: darts, curling, hockey, softball or indoor sports at the recreation hall. A minority of singles were motivated to save a grubstake to reach a specific goal. That meant work, playing sports and keeping to the straight and narrow. But the mainstream singles' social culture was based on drinking, sports and hanging out. The hard physical labour was draining and the competitive nature was fierce. "Work hard, play hard!" was that norm that carried over to the married sector as well (personal communication with Clare Briand-Festel, October, 2012).

In 1981, the workforce numbered 200 when the employees went on strike, closing down UKHM for nine months. When the mine reopened in 1982, employee numbers had dropped to 140. Another temporary closure occurred in 1982-1983. The Elsa mines resumed operation in March 1983, when a major exploration effort, partly funded by flow-through shares, was initiated to increase reserves. The program consisted largely of surface exploration, in particular rotary-percussion drilling to depths of less than 65 yards (60 m). This was followed by the development of adits (tunnels) at poorly defined targets. Little use was made of diamond drilling and almost no exploration was carried out underground adjacent to existing workings. Many of the share owners were workers and managers at UKHM, as they tried desperately to save the mines, their jobs and their way of life.

Prior to 1985, Elsa was a company town and therefore not entitled to government funding for its recreational facilities. However, due to local political pressure, and in order to receive territorial funding, the Elsa camp was registered as a hamlet in 1985 by territorial Order-In-Council 1985/235. Pursuant to the *Municipal Act* (sec. 20[1]), the people of Elsa were to elect an advisory council made up of a chairperson and four council members. The advisory council was responsible for running the day-to-day affairs of the hamlet and advising the provincial minister of Community and Transportation Services on matters regarding the operation of the hamlet.

The locally formed Elsa Recreation Association organized all of the activities in the community, including the building of facilities, with materials supplied by UKHM. During the early 1980s, members of the community lobbied the Yukon government to provide financial assistance to help upgrade the recreational facilities in Elsa, and a commitment was received from government to do so.

UKHM was forced to shut down its mining activities abruptly in 1989 due to falling silver prices and managerial issues. In its last years, UKHM wasn't successful in lowering their production costs enough to counter the declining silver prices. Frequent management turnover exacerbated the problems as the company had a new general manager every two years for its last twenty-three. Despite the closure of the mine, the Yukon government continued with its commitment to provide civic infrastructure to the community and, in 1990, a new curling rink, library and recreation building were completed. The people of Elsa continued to try to find a way to make the mine work and keep the town alive. Some of the management put their own pensions and savings into various schemes to keep things running. The clock continued to tick and, by 1993, many employees and residents had left and buildings were being sold and dismantled. A skeleton crew remained to act as caretakers and manage the water maintenance on the Elsa site.

In 1990, a small lease program by exploration company Archer, Cathro and Associates mined more than 100 tonnes of high-grade ore from open-pits on the Lucky Queen, Keno No. 3 and No. 9 veins.

Falconbridge sold the UKHM company and property, including the Elsa town site, to BLM Mining of New York in 1994. BLM, operating as UKHM Minerals, attempted to reopen the mine by investing $15 million to refurbish the mill and for underground development at Bellekeno and Silver King. They also secured a water-use licence for reopening. Soon after, BLM ended up selling out to another company, which also operated under the name UKHM Minerals.

That company likewise failed to find the financing to reopen the mine. It closed operations, again leaving behind a skeleton crew, ironically composed of many of the same people from the 1989 closure. By

2000, the often unpaid UKHM Minerals care and maintenance crew lost the ability to use the water truck on site. This vehicle was necessary for water-treatment activities; therefore, water treatment ceased. Local Yukon businesses and creditors from other parts of Canada who were owed millions of dollars filed liens under the *Yukon Miners Lien Act* to secure debt owed by UKHM Minerals. These businesses, as well as creditors in Toronto, initiated legal action under their liens to sell the property and assets.

Elsa Declared Type II Mine Site

In January 2001, the Government of Canada declared the UKHM sites, including the Elsa town site, abandoned, under the *Yukon Waters Act*, for failing to maintain water-treatment plans and to ensure local surface waters were protected. The federal Department of Indian Affairs and Northern Development took over management of the site, engaging the First Nation of Nacho Nyäk Dun to undertake care and maintenance to prevent further environmental degradation. Using UKHM Minerals water-licence metals-discharge criteria as a yard stick, the nation hired a local environmental consulting company (Access Consulting) as technical manager and retained a local construction company (Ewing Transport) as site operations contractor.

In October 2001, the Government of Canada, through a process called the Devolution Transfer Agreement, transferred federal responsibilities for land, natural resources and resource management to the Government of Yukon (though the federal government retains the underlying title to land and resources). With regard to federally prescribed Type II mine sites (abandoned mine sites that have or may have unfunded environmental liabilities), the Yukon government was unwilling to take on the environmental liabilities related to mine closure. Therefore, the federal and Yukon governments established general closure and remediation policies for the sites. The closure objectives are to

> protect human health and safety; protect and, to the extent practical, restore the environment, including land, air, water, fish and wildlife; return the mine site to an acceptable state of use that reflects pre-mining land use where practicable; maximize local and Yukon socio-economic benefits; manage long-term site risk

Fig. 11 – Elsa Rec Hall, ca. 1973. Courtesy of M. Mancini, G. D. Sutter collection 4787-3-1.

in a cost effective manner. (Yukon Government Energy Mines and Resources 2011)

Elsa and the other UKHM mine sites were to remain the responsibility of Canada until it was determined that the effects of the hazardous sites had been mitigated. Once the sites were returned to states of repair acceptable to Canada, Yukon and the affected First Nation, properties that were not privately owned would be administered and developed as Yukon territorial land. In essence, with the UKHM properties being declared abandoned mines, Canada became the de facto owner of the mines. As such, the federal government continued to try to sell the assets, while maintaining the historical environmental liabilities. It engaged the brokerage firm Price Waterhouse Coopers to do this.

In 2003, AMT Canada Inc. acquired permission to access the site from the local creditors and Canada in order to do care and maintenance and conduct research-based exploration. However, plans to reopen failed and the property was returned to government control. Similarly, in 2004, Nevada Pacific Gold acquired in court the right to operate the site. They also failed to reopen the mine, and they too returned the property to government control.

In 2004, Auditor General of Canada Sheila Fraser issued a report that condemned the federal government's bookkeeping, in part for its failure to properly account for the liability for remediating environmental impacts from abandoned mines in Canada. The estimated cleanup costs ran to over $6 billion, and since there were no corporate entities left attached to these, she reasoned that the federal government must be liable and that the liability should be reflected in the budget. Following federal budgets incorporated this cost.

This policy change opened the door for the current owner of the mine, Alexco Resources Ltd., to come to an arrangement with the federal government, wherein the new mine owners would be liable for their own impacts but not those from previous owners who deserted their messes (like UKHM). Previous to the auditor general prompting Canada to accept responsibility, the government tried to pin cleanup responsibility for historical environmental impacts to any new operator who wanted to take over an abandoned mine and search for remaining minerals (e.g., AMT Canada, Nevada Pacific Gold), a policy which doomed properties to languish as orphan sites. With these policy changes and modern environmental legislation, there will be no new unfunded abandoned mines in Yukon, as new mines must post security to cover cleanup costs before they open.

In 2005, the Government of Canada obtained a Supreme Court order approving the sale of the Elsa property. In 2006, Alexco Resources Corp, of Vancouver, operating as Elsa Reclamation and Development Company, purchased the property through the Yukon Supreme Court. They took on the obligation of care and maintenance of the sites. A subsidiary agreement, which indemnified Alexco from historic environmental liabilities, allowed for the resumption of mining on a commercial basis under a new regulatory regime called the *Yukon Environmental and Socio-Economic Assessment Act* (*YESAA*), which came into full effect in 2005.

YESAA gets its authority from Yukon First Nations final land-claims agreements (Chapter 12), of which the final agreement for the First Nation of Nacho Nyäk Dun was effectively entrenched into the Canadian Constitution in 1995. *YESAA* is an expanded version of the *Canadian Environmental Assessment Act*, as it includes socio-economic factors in assessing potential impacts of projects in Yukon and recommendations to the regulatory agencies on how to mitigate those impacts. The government objectives of remediation had to consider socioeconomic benefits, including the impact of any project on

Yukon's historical resources. The result was that previously accepted methods of cleanup activities that occurred with Type II mines were no longer acceptable. Prior to 2005, the structures, engineering features and the buildings of mine sites in Yukon were demolished and buried, with the land re-contoured to encourage revegetation, leaving no tangible remains of the activities that had occurred. Since 2005, the public and stakeholders can review and comment on reclamation activities, including identifying those sites that have heritage value to Yukoners. This has potentially changed the way in which mine sites will be remediated.

Alexco was successful in opening its first mine, Bellekeno Mine, on Sourdough Hill northeast of Keno City in 2012. Alexco has built a 400-ton-per-day capacity mill near Keno City, and a camp near Elsa that includes temporary bunkhouses and a mess hall. They currently employ 135 people in their operation and they are using some of the remaining buildings on site in Elsa that are not considered to contain environmental hazards. However, Alexco has the obligation to take every part of their project—building, site reclamation, exploration or development—through the *YESAA* process to be examined for hazardous materials, environmental issues and socioeconomic impacts. The company is undertaking a historical resources impact assessment that will provide organizations and concerned citizens with the opportunity to identify areas or sites that have heritage significance. The Yukon government will also provide input into the process and will identify significant historical resources from the area in the context of Yukon and Canadian history.

Since the new regime for abandoned mine sites has taken effect, making old-style mining towns a thing of the past, it may be that Elsa will come to represent the last abandoned mining town. Future mines will be housed in temporary camps that are designed to be removed. Current and future mines will not leave any record or artifacts behind.

The historic UKHM mining sites in the Keno mining district and Elsa have been photographed, measured and recorded. Management of the historical resources must be meshed with the environmental hazards such as asbestos, chemical and health and safety issues in order to determine which physical structures and historical values can be maintained. The hazards associated with historical mining operations throughout the district include, but are not limited to, open raises and shafts, adits, sinkholes, unstable ground, unstable buildings and open roads. Identification and remediation in high-priority areas of immediate potential threats to safety were addressed in the Physical Hazards Reduction Work Program (2011/12) undertaken by Alexco. On completion of this work program, all high-level threats to safety were demolished or remediated.

Prior to drafting the impact assessment, identification of buildings that may have heritage value, and stakeholder consultation, took place. This included a questionnaire to local businesses, the First Nation and other residents in order to get a wide range of ideas and opinions about how people value these places. At the time of writing, the consultants were still reviewing the returns of this questionnaire and will make recommendations regarding the heritage values. The information gathered from the impact assessment will be used to develop an analysis and heritage management plan.

As of September 2012, all of the residential structures in Elsa pre-dating 1980 have been remediated, except three bunkhouses, the married quarters apartments and the men's staff house. Two log Pan-Abode buildings remain, the geology/engineering office and the cafeteria/snack bar. The mill will be taken down prior to 2020 due to environmental and safety concerns related to the structure and the contaminants that have been found within the building. The assay office, the administration building, power house, boiler house, fire hall, the Elsa portal, ore-thawing shed, the recreation hall, the swimming pool, school, the union shop, light-truck garage, drill-parts warehouse, carpentry shop, framing mill and the first water tank are

Fig. 12 – Elsa 2009. Yukon Government photo.

the existing remains of the Elsa mining camp. There are a number of other buildings scattered at the other sites, and some parts of the tramway still remain.

Conclusion

The tangible remains of United Keno Hill Mines Ltd. reflect the people who did the first prospecting and developed the first silver mines. People worked to acquire a grubstake to mine, and built small log cabins to live in while working their mining claims. The pick axes, hand steel (a chisel-like tool), frozen ground and danger were major parts of a miner's life. Many of the artifacts remain in local museums and at the Elsa site, providing a physical link to the stories and memories created from silver mining in the Yukon.

The evolution of underground mining in Yukon is represented in UKHM mining camps. The ore pulled from the Elsa mine was remarkable in its richness; the ore from the Hector and Calumet mines remarkable for its abundance. The pieces of the Elsa camp that remain are the last vestiges of a largely self-sufficient Yukon mining camp. As noted, the company provided its workers with a place to live, provided their food, their heat, their utilities and communication systems. UKHM was the driver behind the expansion of Yukon's road system, hydro system and communications. UKHM built, or caused to be built, a significant portion of the infrastructure in Yukon.

The mining that occurred in the Keno Hill mining district, and particularly the ore that left the Elsa mill, drove the economic development of Yukon through most of the 20th century. UKHM thus enabled the economy of Yukon to flourish even when mineral prices were down. Because of UKHM, bridges across major northern rivers were built, highways were constructed to connect rural mining towns, an electrification system was developed and, just recently, with the rejuvenation of activities at Elsa, more infrastructure has been constructed, creating a central electrical grid system in Yukon.

The wealth of the ore in the Keno mining district remains a known quantity. As modern mining efficiencies come into play, we can expect to see continued efforts to extract the ore, and we will see the evolution of smaller, portable camps.

Due to environmental regulations, the ease of building portable camps and the mobility of the current Canadian work force, Yukon is unlikely to see another company town like Elsa in the near future. The story of Elsa is iconic in the evolution not only of hard-rock mining in Yukon, but also the development of much of the modern economy. It is a story Yukon is proud to tell.

Notes

1. Hamlet of Elsa fonds. Yukon Archives, Whitehorse, YT. Accession Number 92/64.

2. Float: pieces of rock containing silver and galena, that are typically cobble- or boulder-sized that are found "floating" on or near the ground surface and are not attached to bedrock.

References

Aho, Aaro E. 2006. *Hills of Silver: the Yukon's Mighty Keno Hill Mine*. Madeira Park, BC: Harbour Publishing Co. Ltd.

Bleiler, Lynette, Christopher Burn and Mark O'Donoghue, eds. 2006. *Heart of the Yukon: A Natural and Cultural History of the Mayo Area*. Mayo, YK: Village of Mayo.

Cathro, R. J. 2006. Great Mining Camps of Canada 1. The History and Geology of the Keno Hill Silver Camp, Yukon Territory. *Geoscience Canada* 33 (3). http://journals.hil.unb.ca/index.php/GC/article/view/2686/3104 (accessed September 28, 2012).

Copland, Hugh. 2006. United Keno Hill Mine Closure—A Partnership Approach. Presentation—Best Practises. *National Orphaned/Abandoned Mines Initiative*. http://abandoned-mines.org/pdfs/presentations/UnitedKenoMineClosureCOPLAND.pdf.

Gaffin, Jane. 1982. *Cashing In*. Whitehorse, YK: Nortech Services Ltd.

Hicks, Brodie. [n.d.]. *Yukon Days 1947–1953*. Unpublished manuscript, Mayo Historical Society, Mayo, Yukon.

Service, Robert. 1907. "The Spell of the Yukon." http://www.internal.org/Robert_W_Service/The_Spell_of_the_Yukon (accessed Jan. 17, 2016).

Skuce, Greg. 2011. *Elsa Historic Resources Inventory 2010*. Unpublished report, Historic Sites, Tourism and Culture, Yukon Government.

Yukon Development Corporation 2004. Exploring Keno Hill: Stories of a Silver Deposit. Whitehorse. Environment Yukon. https://www.yukonenergy.ca/media/site_documents/53_keno_brochure_en.pdf (accessed September 20, 2012).

Yukon Government Energy Mines and Resources. 2011. Closure Objectives. Energy, Mines and Resources. http://www.emr.gov.yk.ca/aam/closure_objectives.html (accessed June 29, 2013).

Chapter Seven

Andrew Molloy and Tom Urbaniak

One House: The Bumpy, Hopeful Road to 50 Mechanic Street

Glace Bay is a former coal-mining town on Cape Breton Island's Atlantic coast. There have been no mines for 20 years in this proud but struggling urban community of 17,000 people. Abandoned shops—even a boarded-up post office—and graffiti in the downtown compete with symbols of community spirit and resilience: the old town hall that almost became a parking lot if not for the grit and determination of a small group of citizens; the beautiful and popular Savoy Theatre; and a small park on the main downtown street.

A call centre testifies to economic development schemes that have provided some emergency bandages but that have still not found their mark. The realities of the working poor and of unemployment are not hard to find in Glace Bay: payday loans, recourse to the food bank, public housing complexes. These are set in place with a rich history, a vibrant cultural life and dedicated citizen leaders who try to organize from the ground up. Glace Bay—complex Glace Bay—is a place of rich stories: the immigrant experience; humour in the face of danger; a knack for debunking the latest politicians and promoters.

The hurt of Glace Bay is evident in some of its houses. There are some leafy and stable neighbourhoods, yes, but there is also prolific abandonment. Planners of the Cape Breton Regional Municipality, which includes Glace Bay, have pointed to more than 800 vacant homes in the region of 100,000 people. A fifth to a quarter of these are in or close to Glace Bay.

Abandonment begets abandonment. A typical scenario: The elderly resident of one-half of a century-old company house duplex loses the energy, the skills, the money to make repairs. The resident moves in with relatives or into a "guest home" (seniors/nursing home). The property languishes. Real estate agents are more interested in new homes in the suburban subdivisions (of which there are surprisingly more than a few) than $20,000 fixer-uppers. The municipality starts boarding up the house in response to neighbours' complaints. The cost of doing that work goes on the mounting tax bill. The home is now a liability—its owner hoping that someone will actually acquire it at tax sale. Often, no one does. Nova Scotia's *Municipal Government Act* says you cannot touch a house you bought on tax sale for six months after you buy it.

In the meantime, one-half of such a duplex literally sinks deeper into the ground. A young family in the attached, neighbouring half sees its investment whither too. Might there be a better place to bring up the children?

But why not here? Why not in this established neighbourhood where you can still walk to school, walk for groceries and walk to the downtown? In a place that has housed, and still does, colourful characters and people who look after each other?

A perfect storm linked to imperfect paradigms—paradigms of economic development that leave some regions behind, paradigms that dismiss the value of the old, that plan for cars not pedestrians, that prefer to extend utilities and services to new subdivisions in a region with a declining population, that are maybe too quick to dismiss rehabilitation and renewal of the existing urban fabric.

In 2008, the authors of this article, working with others at Cape Breton University and the Cape Breton Regional Municipality, invited representatives of neighbourhoods, housing organizations, heritage organizations and the three levels of government to a conference—a collective discussion, really—on opportunities for housing revitalization in the regional municipality. Could some of these homes be salvaged, especially when rental vacancy rates were low and when there was a waiting list for public housing? We were joined by people from other Canadian cities who were working to bring some of their old buildings back into a state of repair to address the need for affordable housing.

Local participants agreed that we needed a coordinating group for demonstration projects. From that, the Affordable Housing Renovation Partnership was born. Participants also identified the need for grant or loan programs to help with emergency repairs and for a revolving fund that would accept property donations or buy properties at a low cost, fix them and sell them with covenants to ensure conservation and affordable housing. The desire to set up a Cape Breton chapter of Habitat for Humanity was also identified—but with a focus on renovation or infill development in already-serviced areas.

Implementing even these modest recommendations proved challenging, however. Government support for housing was generally very limited outside narrow criteria. Even getting a hold of properties proved to be difficult. In 2010 the newly established Habitat for Humanity committee asked the council of the Cape Breton Regional Municipality to contribute a property. Council agreed, but staff could not execute the request because almost all of the tax-delinquent and derelict properties were in private hands and had to remain that way until sold at a tax sale, where the bidding often starts at an amount greater than true market value.

The attention turned to doing demonstration projects with private money—with fund-raised dollars. A short-term project called HomeMatch, based at Cape Breton University with personnel support from the federal Homelessness Partnership Initiative, was set up to link three vacant homes with agencies serving people at risk of homelessness. A heritage revolving fund was set up with private donations. It negotiated with an absentee owner to buy the long-vacant Liscombe House in downtown Sydney. And there was the Mechanic Street demonstration project.

This is the story of that one house, "Dominion Coal Company House #734," otherwise known as 50 Mechanic Street. It is one house—purchased at tax sale by one of the authors in order to donate it for a demonstration project that would be of some help to the community in the short term, but also help us to better understand the larger context of policies, planning and problems, a classroom of sorts. But it is also a very human story, a starfish-on-the-beach type of story. This is the story of the MacIntyre family, which lived there for three generations and befriended local songwriters. This home in

Fig. 1 – A back view of the former Dominion Coal Company House – duplex on Mechanic Street, as renovations were getting underway in 2012. This half-company house would undergo an almost complete rebuild. Photo by Joyce Rankin.

the place of industrial Glace Bay, close to the downtown railyards, was a place of friendship and warmth. This is also the story of the family that now owns the home—within walking distance of the call centre and closer to friends and support networks than the public housing complex—thanks to the sweat (literally) and sometimes struggle of Habitat for Humanity. Included in this story are the students of Cape Breton University and Nova Scotia Community College, who met with residents in the early days of the project, who prepared an exhibit on local history and local skills on Mechanic St., who met in teams with technical experts (architects and the owner of a local Indigenous alternative energy company) for three continuous days to come up with designs and costs, and to develop a "statement of significance" so that the circa-1901 home could become the first company house in Cape Breton to receive a heritage designation. This is the story of humble and sincere Cape Breton leaders, like Adrian Wilson (now the chair of the Habitat for Humanity's Cape Breton chapter), Alicia Lake, Joyce Rankin, Debbie McIntyre, Dave MacKeigan, Harold Daigle, Steve Andrea, Rita MacDonald, Paula Michalik, Luca Poloni, Glen Carabin, Vince Carrigan, Becky Dunham, Jimmy O'Handley, Eldon MacDonald, Kim MacDonald, Wade McNeil, Barry Smith, Sandra

Kelly, Deb Murray, Blaine Aitkens and the members of the volunteer and student teams they led, who calmly worked through construction problems on a shoestring budget, even when the project was literally on the verge of collapsing.

It is one house that itself tells a story—a narrative both historical and contemporary.

The Restoration Context: A Municipality in Decline and a Vacant-Building Problem

Why are there hundreds of vacant homes in the Cape Breton Regional Municipality?

One factor is outmigration in a post-industrial region. CBRM is the second largest municipality in Nova Scotia, an amalgamated one-tier entity incorporated in 1995. It covers about a quarter of Cape Breton Island, including most of the former industrial communities: Glace Bay, Sydney, New Waterford, Dominion, North Sydney, Sydney Mines, Louisbourg and the former Cape Breton County. But its population has been declining since 1961 (CBRM 2009: 15). The area's coal and steel industries, which had historically sustained population growth in the region, collapsed entirely in the 1990s. The CBRM witnessed a population drop of 4.7 per cent between 2006 and 2011. During that same period, Canada's population grew by 5.9 per cent (Statistics Canada 2011). According to provincial data, the CBRM's population had shrunk to 97,398 in 2013 (CFNS 2013: 27).

The Cape Breton regional unemployment rate was 17.3 per cent in January of 2016 (Statistics Canada). The CBRM has one of the highest youth-unemployment rates in the country, a rate that has not changed since 2000 (CFNS 2013: 28). According to a 2009 report on the CBRM's Integrated Community Sustainability Plan, the 1996-2006 period witnessed a decline of 35 per cent among those under age five, "while the population between the ages of 20 and 34 years of age declined by 30%" (CBRM 2009: 15).

But population decline is only one factor in the vacant-buildings crisis. Families are smaller, and so the number of households has actually not declined as dramatically as the population. Seniors leave their homes to move into assisted care facilities or with their immediate family members. Some seniors who wish to remain in their homes face the financial challenges of retro-fitting in order to maintain accessibility. "The age of the person responsible for maintaining a home in the CBRM is significantly above the national average" (Whalley 2008: 53). CBRM residents are older than residents in six other comparator Atlantic Canada municipalities (CFNS 2013: 4).

The financial inability of some property owners to maintain their homes is another factor. Poverty rates in the CBRM are considerably higher than the national rates (CFNS 2013: 29). Average income for CBRM residents is 19 per cent below the Nova Scotia average and 40 per cent below the average in the Halifax Regional Municipality, the most populous city in the province (ibid).

CBRM has a higher percentage of private households "in which the total income was below the threshold defining low-income status after tax" than Nova Scotia and Canada as a whole. CBRM homeowners also have to pay "some of the highest residential tax rates in the province" (CFNS 2013: 9).

Renters in CBRM are particularly hard hit by financial challenges, as 53 per cent of those renters "are allocating at least 30% of their annual household income to gross rent and 63% of all lone parent families in the region who rent housing are allocating at least 30% of their annual household income to gross rent" (Whalley 2008: 52). With low vacancy rates for two- and three-bedroom accommodations, there is a demand for safe, affordable housing in the CBRM.

This demand is underlined by municipal auctions, where tax-delinquent properties are purchased at very low prices—less than $10,000 for a home has been common. It is well known locally that some of the buyers have been "slum landlords." Calculating that in some neighbourhoods the value of the property will not appreciate, they rent out premises for as long as tenants will pay. Few repairs are undertaken. Many tenants are unlikely to complain to the municipality about the condition of such properties because they have few affordable-housing alternatives and vacancy rates are surprisingly low (CBC News 2012).

CBRM rental vacancy rates in 2012 ranged from 4 per cent for one-bedroom apartments to 5.3 per cent for apartments with three or more bedrooms (CFNS 2013: 8). These rates placed CBRM in the middle of a six-city Atlantic Canadian group, according to a Community Foundation of Nova Scotia study (CFNS 2013). When tenants or buyers cannot be found for "rundown" buildings, those properties are often simply abandoned.

In a context of declining population and a high rate of poverty, it is unsettling that CBRM has urban sprawl. Around Sydney, new suburban neighbourhoods—Coxheath, Westmount, Hampton Estates—are seeing the extension, not consolidation, of municipal services. Wealthier homeowners build on large lots beside the Mira River or with views of the ocean. A property assessment cap, imposed by the province, is protecting the more affluent properties outside the urban cores (which are increasing in value) from tax increases, further hampering the municipality's ability to deliver services.

The growing number of vacant homes in CBRM has led to frustration on the regional council: It costs between $10,000 and $15,000 to demolish a house (CFNS 2013: 9). The council could not afford to allocate hundreds of thousands of dollars a year to demolitions. The landfill was literally filling up from demolition waste. Properties of historic significance were being erased from the landscape.

Representatives of the municipality worked with Cape Breton University to invite neighbourhood groups, housing organizations, community development groups and heritage organizations to discuss the problem. As noted in the introduction to this chapter, the participants in this problem-solving discussion recommended forming an umbrella steering group to do applied research and link vacant homes with agencies serving people at risk of homelessness, a revolving fund for heritage properties, and the formation of a chapter of Habitat for Humanity that could carry on some rehabilitation projects.

That umbrella group, incorporated in 2010, was the Affordable Housing Renovation Partnership (AHRP). It scanned other efforts across the country. We invited some of the grassroots workers associated with these efforts to meet with people in Cape Breton. AHRP also studied the history of projects that had been undertaken locally in Cape Breton. In short, it set out to determine what is possible and to create an appropriate business plan.

We looked at Winnipeg. In 1978, that city established the Winnipeg Housing Rehabilitation Corporation to take over, or purchase, derelict buildings for resale or lease as affordable dwellings. That city-wide entity inspired neighbourhood social enterprise corporations, which could acquire properties from the central corporation or tap into staff expertise available through the central corporation.

Winnipeg's North End Housing Project was one of the major initiatives. Lawrence Deane was actively involved as a board member and as a faculty member in social work at the University of Manitoba. We invited him to visit Cape Breton to share the experience. In *Under One Roof*, Deane (2006) describes the North End of Winnipeg as being an "at-risk" area, with high rates of poverty, crime and dereliction. The North End Housing Project worked with residents, the Canada Mortgage and Housing Corporation, credit unions, local entrepreneurs and post-secondary institutions. Even some low-income persons on social assistance were given the opportunity to become homeowners, not just permanent renters, usually through rent-to-own schemes. This initiative in turn spawned the development of a veritable social infrastructure for the neighbourhoods, including crime-prevention efforts, addiction treatment and training programs. Meanwhile, a new renovation company (a social enterprise), Inner City Renovations, hired unemployed local residents.

Deane reported that by creating micro-economies where neighbourhood social enterprises feed off the original objective of fixing derelict homes, the bleeding of local resources could be slowed. He carefully examined inputs and outputs and found a positive return on investment.

Another housing-revitalization story that we studied was Saskatoon's Quint Development Corporation. That social enterprise was set up in 1995, with the active assistance of two city councillors. It focused on five targeted neighbourhoods (Caledon Institute of Social Policy 2001). These older "core" neighbourhoods had seen decline and physical deterioration. Poverty had increased. An account from Quint's early days reported that the "housing stock is aging, many houses are vacant, residents experience higher unemployment levels, and subsequently greater numbers of families are on social assistance than in other Saskatoon neighbourhoods" (ibid: 1). Groups of homes purchased by the corporation for rehabilitation became co-ops. The residents became part owners of the co-op, and Quint helped to arrange or provide support services to help residents make the transition from social assistance to stable employment, and to prepare them for home ownership. After five years, residents could assume outright ownership of a property and pay mortgage based on Quint's original purchase price. The co-op fees are then counted as if they had been mortgage payments.

A third housing revitalization case study began with a single property and took off from there. The organization Homegrown Homes,
in Peterborough, Ontario, renovates derelict buildings, usually one at
a time, to create affordable housing. The city owned a derelict heritage building that it had acquired to make room for a road-widening
project that never happened. The nascent Homegrown Homes asked
for that building, plus the $10,000 that the city would have spent to de-
molish it. After that first housing-revitalization project was completed
as affordable rental housing, the city's planning department ensured
that whenever vacant homes fall into municipal hands, Homegrown
Homes would be approached. The publicity generated by the one
project was crucial to changing the local paradigm in Peterborough.
In this manner, the municipality became more involved in affordable
housing while improving property standards.

In Nova Scotia, affordable housing and community development
have close historical ties. This is thanks in part to the Antigonish
Movement, which was most active from the 1920s to the 1950s. Leaders
of that movement included progressive Cape Breton Catholic priest-
professors Jimmy Tompkins and Moses Coady (Alexander 1997). In
part through their adult-education university-extension department
at St. Francis Xavier University, Tompkins and Coady promoted
grassroots development, sparked locally through "study clubs." This
led to co-operatives, credit unions, libraries and other forms of collective entrepreneurship organizing (Coady 1939).

Housing development was viewed by the Antigonish Movement
as a particularly useful form of community education and better-
ment. It required an examination of poverty and economic disparities
within the context of existing economic and political systems; it used
the skilled trades; it called for pooled investments and a great deal
of organizing. Housing was a linking issue, a way to bring together
divergent interests and resources to begin to address grave social
conditions while creating locally owned enterprises.

One of the first co-operative housing-development projects was
Tompkinsville (as it would later be dubbed), in Reserve Mines, less
than 10 km from Mechanic Street, Glace Bay. The housing was meant
to be aesthetically pleasing. Decrying the "ugly and mean little dwellings" that marred the beautiful natural settings of Atlantic Canada,
Moses Coady extolled the virtues of artistic homes, which would

uplift the lives of the workers and the communities in which they were situated (Coady 1939).

The local study groups that got Tompkinsville off the ground were assisted by Mary Arnold, a member of the Cooperative League of the U.S.A. (Harris 2001: 108). At the outset, she and the study groups did "planning, organizing, book-keeping and building cardboard models of the homes" (MacKinnon 2009: 148). The Nova Scotia Housing Commission agreed to make available construction loans to co-operatives and to accept labour-in-kind as part of a miner's family's down payment on a home (Harris 2001: 110). The completion of Tompkinsville in 1938 played a major role in spurring co-operative-housing efforts for low-income families in Nova Scotia. It was also considered to be an original housing initiative that "was codified as a plan which was taken up by groups in various settings" (ibid: 103). The plan, detailed in a manual, was cost-effective and helped the commission oversee the building of 5,475 homes in Nova Scotia between 1940 and 1973 (ibid). The cost-effectiveness of this model was noted in a comparative costing of co-op housing projects and public-housing units in Halifax and Sydney. Co-op housing was noticeably cheaper to develop (ibid: 117).

Although it has been argued that an affordable owner-occupant model might have gained even more traction (ibid: 104), the lessons of Tompkinsville and the Antigonish Movement included carefully identifying the needs and opportunities, developing policy and execution capacity through an appropriate organizational vehicle, bringing on community partners and eventually obtaining some government financial support.

However, AHRP quickly discovered important obstacles to launching a modern program that could link salvageable vacant properties with affordable housing (Harker Associates 2010).

As noted, it was actually hard to get vacant properties. Many of these were tied up in a cumbersome tax sale process that required bidding to start at the amount owing and that delayed any work on a property for six months after the successful bid. Provincial funding was almost designed not to fund vacant and reclaimed properties: New builds and already-inhabited properties were the focus. And the municipality was reluctant to ambitiously engage in a negotiated housing program with the province. For the CBRM, this was a time of major conflict with the government of Nova Scotia.

That conflict started in 2004, when the CBRM launched an unsuccessful lawsuit against the province (CBC News 2008). The municipality, led by then-Mayor John Morgan, argued that the province was not living up to its constitutional responsibilities (section 36 of the *Constitution Act*, 1982) to "provide reasonably comparable levels of public services at reasonably comparable levels of taxation." Without such funding, the mayor argued, the CBRM is kept in a position of deliberate economic underdevelopment while the Halifax Regional Municipality, the provincial capital, remained the chosen engine of economic growth.

Because the unsuccessful lawsuit, which carried on in one form or another for seven years, was viewed by the mayor as "the only" option for the survival of the CBRM, new pilot projects or new initiatives were discouraged. Local governments wanted to demonstrate that the municipality was, in fact, not sustainable (CBC Radio 2008). Mayor Morgan was wary of what he called a "tyranny of positive speaking," whereby "we are encouraged and demanded to speak positively even when the plain facts, the statistical circumstances, say we ought not to speak positively" (McNeil 2010).

In such an atmosphere, efforts like those of the Affordable Housing Renovation Partnership (AHRP) were viewed as offering "band-aid" solutions to serious economic problems. From this perspective, it is supposedly better instead to let the region's economic situation worsen and force senior levels of government to respond.

But AHRP members believed that they could still play a constructive role by prompting demonstration projects that show what might eventually be possible on a larger scale, by researching the successes and failures of previously attempted housing revitalization initiatives, locally and elsewhere, by drafting revitalization-friendly policies, and by doing need-and-demand studies in areas where there was a chance for movement.

AHRP thus took on three short-term projects:

HomeMatch—to do some of the funding work to link three vacant properties with agencies serving people at risk of homelessness

Help to get the heritage conservation revolving fund off the ground.

Help to get the Habitat for Humanity chapter off the ground, with a home to rehabilitate.

The revolving fund was greatly helped by a donation of $10,000 by Donald and Grace Arseneau and support from the Old Sydney Society. A non-profit organization, the Sydney Architectural Conservation Society, was incorporated to administer it. The society obtained a loan and bought the historic Liscombe House (1860) near downtown Sydney, which had been vacant for seven years. It was one of the few Italianate homes in Sydney. Some renovation work was done and a request for proposals was put out to local developers. The home was then sold under a perpetual preservation covenant, the proceeds of the sale went back into the fund, and were used to work on a second property, on Victoria Road in Whitney Pier. The developer, Kenneth MacKeigan, converted Liscombe House into two beautiful rental units. It is hoped that the fund can continue to revolve in perpetuity.

AHRP members, working with students at Cape Breton University, helped to start the local Habitat for Humanity committee. Nova Scotia Community College's Marconi campus quickly came on board. Fundraising began. But because of the previously mentioned difficulty of actually securing a site, one of the authors purchased

Fig. 2 – The Liscombe House. Photo by Joyce Rankin.

a vacant home at tax sale for $8,600 and offered it as a donation to Habitat for Humanity. It was 50 Mechanic Street, Glace Bay.

50 Mechanic Street

Why 50 Mechanic Street? Here was an already-serviced lot. It was easy walking distance to schools, shopping and downtown. The Glace Bay-Sydney transit line runs nearby. The home was a duplex, and the other half was well cared for but at risk if something was not done. And 50 Mechanic Street was part of an important cultural landscape. In a 1997 report commissioned by the Historic Sites and Monuments Board of Canada, William Wylie (1997) characterized Glace Bay's company-house neighbourhoods as being among the country's most significant cultural-industrial landscapes.

The homes of Mechanic Street and, behind it, Foundry Street, were built for workers of the Sydney and Louisburg Railway. Begun in 1895, the railway transported coal to ports in Cape Breton, where it was then shipped across the world.

Before Mechanic and Foundry Street were named for the mechanics and forgers (blacksmiths) who lived there, the streets were called the "Dominion Rows." The railway carried coal belonging to DOMCO (company) just metres from the homes. In one of a series of interviews conducted with long-time Mechanic Street residents by Cape Breton University student Charlotte Deane in the spring and summer of 2011, one respondent recalled how women hanging their white laundry outside would shake their fists at the black smoke and soot coming from the passing coal trains (The Healthy Home 2011).

The DOMCO offices were on Union Street, next to Mechanic Street. A machine shop, a forgery, a pattern shop, a coal yard, a railway station, railway roundhouses and a repair shop provided steady employment. One long-term resident of Foundry Street recalled how he could get work anywhere when he was a teenager (ibid). A long-time business owner in the community estimated that two thousand people were employed in this small area at one time.

The company houses on Mechanic and Foundry Streets were constructed so that the workers would be close at hand for their shifts. Although these homes are almost universally referred to as company houses, early 20th-century architectural drawings refer only to managers' premises as "houses." The workers had "cottages."

As noted by Richard MacKinnon (2009: 128), the Cape Breton company house comes in several forms: as long rows (the best current examples are the "Red Row" houses in Sydney Mines), as small detached singles and as various duplexes, including the gabled Gothic Revival kind. The latter are especially intriguing because the Gothic Revival style was seen as part of a reaction against the mechanistics of the Industrial Revolution.

Fifty Mechanic Street was part of the series of ten duplexes built on that street (ibid). Foundry Street had twenty duplexes. The original dimensions of all the homes on the streets were the same. The homes were built on symmetrical 40 x 100-foot (12 x 30 m) lots. One-half of a duplex was "24 by 24 feet (7.3 by 7.3 m) in size and possessed a front room with a fireplace (called a living room in the original plan), a kitchen and a pantry on the ground floor, plus four small bedrooms on the second floor" (ibid). There were no foundations for the homes; they were built on sills.

The construction of 50 Mechanic Street—Dominion Coal Company House 734—took place in 1901. Conforming to a standard plan prepared by the firm Rhodes and Curry, it was built using ready-made materials. One neighbourhood resident told the story of a man sorting out all the boards that would later be used in constructing the frame of a company home. He was sorting them out by size and length

Fig. 3 – Miners' double cottage pitched-roof house plan, 1905. Dominion Coal Company Limited, 264-Y. Beaton Institute, Cape Breton University.

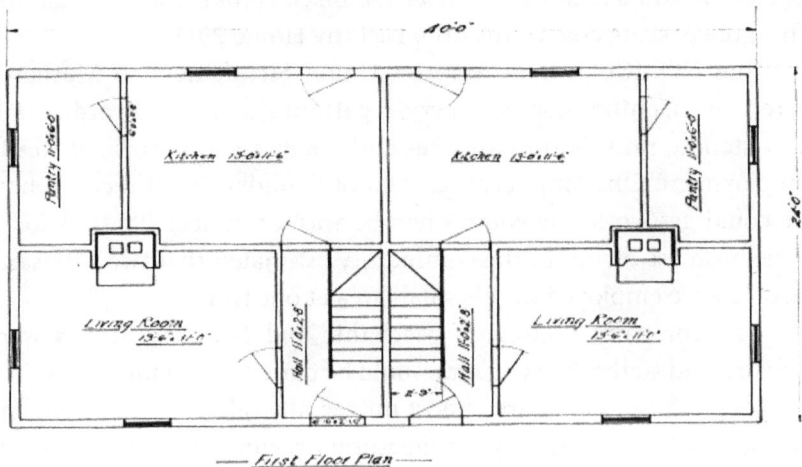

First Floor Plan

so that the men would know what boards they would need to grab for consistency in every wall. Another man came along and asked what he was doing, so he told him he was sorting out the boards. That man told him not to worry about it, that's the plasterer's problem (The Healthy Home: 2011).[1]

DOMCO employed a maintenance crew that was responsible for the company houses. Because of the standard plan for the homes, minor work could be done quickly. As all the windows were the same, boards would be attached over the windows and the house was simply spray-painted to a "dark brown hue" through the use of oil and oakum (MacKinnon 2009: 126). The boards would then be removed and the same process would be repeated with another home.

Most of the homes had small gardens in the back, which were used to grow vegetables like carrots, potatoes, peas, beans and onions. Because of the small size of the lots, however, most gardens were never big enough to produce enough food for the winter. Interview respondents did remember one large garden on Mechanic Street and recalled carrots being grown there, along with apple trees, and kids sneaking away with that produce. One neighbour in the area was known to use toilet waste to fertilize a garden, and as a theft deterrent (The Healthy Home 2011).

A gathering place for children was a large field behind Foundry Street. Baseball was played in the summer, hockey in the winter, and football year-round. Mechanic and Foundry streets also had hockey teams, and the teams played against each other and other street teams. Hockey sticks and gloves were shared (ibid).

Until it was vacated in 2008, 50 Mechanic Street had been home to the MacIntyre family. According to 1901 census data, the family was Catholic and of Scottish origin. Allan MacIntyre and his son Francis were railway foremen and tenants of DOMCO. In March 1929, the family was making weekly payments of $2.54 in support of an $11-a-month company lease. According to the house lease, the tenants were required to "keep the said house and premises clean and tidy, and not in any way to cause or allow them to be damaged beyond reasonable wear and tear" (Dominion Coal Company 1929). They were not allowed to keep pigs (ibid). In 1946, Francis MacIntyre finally purchased the home from the company for $597.55. This purchase was actually made eleven years after the company sold the other half of the duplex. When Francis MacIntyre died in 1988 the home passed to his wife,

Katherine Marie. Her children inherited it after her death in 1999. One of them described growing up in 50 Mechanic Street as

A very pleasant experience. There was always a warm and nurturing feeling in the home that expanded out to residents in the neighbourhood. Children in the community would often stay for supper with the MacIntyres, as their parents felt their children were safe staying with the family. Although the family never owned a car, the location of the home was in very close proximity to downtown Glace Bay and Francis's workplace, the railroad. Even though the home was close to a railway station, the disruptions of the train driving through town (upwards of 20 times a day) were something you got used to. (Qtd. in Lahey 2011)

In addition to being a welcoming place on a bustling street, the home also has a musical heritage that spanned three generations. This tradition began when Francis purchased a piano after he started working for the railway. Cape Breton kitchen parties were held at the

Fig. 4 – Imelda and Allan MacIntyre, shown in this undated photograph in front of the Mechanic Street Home, were the children of Francis and Katherine Marie MacIntyre (married in 1937). Francis was the son of Allan Francis and Flora MacIntyre, who made this company house a home at the turn of the 20th century. Photo courtesy of Imelda (MacIntyre) Crosby.

home with fiddlers, dancers and singers, often from Inverness, on the western side of the island. Francis's son, Allan, carried on the musical tradition and actually became good friends with such musical notables as Burton Cummings, Don McLean, Gary and Blair MacLean, Rodger Young and Allister MacGillivray in the 1960s. MacGillivray, who was a frequent visitor to the home, characterized these gatherings as good opportunities to enhance one's learning of musical theory, expand repertoires and develop a network of fellow musicians (ibid). Many of the songs played "were songs of protest, giving songwriters the opportunity to take a stand and voice their opinion on public issues" (ibid). When the home was first opened up after the tax sale, a piano was still in the living room.

Rebuilding a Company House

At the time of the tax-sale purchase, 50 Mechanic St., though vacant, was filled with furniture. In addition to the piano, there was a china cabinet, beds and heavy dresser drawers.

There was no water intrusion or mould, but the sill plates were rotting. In fact, the home was sagging dramatically, and the den attached to the back of the kitchen seemed to be unsalvageable. In neighbourhood interviews, owners discussed the methods they used to fix the sills. Sill work was apparently not carried out by the company maintenance crews and the owners could typically not afford to put in a proper foundation. Instead, digging would have to be done around the existing posts, and then the rotted uprights near the posts would be removed and replaced. At 50 Mechanic St., none of this had been done in a long time.

The backyard had received no maintenance and had become seriously overgrown. The shingles on the roof and on the sides needed to be replaced, along with the plumbing and wiring.

Shortly after Dominion Coal Company House #734 was offered as a donation for a demonstration project, AHRP convened a community focus group meeting. It was held near the home. In addition to local residents, attending were the local councillor, MLA, representatives of the downtown business association and a local historian. Twenty people were present.

Attendees agreed that there was potential here for a viable demonstration project. It was a visible location in a core-area neighbourhood

Fig. 5 – The fireplace, mantle and piano from 50 Mechanic Street. Photo by Joyce Rankin.

that could and should see improvement. People even talked about the National Trust for Canada's decision in 2010 to put "the company houses of industrial Cape Breton" on its list of the ten most endangered historic places in Canada. Here was an opportunity to show that some of the vacant company homes might have a future—that there might be some opportunities to use existing infrastructure, spruce up neighbourhoods, provide decent housing and maybe create an opportunity for a modest-income family to own a home.

But some practical problems were discussed, too: A foundation or new sills would have to be put in while not disrupting the neighbouring half of the duplex. Any major renovation would require a new fire wall between the two halves. And a way would have to be found to make the home energy-efficient.

In short, this would take some thought, some creativity, some consultation, some design and some fund-raising. It would be a "learning home." We thought that a good way to generate some of that creativity and problem-solving would be through a multi-day student design competition. We starting planning it in January 2011 and scheduled it for the end of March.

No one area of study could solve these problems. And so we imagined four mixed teams of Cape Breton University students from the social sciences and Nova Scotia Community College students (various campuses) in several disciplines, including carpentry and electrical.

Our Political Science students started studying the neighbourhood and nearby neighbourhoods; we wanted to be guided by local wisdom as much as possible. The Glace Bay Heritage Museum gave us space for an exhibit, to run concurrently with the design competition. The exhibit was called "Homes and Gardens: How Our People Survived." With interpretive panels and artifacts, the students recounted how local elders used seaweed and clothing for insulation (both were found in the walls of 50 Mechanic Street), how everything was recycled and how sill repairs were done painstakingly by hand.

At the design competition, we asked some specific questions: For example, what skilled trades will be required? Should the home be lifted for a new foundation? What features would you try to retain and how? How will you make the home energy efficient? Approximately how much will it cost? (The estimates were in the range of $55,000 to $65,000, which, as we shall see, turned out to be low.)

We wanted the teams to have resources at hand, ways to get plausible answers. Not only did that mean continuous access to the site but access to local and other experts in architecture, alternative energy and design. Several CBU and Nova Scotia Community College faculty agreed to be present. ICOMOS Canada (the Canadian committee of the International Council on Monuments and Sites) offered heritage architects Allan Killin and Tony Gillis, who joined us on site. Karlena Johnson, president of Mi'kmaw Alternative Energy, joined us for the three days as well as Charlie Aucoin from the Canada Mortgage and Housing Corporation.

The results were creative but practical. Lifting the house was not recommended, but a new foundation could be dug with sonotubes. Solar power could be introduced for under $5,000. A rain barrel for the toilet would be a practical addition. New floor joists, windows and completely new electrical would be required.

Fig. 6 – Participants in the Mechanic Street student design competition take measurements. Photo courtesy of Joyce Rankin.

Transfer of the property to Habitat for Humanity was finalized shortly after the design competition. At the same time, based on CBU student Michelle Lahey's work, and recommendations from the student design teams, the home was designated a municipal heritage property by the council of the Cape Breton Regional Municipality—the first former company house to be so registered. The municipality's statement of significance came directly from Lahey's work and also drew on some of the information gathered by the teams in the design competition.

At first it seemed to go quickly and well. Even Governor General David Johnston stopped by to work on the renovations during a visit to Cape Breton. But we soon ran into problems: foundation repairs needed more specialized expertise. The on-site volunteers were worried that the structural problems were greater than anticipated.

We referred this problem to a working group that was already scheduled to spend two weeks in Cape Breton with AHRP and CBU. It consisted of two architecture faculty members and two graduate students from Southern Illinois University, who had recently worked on turning a derelict historic worker's "shotgun house" in the economically struggling small city of Cairo, Illinois, into an affordable home. Joining them were six other students from CBU, Dalhousie University, Université de Montréal and University of Ottawa. They formed a problem-solving team, met with a local engineering firm and architect, and with Nova Scotia Community College faculty.

They drafted detailed plans for this company house. These plans served as a resource for NSCC faculty to develop a revised building permit application. The municipality was understandably concerned. The project was at risk.

There followed almost two years of painstaking work—some trial and error, lots of student engagement. Habitat for Humanity volunteers, NSCC and CBU raised funds, trained volunteers and used the home as a laboratory of sorts. Work had to slow at various periods as more funds were raised. The persistence of a build committee, led by Alicia Lake and then Adrian Wilson, was exemplary. They were not going to let the community down.

About $95,000 was needed in addition to the volunteer labour. The fund-raising took many forms. Local artist Diane Lawrence did a watercolour of the house, and prints were sold. Local businesses and philanthropists were invited to contribute $734 (because it was

Dominion Coal Company House #734). The volunteer team salvaged valuable items from the to-be-demolished St. Anne's rectory in Glace Bay and sold them. The local Home Depot gave us surplus products that would have been discarded because it was too expensive to send them back. Some were used in the home, others were sold to raise funds. The Cape Breton Regional Municipality provided $8,000 from its heritage conservation fund. Joyce Rankin, experienced in community development, played a coordinating role in this. It became about community pride, engagement and creative recycling almost as much as it was about the one home.

The work seemed to go more quickly once a family was selected and began to work on the project. A Habitat for Humanity family selection committee considered ability to pay, current housing condition and willingness to do "sweat equity" (volunteer work on the project) in exchange for no down payment and an interest-free mortgage. On October 6, 2013, the family and the volunteers gathered to celebrate the completion of the home through a "key ceremony."

The Energuide rating went from 0 to more than 80, which is almost unheard of for a former company house. And if you look very closely you will see that the solar panel is made from recycled pop cans.

Fig. 7 – The "pop can" solar panel can be seen in the right corner of the home. Photo by Joyce Rankin.

The final appraised market value was $72,000. The effective age was "zero." Dominion Coal Company House #734—this regenerated heritage property—was a modern home.

The community benefits of bringing this house back to life made the extra investment worthwhile. And we certainly believe that it would make sense for public policy to support this kind of effort. The neighbouring half of the duplex did not have to be abandoned. An overgrown eyesore became a beautiful home.

Lessons Learned

We learned a great deal about the obstacles to doing this work on a larger scale, but we also saw how it could be possible. We saw clearly a need and a demand, an enthusiasm and a local appreciation.

These are some lessons we learned:

The Habitat for Humanity model, although it comes with a great brand, does not provide a full revolving fund. Although the new family owns the home, the funds from the sale are not available *lump sum* to start the next project. That is because Habitat for Humanity finances its own mortgages. The local chapter needed to raise another $75,000 to start the next build. Costs above that would be covered by the provincial affiliate, which was gradually getting the proceeds from the mortgage payments. We need to find ways to build up additional local revolving funds that allow organizations to realize the value of their completed real estate and move quickly to the next project.

The municipality needs a central system to manage the vacant properties and get them into willing hands before the properties deteriorate too seriously. In the case of 50 Mechanic Street, the previous owner had long since walked away and stopped paying taxes. A housing revitalization corporation could take property donations, sell some, fix others and use profits for those properties that require demolition or subsidized work.

It is important to try to work in clusters as in Winnipeg and try to stabilize neighbourhoods through coordinated interventions by several organizations rather than "one-off" and scattered housing projects.

The difficulty accessing technical expertise was apparent, and the project would have been impossible without the involvement of

Nova Scotia Community College. We need an accessible bank of such expertise.

A renovation assistance service would help many modest income or mobility challenged residents to stay in their homes longer. During our work on this and other projects, we heard constantly how difficult it was to access labour—carpentry, plumbing, electrical—in the community. Paid contractors were looking for bigger work and getting it—either locally or in Alberta.

Conclusion

Fifty Mechanic Street represents a living heritage—an approach to heritage conservation that is pragmatic, that is focused on social needs of a community, that engages people of all walks of life, that builds relationships and support networks, and that builds community. Conserving Dominion Coal Company House #734 meant *changing* it into a modern affordable home. It meant learning from mistakes. It meant affirming that "heritage" is not just the ornate or the work of specialists. It meant breaking down the barriers between disciplines and subject areas at the university and community college.

But it also reinforced the persistent needs of one of Canada's most economically disadvantaged regions. The solution will arguably not lie in grand industrial schemes but in providing the conditions, the policy environment, the (de-)regulations, the seed funds and the access to advice that will allow social entrepreneurship to flourish. The coal and steel companies came with their bosses, their plans—and their houses. They are long gone.

The leadership must now be driven locally. New kinds of "bosses" must keep emerging—collaborative, entrepreneurial, creative and inter-disciplinary. They must start small and scale up, but never get detached from the stories, the sorrows or the unique opportunities. They must be generous with their time and insights. They must be "servant leaders."

And they must be learners. There was something very humbling about this project and others like it. For us, there was—there is still is—so much to learn about skilled trades, about local cultures, about the needs and interests of our neighbours, about getting things done in a complex environment.

Ethically and practically, we needed to be outside the classroom.

Note

1. The authors would like to thank Charmaine Deane for conducting project interviews with neighbourhood residents.

References

Alexander, Anne. 1997. *The Antigonish Movement: Moses Coady and Adult Education Today.* Toronto: Thompson Education Publishing.

Caledon Institute of Social Policy. 2001. *Quint: CED and Affordable Housing in Saskatoon.* Ottawa: Caledon Institute of Social Policy.

Coady, M. M. 1939. *Masters Of Their Own Destiny.* New York: Harper and Brothers.

CBC News. 2008. Court rejects CBRM lawsuit against province. CBC.ca. http://www.cbc.ca/news/canada/nova-scotia/story/2008/04/24/cbrm-dismiss.html?ref=rss (accessed June 12, 2014).

———. 2012. Sydney tenants in slum rentals urged to speak out. CBC.ca. http://www.cbc.ca/news/canada/nova-scotia/story/2012/02/15/ns-cbrm-slum-rentals-acorn.html (accessed June 20, 2014).

———. 2016. Nova Scotia population rises just a touch as Halifax grows. CBC.ca. http://www.cbc.ca/news/canada/nova-scotia/nova-scotia-population-slight-increase-1.3444594.

CBC Radio 2008. *Information Morning* Cape Breton, April 24, 7:45 a.m.

CBRM (Cape Breton Regional Municipality). 2009. CBRM's Integrated Community Sustainability Plan—A Discussion Paper. Presented to Council on September 15, 2009. http://www.cbrm.ns.ca.

CFNS (Community Foundation of Nova Scotia). 2013. *Cape Breton Regional Municipality's Vital Signs.* Taking the pulse of our municipality. http://www.cfns.ca (accessed November 20, 2014).

Deane, Lawrence. 2006. *Under One Roof: Community Economic Development in the Inner City.* Halifax, NS: Fernwood Books.

Dominion Coal Company, Limited. 1929. House Lease for House No. 734 between the Dominion Coal Company, Limited and Allan MacIntyre.

Harker Associates. 2010. AHRP 2010-15 Business Plan. Sydney, Nova Scotia.

Harris, Richard. 2001. Flattered But Not Imitated: Co-operative Self-Help and the Nova Scotia Housing Commission, 1936-1973. *Acadiensis* 31 (1).

Lahey, Michelle. 2011. Planned Panels and Visuals for Architectural Design Workshop. In *Houses and Homes: How Our People Survived* (student exhibit).

MacKinnon, Richard. 2009. *Discovering Cape Breton Folklore*. Sydney, NS: Cape Breton University Press.

McNeil, Greg. 2010. CBRM council approves sustainability plan. *Cape Breton Post*, March 25. http://www.capebretonpost.com/News/Local/2010-03-25/article-964425/CBRM-council-approves-sustainability-plan/1 (accessed February 23, 2015).

Statistics Canada. 2011. The Canadian Population in 2011: Population Counts and Growth. https://www12.statcan.gc.ca/census-recensement/2011/as-sa/98-310-x/98-310-x2011001-eng.cfm (accessed July 23, 2014).

———. 2016. Table 282-0122, Labour force survey estimates (LFS), by provinces and economic regions based on 2011 Census boundaries, 3-month moving average, unadjusted for seasonality. http://www.statcan.gc.ca/start-debut-eng.html.

The Healthy Home: An Accessible Inventory of Practical Renovation and Food Gardening Skills in a Glace Bay Neighbourhood. 2011. Unpublished.

Whalley, John. 2008. CBRM Overview 2008. Report prepared for the Cape Breton Regional Municipality. http://www.cbrm.ns.ca/images/stories/reports/CBRM_Overview_2008_J_Whalley.pdf (accessed April 3, 2014).

Wylie, William Newman Thomas. 1997. *Coal Culture: The History and Commemoration of Coal Mining in Nova Scotia*. Ottawa: Historic Sites and Monuments Board of Canada.

Conclusion

New and Renewed Vocations for Post-Industrial Communities

About 30 kilometres to the east of the thriving community of Kaszuby, Ontario, is the ghost town of Foymount. In its heyday, it was a strategically located settlement serving the North American Air Defence System (NORAD): This use made sense for the highest point in southern Ontario, until improved technology made it obsolete. There are still inhabited homes on the periphery of the ghost town, and some storage buildings are being used by the Township of Bonnechere Valley, but the 1950s-era apartments and hangars have barely been touched since they were abandoned in 1974. Even vintage trucks and trailer hitches dot the landscape. It is rather surreal.

Foymount was an intentional community, but it now lacks vocations. Nor is it a bedroom community for another place. Its survival and renewal would have required determined leadership and entrepreneurship—of leaders and entrepreneurs who know the community, celebrate diversity and see opportunities for new business and affordable housing. Moreover, smart public policy can create better soil for such new growth and help to recycle the historic environment. Company towns were founded as intentional communities, and, in some ways, they need to be cultivated with intent now.

The idea of Arvida as a model community was inscribed into the town's sense of itself by the original leaders. This notion has been picked up by today's champions. Meanwhile, post-industrial Marysville benefitted from friends in high places at critical moments as well as its proximity to Fredericton. Cape Breton and Bell Island are still absorbing the shock of industrial collapse and still trying to determine where to land in the post-industrial era. A new generation of local leadership and new local narratives are struggling to emerge.

For these communities, conservation is not a matter of staying one step ahead of the developers. It's about *being* the developers. Developers of cultural opportunities—and multicultural opportunities. Developers of affordable housing. Developers of creative financial instruments to raise capital. Some of the examples are described in this book. Others are emerging.

In Sydney Mines, Cape Breton, the Red Brick Row Investment Cooperative rescued a prominent collection of company houses by selling shares that entitled investors to a tax credit under Nova Scotia's program of Community Economic Development Investment Funds (CEDIFs). The Affordable Housing Renovation Partnership supported this project financially by selling an unused vacant lot in Sydney Mines, which was then used by the new owners to build an inexpensive home, and donating the money from the sale to the cooperative. This experiment was called "lot leveraging." Arvida promoted itself as unique in the world and thus reinforced civic pride and attracted creative civic projects. Marysville benefitted from the provincial government deciding to locate its offices in historic buildings, and retrofit them accordingly, rather than in a new office building or suburban strip plaza.

The problem of the adaptive re-use of former company towns is often the problem of regional economic development. What public policies will generate opportunities for communities that need a new economic vocation? Regions in the European Union have been establishing special economic zones, with tax incentives and investment advice for entrepreneurs who may wish to put down some roots in economically struggling regions. Poland's Mielec Special Economic Zone, for example, was established in 1995, after this small city went into decline: there was no longer a need to manufacture Soviet-era aircraft. Old plants and homes were abandoned. With a combination of tax incentives, special subsidies, land reclamation projects and coordinated marketing, the local administration reports private investments equivalent to about $2 billion and the creation of more than 20,000 jobs (Ernst and Young 2013).

But government agencies may be prone to pick the wrong "winners," to focus too much on finding the one big investor, or to favouritism. The federal Enterprise Cape Breton Corporation was disbanded by an Act of Parliament precisely because of these concerns.

Sometimes it will take civil-society leaders with unusual foresight and vision.

One such example is Holden Village in Washington State, USA. The former copper mining town was abandoned in 1957. No roads— only a passenger ferry—linked it directly with the outside world. Wes Prieb, who was active in Trinity Lutheran College, envisioned it as a Lutheran Retreat Centre, and took it over for one dollar. It became that, with a lot of work from volunteers. It has been successful, although mine remediation remains a constant burden. Its official literature reports that, "Some people visit for just a few days, most for at least a week, and some stay for years. All are Villagers. All are embraced by the community, encouraged to share in meals, worship and the wide range of activities" (Holden Village 2015).

In 1964, the International Council on Monuments and Sites passed the Venice Charter. It remains a short, clear, widely accepted statement of principles on the conservation of heritage. Article 1 says:

> The concept of a historic monument embraces not only the single
> architectural work but also the urban or rural setting in which
> is found the evidence of a particular civilization, a significant
> development or a historic event. This applies not only to great
> works of art but also to more modest works of the past which
> have acquired cultural significance with the passing of time.
> (ICOMOS 1964)

Our company towns have such significance. They speak to social conflict and change, to cultural diversity and economic history. They reflect our vernacular architecture and philosophies of community and ideas about development that had import at particular points in time. Living landscapes tell stories, often better than books and museums.

United States Executive Order 13006, signed by President Bill Clinton in 1996, requires the federal government to look first to meet its real estate and rental needs in historic buildings or downtown areas. This could be replicated in Canada. Arbitrary affordable housing subsidy policies that exclude renovation in favour of new construction should be eliminated. A general tax credit for renovations would help as well. The National Trust for Canada has recommended an "eco-historic tax credit," similar to the 2009 home renovation tax credit, which was claimed by about three million Canadians for the short time that it remained in force (National Trust for Canada: 2016).

In partial response to a study by Cape Breton University and the Affordable Housing Renovation Partnership (Leviten-Reid et al. 2014), the Province of Nova Scotia has launched a program of easily accessible micro-grants of up to a few thousand dollars for owners for former company houses in Glace Bay's New Aberdeen neighbourhood. It's touted as a pilot—a kind of small spark, and it is worth watching (Cape Breton Post, 2015).

But at a time when governments are sputtering, and when citizens have less confidence in public bodies to solve or own problems, we are back again to civil society. The National Trust for Canada's recent "This Lighthouse Matters" program, consisting of crowd-funding and philanthropically sponsored on-line voting, helped to rescue rural lighthouses that would likely otherwise have lost their chance to endure another generation. It also helped to cultivate a new generation of community organizers. It set the stage for a broader program called "This Place Matters." The Trust's Regeneration Works program is also expanding its reach, reaching out more explicitly to "areas of deprivation."

Revolving funds have taken off in many American jurisdictions. The first, in Charleston, South Carolina, was established in 1947. It has saved that city's historic fabric (cf. Weyeneth 1997). Early visionaries used fund-raised dollars to buy properties at a low price, fix them, market them far and wide, and sell them, often with a stated social purpose. In the small city of Paducah, Kentucky, a nationally advertised "Artist Relocation Program" has helped to fill many vacant buildings.

A revolving fund on a smaller scale is now being tried in Cape Breton, as mentioned in Chapter 7. A recent project was a 55-square-metre (600-sq-ft) former steelworker's home on Victoria Road in Whitney Pier. The vacant home, donated by the estate of James Antle, was restored, and is subject to a covenant on title requiring that future owners not tear it down. They must use it for affordable housing for at least ten years, citing criteria of the Canada Mortgage and Housing

Corporation. The project actually generated net revenue for the fund, some of which is being used to develop a parkette in the same neighbourhood celebrating the contribution of immigrants.

On July 9, 2015, hundreds of people in that Whitney Pier neighbourhood gathered at the Polish Village Hall for the release of a board game about the community. The steel plant was gone. Many storefronts are vacant. But local pride and determination remain. Just a block away, thanks to community solidarity, the historic St. Mary's Polish Church, the only Polish church in Atlantic Canada, was literally rising from the ashes—it was being rebuilt following a fire the previous November. Now, the area churches and mosque had worked together on the game, with proceeds going to build an infill Habitat for Humanity home in the neighbourhood. The inscription on the box says, "Build affordable homes. Know the community. Celebrate diversity. Care for others."

That could well be the motto for the regeneration of company houses and company towns.

References

Cape Breton Post. 2015. New look for New Aberdeen, May 4.

Ernst and Young. 2013. *Poland: A True Special Economic Zone.* http://www.ey.com/Publication/vwLUAssets/Raport_EY_Poland_-_a_true_special_economic_zone/$FILE/Raport-Poland-a-true-special-economic-zone.pdf (accessed September 1, 2015).

Holden Village. 2015. "Village Life." Official website of Holden Village: http://www.holdenvillage.org/village-life/ (accessed September 1, 2015).

International Council on Monuments and Sites. 1964. *The Venice Charter: International Charter for the Conservation and Restoration of Monuments and Sites.*

Leviten-Reid, Catherine et al. 2014. *Housing Need and Demand Study for a Neighbourhood in Glace Bay* (Prepared for the Cape Breton Regional Municipality). www.homematchcapebreton.com.

National Trust for Canada (2016). *Brief to House of Commons Standing Committee on Finance—Recommendations for Budget 2017.*

Weyeneth, Robert. 2000. *Historic Preservation for a Living City:* Historic Charleston Foundation, *1947-1997.* Columbia: University of South Carolina Press.

Contributors

LYN BLEILER's family mined placer gold on Highet Creek near Mayo for more than a hundred years. She is the principal author of several books of local history.

ALEX FORBES has a Master's Degree in Urban Planning from Dalhousie University and a Master's degree in Business Administration from the University of New Brunswick. He was employed from 1991 to 2013 as a City Planner with the City of Fredericton. Early in his career his work required him to undertake research on Marysville, which led to a long-term interest in the town and in particular its founder, Alexander "Boss" Gibson.

BARBARA HOGAN has been involved with the research and documentation of the UKHM properties since 2004, working with community members of Keno and with Access Consulting, a subsidiary of Alexco Resources Ltd, to develop a plan to manage the UKHM historic resources. Barbara is currently the manager of historic sites, Yukon Government.

MARC JOHNSTON is a Yukon heritage worker, president of the Yukon Historical Museums Association and a member of the board of governors of the National Trust for Canada.

ANNE LECKIE is a geographer who has worked with the First Nation of Nacho Nyäk Dun on land-claims issues for over thirty years, worked as their lands director, executive director and political adviser. Along with Bleiler, she has been a contributor to several books on area local history.

JESSICA MACE is an architectural historian and SSHRC Postdoctoral Fellow (York University) with the Canada Research Chair in Urban Heritage at the Université du Québec à Montréal. Her current research focuses on the domestic architecture of Canadian company towns.

RICHARD MACKINNON is the former Tier One Canada Research Chair in Intangible Cultural Heritage at Cape Breton University, where he teaches folklore in the Department of History and Culture and directs the Centre for Cape Breton Studies. His research interests include all aspects of Atlantic Canada's culture including oral traditions, music, language, material culture and vernacular architecture.

ROB MCINTYRE is an engineer and was the principal of Access Consulting, the company that had the care and maintenance contract at Elsa after the mine closure of 1989. He is a vice-president of Alexco Resources.

ANDREW MOLLOY is Professor of Political Science and a member of the teaching faculty in the MBA CED (Community Economic Development) program at Cape Breton University. His areas of academic specialization include public policy and public administration, community economic development, Canadian government and politics and applied research methodology.

LUCIE K. MORISSET is professor of Urban and Touristic Studies at Université du Québec à Montréal and Canada Research Chair in Urban Heritage. She has been leading research on the morphogenesis and the semiogenesis of the built landscape and on the relations between identity and culture as they are manifested throughout the practices and discourse of heritage production. She is Fellow of the Royal Society of Canada.

TOM URBANIAK is Associate Professor of Political Science at Cape Breton University. He is the past chair of the board of governors of the National Trust for Canada and is active in many non-profit organizations. He chairs the parish council of St. Mary's Polish Church in the multicultural, post-industrial community of Whitney Pier, Cape Breton, where he resides. He is the author of four books, including *Her Worship: Hazel McCallion and the Development of Mississauga* and *Action, Accommodation, Accountability: Rules of Order for Canadian Organizations*.

GAIL (HUSSEY) WEIR, is the daughter and granddaughter of two generations of iron-ore miners on Bell Island, NL, who worked in the Wabana Mines when they were at their zenith. She is the author of *The Miners of Wabana* (Breakwater Books, 1989 & 2006). A former archivist with Memorial University Library's Archives and Special Collections, she is spending her retirement years on research and writing.

www.ingramcontent.com/pod-product-compliance
Lightning Source LLC
Chambersburg PA
CBHW020659270326
41928CB00005B/190